FOOD LOVERS'
GUIDE TO
THE HUDSON VALLEY

FOOD LOVERS' SERIES

FOOD LOVERS'
GUIDE TO®
THE HUDSON VALLEY

The Best Restaurants, Markets
& Local Culinary Offerings

1st Edition

Sheila Buff

Guilford, Connecticut

All the information in this guidebook is subject to change. We recommend that you call ahead to obtain current information before traveling.

Editor: Amy Lyons
Project Editor: Lauren Szalkiewicz
Layout Artist: Mary Ballachino
Text Design: Sheryl Kober
Illustrations by Jill Butler with additional art by Carleen Moira Powell and MaryAnn Dubé
Maps: Trailhead Graphics, Inc. © Morris Book Publishing, LLC

ISBN 978-0-7627-8153-9

Printed in the United States of America

10 9 8 7 6 5 4 3 2 1

Contents

Introduction: The Hudson Valley Foodshed, 1

    How to Use This Book, 3

    Keeping Up with Foodie News, 5

Putnam County, 9

  Cold Spring, 11

    Foodie Faves, 11

    Cafes & Quick Bites, 15

    Farm Bounty, 17

  Garrison, 20

    Foodie Faves, 20

    Farm Bounty, 23

  Putnam Valley, 23

    Farm Bounty, 23

Dutchess County, 25

Amenia, 26

 Foodie Faves, 26

 Cafes & Quick Bites, 27

 Specialty Stores & Producers, 28

 Farm Bounty, 28

Beacon, 29

 Foodie Faves, 29

 Cafes & Quick Bites, 35

 Specialty Stores & Producers, 38

 Farm Bounty, 42

Clinton Corners, 42

 Specialty Stores & Producers, 42

 Farm Bounty, 42

Dover Plains, 44

 Farm Bounty, 44

Fishkill, 45

 Foodie Faves, 45

 Cafes & Quick Bites, 48

 Specialty Stores & Producers, 48

 Farm Bounty, 49

Hopewell Junction, 49

    Foodie Faves, 49

    Farm Bounty, 50

Hyde Park, 52

    Foodie Faves, 52

    Cafes & Quick Bites, 57

    Farm Bounty, 57

LaGrangeville, 57

    Farm Bounty, 57

Milan, 58

    Foodie Faves, 58

    Specialty Stores & Producers, 58

    Farm Bounty, 59

Millbrook, 59

    Foodie Faves, 59

    Cafes & Quick Bites, 61

    Specialty Stores & Producers, 62

    Farm Bounty, 64

Millerton, 66

    Foodie Faves, 66

    Cafes & Quick Bites, 67

Specialty Stores & Producers, 68

Farm Bounty, 69

Pawling, 72

Foodie Faves, 72

Pine Plains, 73

Foodie Faves, 73

Cafes & Quick Bites, 74

Specialty Stores & Producers, 74

Farm Bounty, 78

Pleasant Valley, 79

Specialty Stores & Producers, 79

Farm Bounty, 79

Poughkeepsie, 80

Foodie Faves, 80

Cafes & Quick Bites, 91

Specialty Stores & Producers, 95

Farm Bounty, 99

Red Hook, 100

Foodie Faves, 100

Cafes & Quick Bites, 102

Specialty Stores & Producers, 105

Farm Bounty, 106

Rhinebeck, 110

Foodie Faves, 110

Cafes & Quick Bites, 120

Specialty Stores & Producers, 122

Farm Bounty, 125

Salt Point, 127

Foodie Faves, 127

Farm Bounty, 128

Staatsburg, 129

Foodie Faves, 129

Farm Bounty, 129

Stanfordville, 130

Foodie Faves, 130

Farm Bounty, 131

Tivoli, 132

Foodie Faves, 132

Specialty Stores & Producers, 135

Farm Bounty, 135

Wappingers Falls, 136

Foodie Faves, 136

Cafes & Quick Bites, 138

Specialty Stores & Producers, 138

Farm Bounty, 140

Wingdale, 140

Foodie Faves, 140

Columbia County, 143

Ancram, 144

Foodie Faves, 144

Cafes & Quick Bites, 144

Specialty Stores & Producers, 145

Farm Bounty, 146

Chatham, 148

Foodie Faves, 148

Specialty Stores & Producers, 150

Farm Bounty, 151

Claverack, 152

    Foodie Faves, 152

    Farm Bounty, 153

Clermont, 155

    Farm Bounty, 155

Copake, 155

    Foodie Faves, 155

    Farm Bounty, 156

Germantown, 157

    Specialty Stores & Producers, 157

    Farm Bounty, 159

Ghent, 160

    Specialty Stores & Producers, 160

    Farm Bounty, 162

Hillsdale, 164

    Foodie Faves, 164

    Cafes & Quick Bites, 165

    Farm Bounty, 165

Hudson, 166

    Foodie Faves, 166

    Cafes & Quick Bites, 175

    Specialty Stores & Producers, 180

    Farm Bounty, 182

Kinderhook, 185

    Foodie Faves, 185

    Farm Bounty, 185

Livingston, 187

    Foodie Faves, 187

    Farm Bounty, 187

Old Chatham, 188

    Cafes & Quick Bites, 188

    Specialty Stores & Producers, 189

Philmont, 189

    Foodie Faves, 189

    Farm Bounty, 191

Stuyvesant, 191

    Farm Bounty, 191

Valatie, 192

    Specialty Stores & Producers, 192

    Farm Bounty, 192

Orange County, 195

Cornwall, 196

    Foodie Faves, 196

    Cafes & Quick Bites, 198

    Farm Bounty, 199

New Windsor, 200

    Foodie Faves, 200

    Specialty Stores & Producers, 201

    Farm Bounty, 201

Newburgh, 202

    Foodie Faves, 202

    Cafes & Quick Bites, 210

    Specialty Stores & Producers, 211

    Farm Bounty, 212

West Point/Highlands, 214

    Foodie Faves, 214

    Farm Bounty, 215

Ulster County, 217

Clintondale, 218

Foodie Faves, 218

Farm Bounty, 219

High Falls, 219

Foodie Faves, 219

Cafes & Quick Bites, 224

Farm Bounty, 224

Highland, 225

Foodie Faves, 225

Cafes & Quick Bites, 226

Specialty Stores & Producers, 226

Farm Bounty, 227

Kingston, 229

Foodie Faves, 229

Cafes & Quick Bites, 237

Specialty Stores & Producers, 244

Farm Bounty, 248

Marlboro, 248

Specialty Stores & Producers, 248

Farm Bounty, 250

Milton, 250

    Foodie Faves, 250

    Farm Bounty, 251

Modena, 252

    Farm Bounty, 252

New Paltz, 253

    Foodie Faves, 253

    Cafes & Quick Bites, 257

    Specialty Stores & Producers, 260

    Farm Bounty, 264

Rosendale, 268

    Foodie Faves, 268

    Cafes & Quick Bites, 269

    Specialty Stores & Producers, 270

    Farm Bounty, 271

Saugerties, 271

    Foodie Faves, 271

    Cafes & Quick Bites, 275

    Specialty Stores &
    Producers, 277

    Farm Bounty, 280

West Park, 281

Foodie Faves, 281

Specialty Stores & Producers, 282

Greene County, 283

Athens, 283

Foodie Faves, 283

Farm Bounty, 285

Catskill, 286

Foodie Faves, 286

Cafes & Quick Bites, 287

Specialty Stores & Producers, 288

Farm Bounty, 288

Climax, 289

Farm Bounty, 289

Coxsackie, 289

Foodie Faves, 289

Farm Bounty, 290

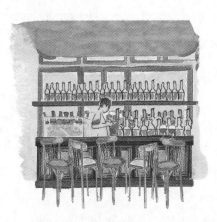

Hudson Valley Farmers' Markets, 291

    Putnam County, 292

    Dutchess County, 292

    Columbia County, 295

    Orange County, 296

    Ulster County, 297

    Greene County, 298

Food Events, Festivals & Celebrations, 299

Recipes, 311

Glynwood Apple Soup, 312

Magic Soup, 314

Spaghetti Squash Gratin, 315

Sour Cream Onion Dip, 316

Sour Cream Pancakes, 317

Basil Pesto, 318

Bootlegger's Swizzle, 319

Fire Cider Margarita, 320

Frozen Raspberry Mojito, 321

Hawthorne Valley Farm Rye Strudel, 322

Hudson Valley Raclette, 324

Porcini Mushroom Sauce, 325

Simple Fresh Garden Pasta Sauce, 326

Adams's Own Tattooed Rosemary Potatoes, 327

Crown Maple Blackberry Pork Chops from Madava Farms, 328

Appendices, 329

Appendix A: Eateries by Cuisine, 330

Appendix B: Specialty Producers & Shops, 336

Appendix C: Farm Bounty, 341

Appendix D: Land Trusts, 346

Index, 350

About the Author

Sheila Buff has been a resident of the small town of Milan, in the mid–Hudson Valley, since 1987. She is a founding member of her local community-supported organic farm, where she is head vegetable washer and teaches classes in pickling, preserving, and cheesemaking. In addition to her extensive work as a medical writer, she is the author of several books about the Hudson Valley and the outdoors, including *Birding for Beginners* (Falcon Guides), *Insiders' Guide to the Hudson River Valley* (Globe Pequot Press), and *Traditional Country Skills* (Lyons Press). She is also the editor of the revised edition of *Exploring the Appalachian Trail: Hikes in the Mid-Atlantic States*.

Acknowledgments

Over the years, many friends, acquaintances, and friends of friends have shared their love of good, locally produced food and favorite local restaurants with me. They've revealed their favorite rural farm stands. They've shared their knowledge of hidden specialty shops and eateries and debated the merits of local bakeries and food trucks. They've gone on winery tours, visited distant farmers' markets, and driven many miles to check out rumors of good ethnic food. They're too numerous to be named here, but they know who they are. I'm grateful for their help and companionship on eating expeditions across six counties.

I'd also like to thank the many farmers, cheesemakers, distillers, brewers, chocolatiers, and other staunch food artisans who are keeping local agriculture not only alive but thriving in the region. They were endlessly patient about answering my questions and generously guided me to many of the producers included in this book.

Books like this are just fun to research and write, even if they do make you feel hungry all the time. Adding to the pleasure of this project was once again working with Amy Lyons and the crew at Globe Pequot Press.

Introduction: The Hudson Valley Foodshed

In the summer of 1609, when Henry Hudson sailed up the unknown river that came to bear his name, he saw a beautiful new world. The Native Americans of the region fished in the river, hunted the deer and other game in the woods that lined it, and cultivated corn, beans, and squash. Hudson wrote in his log, "The land is the finest for cultivation that I ever in my life set foot upon, and it also abounds in trees of every description."

Henry got the cultivation part right. By the 1620s, European settlement had begun in the Hudson Valley. By the 1660s, French Huguenots fleeing religious persecution in Europe had brought their wine-making skills to the area that is now New Paltz in Ulster County. The legacy of the vineyards they planted lives on at places like Benmarl Winery in Marlboro, the oldest vineyard in America. Today, the Hudson Valley is the oldest winemaking region in the country, and is also one of New York's major wine-producing regions, with over 20 operating wineries.

Henry was right about the trees, too. The Hudson Valley quickly became known for its many productive orchards, and particularly for its apples. The legacy of 400 years lives on—farmers in the eastern and western Hudson Valley grow nearly half of the 29 million bushels of apples produced every year in New York. And recent changes to New York law mean that the production of hard cider from those apples is now once again a thriving regional enterprise.

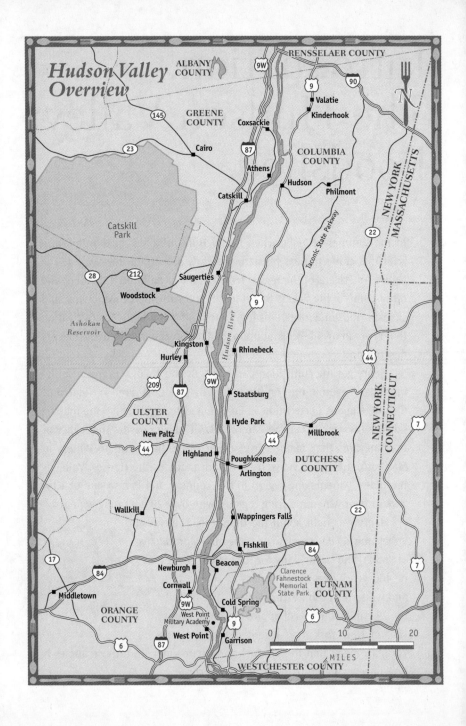

Hudson Valley Overview

ALBANY COUNTY

9W

RENSSELAER COUNTY

9

90

N

145

GREENE COUNTY

Valatie

Kinderhook

Coxsackie

23

Cairo

87

COLUMBIA COUNTY

Athens

Hudson

Philmont

Catskill

Catskill Park

Taconic State Parkway

22

28

212

Saugerties

Woodstock

Hudson River

9

Ashokan Reservoir

Kingston

Rhinebeck

Hurley

44

209

87

9W

Staatsburg

ULSTER COUNTY

Hyde Park

Millbrook

NEW YORK CONNECTICUT

New Paltz

44

7

Highland

Poughkeepsie

44

Arlington

DUTCHESS COUNTY

Wallkill

Wappingers Falls

22

Fishkill

84

17

Newburgh

Beacon

Clarence Fahnestock Memorial State Park

7

84

Middletown

Cornwall

PUTNAM COUNTY

Cold Spring

9W

West Point Military Academy

6

ORANGE COUNTY

9

0   10   20

6

87

West Point

Garrison

MILES

WESTCHESTER COUNTY

In recent years the huge demand for fresh, locally grown food has led to an amazing resurgence in farming in the Hudson Valley. Bustling local farmers' markets, community-supported agriculture, pastured meat, and artisan food and drink of all sorts have made the region into a food lover's paradise.

The presence of the famed Culinary Institute of America in Hyde Park (Dutchess County) has been the catalyst for the remarkable growth in truly excellent restaurants across the region. Students at the CIA come to appreciate the wonderful bounty of Hudson Valley farms and grow to love the area. Many decide to stay, honing their skills in the kitchens of others and eventually opening their own restaurants. In a virtuous circle, the presence of great ingredients leads to great cooking, which attracts visitors from the region, from the greater New York City area, and from everywhere else—which leads to even more demand for farm-fresh produce and restaurants that know how to use it. It's all led to an amazing number of really good restaurants across the foodie spectrum, from high-end contemporary American to a broad range of ethnic restaurants to food trucks that boast about using local ingredients.

How to Use This Book

The mid-Hudson River Valley region covered by this book is very large—parts of six counties stretching for 90 miles along the river. The region is divided by the Hudson River itself. On the east side of the river are, from south to north, Putnam, Dutchess, and Columbia counties. On the west side of the river are, from south to north, Orange, Ulster, and Greene counties. Within the counties, this book focuses on the places that are most closely linked to the Hudson River, either by geography or history. The restaurant-filled river towns that line the banks are covered extensively, of course. In the Hudson Valley, the countryside isn't ever very far away, and this book also travels inland to take in the many farms, artisans, and restaurants that abound among the rolling hills. Many a scenic country road winds through fields and orchards and leads to a world-class restaurant, an internationally famed winery, a maple syrup sugar house, or a farm stand overflowing with seasonal produce.

But because the region is so large, some areas in each county simply couldn't be included—apologies to those towns that are just too far to the east or west to be considered part of the Hudson River region.

Each chapter of this book covers a county, starting on the east side of the river and moving north, and then crossing to the west side and again moving north. Each chapter is subdivided alphabetically by town. Within each town, the information is broken down into subsections, including:

Foodie Faves

This section lists sit-down restaurants worth visiting—they represent the best cuisine the Hudson Valley has to offer.

Cafes & Quick Bites

A subcategory of Foodie Faves, this section covers great food that's served in coffee shops, bakery cafes, and other less formal places—including ice cream stands and sandwich shops.

Specialty Stores & Producers

This section is devoted to outstanding bakeries, chocolatiers, wine shops, ethnic groceries, and other places that provide wonderful things to eat and drink. It also includes wineries, breweries, and distilleries.

Farm Bounty

In this section, the book lists farmers' markets, farm stands, pastured meat growers, cheesemakers, and other artisan food producers. This is also the place to find pick-your-own orchards and farms.

Restaurant Price Key

Each restaurant, cafe, and quick place to eat carries a price code to give you a rough approximation of what you will spend. For restaurants, the code is based on dinner entree prices; for Cafes & Quick Bites, the price is based on a popular basic menu item, such as an ice cream cone. As a general rule at a restaurant, double the figure to estimate the cost of a three-course meal with a glass of wine. The codes represent the majority of dinner entrees; most restaurants will have a few dishes that are less expensive and a few that are more expensive. The cost of lunch is almost always lower.

$	under $15
$$	$15 to $25
$$$	$25 to $40
$$$$	more than $40 or prix fixe

Keeping Up with Foodie News

The Hudson Valley food scene today is very lively—throughout the region, new restaurants and specialty stores are opening (and sometimes closing). Fortunately for foodies, the region also has a useful set of informative magazines and websites that track developments.

Magazines

Edible Hudson Valley, **PO Box 650, Rhinebeck, NY 12572; (845) 688-6880; ediblehudsonvalley.com.** This quarterly magazine, published on recycled paper, looks at local foods in the Hudson Valley and Catskills. The articles are always interesting, with a lot of focus on farms and other producers and not much emphasis on restaurants.

WHAT DOES ORGANIC MEAN?

For a food to carry the official United States Department of Agriculture (USDA) National Organic Program (NOP) seal, it has to be produced without using conventional pesticides, petroleum-based fertilizers, sewage sludge fertilizers, genetic engineering, or irradiation. Organic meat, poultry, eggs, and dairy products must come from animals that are given no antibiotics or growth hormones. Before a product can be labeled organic, a federally approved certifier inspects the farm to make sure the farmer is following the strict USDA organic standards. The complexity and cost of the process is such that only the largest farms in the region can obtain USDA NOP certification. In addition, many small organic farmers disagree with some of the practices the USDA allows for NOP certification.

In the Hudson Valley, many organic farms work with the nonprofit Northeast Organic Farming Association of New York (NOFA-NY), a USDA-accredited certifying agency, to get their certification of organic production and handling operations. These farms are allowed to use the NOFA-NY seal (see nofany.org for details). The process for NOFA-NY certification is also complex and costly, though much more manageable than the USDA process. Other farmers prefer to work with Certified Naturally Grown (CNG), a

Edible Hudson Valley is the sponsor of the **Festival of Farmers' Markets** (see p. 300). Rotating participants at weekly markets host special events, live music, cooking demonstrations, and other events throughout the season. Subscriptions are $28 a year.

***Hudson Valley*, 2678 South Rd., Poughkeepsie, NY 12601; (845) 463-0542; hvmag.com.** A glossy monthly covering all aspects of life in the region, *Hudson Valley* has excellent coverage of the food scene. *Hudson Valley* sponsors the annual Best of the Hudson Valley contest, which of course includes the important categories Best Restaurants, nonprofit organization (naturallygrown.org) offering certification tailored for small-scale, direct-market farmers and beekeepers using natural methods. The CNG certification encourages collaboration, transparency, and community involvement. CNG farms don't use any synthetic fertilizers, pesticides, herbicides, fungicides, or GMO seeds, just like organic farms. Certified Naturally Grown is an independent program not affiliated with the NOP.

Many organic farmers in the region don't have NOFA-NY or CNG certification, however. That's not a reason to avoid their products. These farmers are still using organic and sustainable farming methods that improve the productivity of the land by encouraging and enhancing natural biological processes.

How can you know if your local farmer is using good organic farming methods? At the farmers' market or farm stand, ask. Organic farmers love to talk about their farms and will be happy to tell you all about their crop rotation methods, integrated pest management, high tunnels, how they compost the manure, and pretty much anything else. If you're a CSA member, volunteer on the farm to get a firsthand look at the organic methods in use. And remember that buying from your local farmer is the best way of all to support local agriculture and open space.

Best Food, and Best Drink. Readers vote on their favorites by county, cuisine, and atmosphere. The voice of the people is rarely wrong—winners proudly display their plaques. The free e-newsletter Corner Table, sent out every Friday, includes restaurant reviews, recipes, and local events. The website has lots of great information about restaurants, farms, and food events. The magazine is available at most newsstands and magazine racks in the region. Individual issues are $4.99; subscriptions are $18 a year.

Hudson Valley Wine, Box 353, Coxsackie, NY 12051; (518) 731-1332; hvwinemag.com. Published twice a year, this large-format, glossy magazine printed on recycled paper covers the burgeoning wine industry in the region (also breweries and distilleries). It's distributed free through wine shops, liquor stores, and other selected sites, but copies always seem to be very scarce. Fortunately, it can be read on the website.

The Valley Table, 125 Powelton Circle, Newburgh, NY 12550; (845) 561-2022; valleytable.com. This excellent magazine focuses on Hudson Valley farms, food, and cuisine. It puts special emphasis on sustainable agriculture and the links among producers, restaurants, and consumers. The magazine is also the driving force behind the annual **Hudson Valley Restaurant Week** (see p. 300). The website is a great source of information, especially about upcoming events. *The Valley Table* is published quarterly. It's distributed free at selected sites in the region, but copies always get snatched up so quickly that it can be hard to find; subscriptions are $20 a year.

Websites

Hudson River Valley National Heritage Area, hudsonrivervalley.com

Hudson Valley Bounty, hudsonvalleybounty.com

Hudson Valley Food Network, hvfoodnetwork.com

Hudson Valley Good Stuff, hudsonvalleygoodstuff.com

Hudson Valley Tourism, travelhudsonvalley.com

Putnam County

The smallest of the counties covered in this book, Putnam County is only 246 square miles. The historic river towns of Garrison and Cold Spring are separated from the interior of the county by the rugged hills of the Hudson Highlands. The geography means that for the purposes of this book, only these two towns and the area around them are truly in the Hudson River valley. That still gives a lot of scope for discussion, because some of the finest and most innovative cooking in the region takes place here at farm-to-table restaurants such as Valley at the Garrison, perched high in the hills overlooking the river. The very walkable and very accessible town of Cold Spring (easily reached by Metro-North trains) has half a dozen worthwhile restaurants and lots of fun foodie places. Because Putnam County today is largely a commuter suburb of New York City, and because much of the rugged terrain isn't really suitable for farming, the agriculture scene is considerably smaller here than the other locales in this book. Several farmers' markets serve the area, and a lot of innovative thinking about farming is taking place at Glynwood Farm.

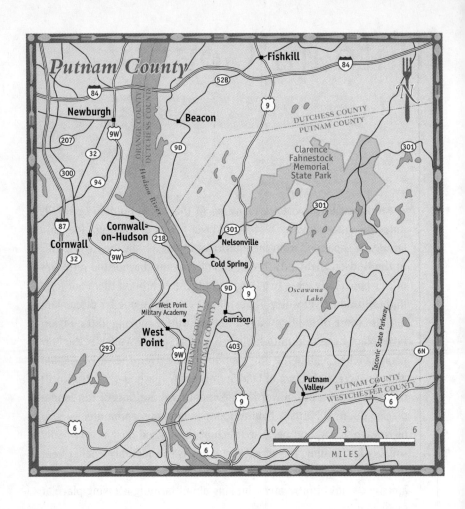

Putnam County

Fishkill

Newburgh

Beacon

ORANGE COUNTY
DUTCHESS COUNTY

DUTCHESS COUNTY
PUTNAM COUNTY

Clarence
Fahnestock
Memorial
State Park

Hudson River

Cornwall-
on-Hudson

Nelsonville

Cornwall

Cold Spring

Oscawana
Lake

West Point
Military Academy

Garrison

Taconic State Parkway

West
Point

Putnam
Valley

PUTNAM COUNTY
WESTCHESTER COUNTY

ORANGE COUNTY
PUTNAM COUNTY

0   3   6

MILES

Cold Spring

Foodie Faves

Brasserie le Bouchon, 76 Main St. (Fair Street), Cold Spring, NY 10516; (845) 265-7676; French $$. Brasserie le Bouchon is a local favorite for its traditional menu of well-prepared classic bistro dishes, such as *steak grillé maître d'hôtel* (grilled steak with house butter and outstanding house-made *frites*), cassoulet, *moules au curry,* and the house-made country pâté. In true French fashion, and starting before it became fashionable, the bistro sources ingredients locally, including Valley-raised duck and chicken. In warm weather, ask to be seated on the charming front porch and watch the world go by on Cold Spring's lively, shop-lined Main Street. Cozy and casual, Le Bouchon is located in a century-old house turned restaurant. It's a bit on the small side and it can get crowded during the dinner rush. Reservations recommended.

Cathryn's Tuscan Grill, 91 Main St. (Fair Street), Cold Spring, NY, 10516; (845) 265-5582; tuscangrill.com; Italian; $$$. Open every day of the night and week for both lunch and dinner (Champagne brunch on Sundays), Cathryn's Tuscan Grill is tucked away in the far corner of a courtyard just opposite the corner of Main and Fair Streets. This casually elegant cafe is worth looking for to sample the wide-ranging menu of intriguing Italian specialties, along with the extensive Italian wine list. A signature dish from the dinner menu is *pappardelle all'uva e coniglio,* or fresh pappardelle pasta with pulled rabbit meat in a grappa sauce. This may be a common dish in Tuscany, but it's a rare—and delicious—option in the Hudson Valley. The lunch menu offers a

good selection of salads and pastas along with a daily sandwich special. Reservations are suggested for dinner.

Cold Spring Depot, 1 Depot Sq., Cold Spring, NY 10516; (845) 265-5000; coldspringdepot.com; Traditional American; $$. One of the pleasures of visiting Cold Spring is that the charming town is easily accessible by taking a Metro-North train from Grand Central Terminal. The station is at the foot of Main Street; most of the restaurants and shops are within easy walking distance. (You can also bring your bike on the train.) At the foot of Main Street just next to the station is Cold Spring Depot, a handy place to watch the trains go by while enjoying a really well-prepared burger and a great Bloody Mary. If you're with the kids, so much the better. Kids love the trains (nearly 70 go past in a day) and the restaurant has an attached ice cream shop. Live music is on tap most weekends at this very family-friendly restaurant. On Sunday in the summer, a Dixie band plays in the gazebo on the lawn. In the warmer weather, Friday night is all-you-can-eat barbecue night, one of the better values in the area. Cold Spring Depot has events year-round, including Oktoberfest weekends in Sept and Oct.

Hudson House River Inn, 2 Main St., Cold Spring, NY 10516; (845) 265-9355; hudsonhouseinn.com; Traditional American; $$$. The Hudson House Inn was built in 1832 and has been in continuous operation as a hotel ever since. The historic building, perched right on the waterfront, is on the National Register of Historic Places. The River Room is just a hundred feet from the Hudson River and has stunning views, as does the more casual Tavern Room. Hudson House River Inn offers a good lunch menu, a very nice prix-fixe Sunday brunch, and an outstanding wine list. Even so, the real reason to eat here at dinner is the steak. They've been cooking beef at the inn for more than a hundred years. Practice makes perfect, and in this case, practice means perfect steaks. The steaks here are dry-aged, hand-cut prime beef, broiled exactly to your specifications and served on a heated plate. Choose the perfect homemade steak fries as a side dish. You don't have to order steak here—well-prepared fish and pasta entrees are also options, but this isn't the place for a vegetarian. Hudson House offers excellent value in a prix-fixe dinner menu that includes a steak option (also really good desserts, including apple strudel). Dinner reservations strongly suggested; reservations for lunch and brunch only for parties of six or more.

Plumbush Inn at the Parrott House, 1656 Rte. 9D, Cold Spring, NY 10516; (845) 265-3904; plumbushinn.com; Traditional American; $$$$. The elegant Plumbush Inn is housed in the ornate Parrott House, a Victorian mansion built in 1867 as the residence of Robert Parker Parrott, inventor of the Parrott gun, the rifled cannon that came into use during the Civil War. It was later the residence of Marquise Agnes Rizzoli dei Ritii, who began life as the American-born Agnes Shewan (that's her portrait hanging over the mantel in the Rose Room), and became an inn and restaurant after her death in the 1970s. The mansion has been authentically restored and sits among beautifully maintained gardens and lawns. The Plumbush Inn is primarily a destination spot for weddings, corporate meetings, and other events. The restaurant, however, is open to the public Wed through Sun for lunch, dinner, and Sun brunch. The lovely dining rooms are great places for that special celebratory meal. The cuisine here is rustic American, which means the menu features seasonal, fresh foods in traditional dishes. Signature dishes here are whole-grain mustard and maple-glazed Alaskan salmon with Egyptian lentil stew and the Plumbush Inn beef Wellington.

Riverview Restaurant, 45 Fair St., Cold Spring, NY 10516; (845) 265-4778; riverdining.com; New American; $$. As the name suggests, Riverview Restaurant is located right on the Hudson, with spectacular views of Storm King Mountain and the beautiful Hudson Highlands. This casually elegant eatery offers full lunch and dinner menus with a strong selection of well-prepared seafood dishes. Riverview also has a wood-fired brick pizza oven that turns out imaginative variations on the basics, such as the Parisian pizza topped with smoked ham, brie, and fresh thyme. The scenery inside Riverview is as attractive as outside—the restaurant is also a gallery featuring rotating exhibits of work by outstanding local artists. The works are displayed in seven different locations throughout the airy restaurant. Dinner reservations recommended. A word of warning: The restaurant does not accept credit cards.

RoundUp Texas BBQ, 2741 Rte. 9, Cold Spring, NY 10516; (845) 809-5557; rounduptxbbq.com; Barbecue; $$. Don't be put off by the unassuming appearance of RoundUp Texas BBQ. In fact, with its order window, picnic-table seating, large cold-beer sign, and parking lot that's often filled with motorcycles, this restaurant definitely qualifies as a joint. The authentic barbecue, prepared in a separate smoker by a couple of warmhearted expatriate Texans, easily overcomes the lack of anything close to ambience. The entrees are all prepared with dry rubs and smoked until the meat falls off the bone; the brisket takes a full 18 hours to prepare. Also on the menu are chicken, sausage, and even smoked hot dogs. The traditional sides of potato salad, coleslaw, corn bread, and ranch beans are all freshly made and are as carefully prepared and seasoned as the meat. The combination platters, offering two meats and two sides, or even three meats and three sides for hearty eaters, are the best way to sample the full range of flavors. This restaurant is very kid- and dog-friendly.

Cafes & Quick Bites

Cold Spring Coffee Pantry, 3091 Rte. 9, Cold Spring, NY 10516; (845) 265-2840; coldspringcoffeepantry.com; **Coffeehouse; $.** Featuring a rotating menu of international coffees from great roasters (including **Irving Farm** in Millerton—see p. 67), Cold Spring Coffee Pantry also offers gourmet croissant sandwiches and a good range of fresh, locally made pastries. The coffee is good and hot, the food is good, the people are friendly, and the Wi-Fi is free. A great spot for a quick breakfast, lunch, or break. The shop may be a bit hard to find—it's inside **Vera's Philipstown Fruit and Vegetable Market** (see p. 17). Open every weekday from 6:30 a.m. to 6:30 p.m.; 7:30 a.m. to 6:30 p.m. on weekends.

Frozenberry, 116 Main St., Cold Spring, NY 10516; (845) 809-5323; frozenberry.net; **Yogurt; $.** Frozen yogurt is the main attraction at this storefront cafe. The self-service approach lets you mix and match yogurt flavors and toppings to create your own specialty. Frozenberry also offers a quick menu of freshly prepared salads, paninis, and wraps, along with smoothies and a full coffee bar. **Additional location:** 6 Broad St., Fishkill, NY 12524; (845) 897-0615.

Go-Go Pops, 64 Main St., Cold Spring, NY 10516; (845) 809-5600; facebook.com/go-go-pops; **Ice Cream; $.** Go-Go Pops started out selling their handmade fresh fruit ice pops at local Hudson Valley greenmarkets. The shop offers the pops along with handmade baked goods, fresh juices, smoothies, bubble tea, Go-Go Joe (fair-trade organic coffee), cocoa with handmade marshmallows, and great soups. When the kids need a break from exploring Cold Spring, or when it's time for lunch, this is a good stop for them and their accompanying adults. In addition to more traditional flavors such as fudge, orange cream, and raspberry lemon, the shop offers imaginative combinations such as banana pudding, cucumber chile, and the very surprising Green Fairy pop, made with avocado.

Moo-Moo's Creamery, 32 West St., Cold Spring, NY 10516; (845) 204-9230; facebook.com/moomooscreamery; Ice Cream; $. Moo-Moo's Creamery makes some of the very best ice cream in the region, and serves it in really big scoops. The ice cream is made fresh every day; the shop offers over a hundred different flavors, with 17 available on any given day. The flavors rotate, so the fabulous banana walnut, Mexican chocolate, and caramel cashew may not be available that day. Just go with some other house specialty instead, like hazelnut gelato or coffee. Moo-Moo's is very popular, especially in the summer. Friendly and efficient service keeps the line moving. Moo-Moo's is a bit hard to find because it's right on the waterfront on the far side of the railroad tracks. From the foot of Main Street in Cold Spring, look toward the Hudson for the sign saying "To River," which leads to a tunnel under the tracks. Emerge onto the extension of Main Street, follow it for another block, then turn right onto West Street. Enjoy your ice cream and the views in nearby Dockside Park. Closed during the winter months.

Silver Spoon Restaurant and Bar, 124 Main St., Cold Spring NY 10516; (845) 265-2525; silverspooncoldspring.com; Traditional American; $$. The Silver Spoon is an informal, reasonably priced oasis for the hungry. If you're planning to hike or bike nearby Breakneck Ridge or Mt. Taurus, the Silver Spoon is the right spot to fortify yourself with an outstanding breakfast, starting at 9 a.m. Later in the day, sandwiches, wraps, and burgers are the popular choices; there's a full dinner menu.

Farm Bounty

Cold Spring Indoor Farmers' Market, Philipstown Recreation Center; 107 Glenclyffe Dr., Garrison, NY 10524; csfarmmarket
.org. Sat. from 8:30 a.m. to 1:30 p.m., mid-Nov. to early May.

Cold Spring Outdoor Farmers' Market, Boscobel House &
Gardens, 1601 Rte. 9D, Garrison, NY 10524; csfarmmarket.org. Sat.
from 8:30 a.m. to 1:30 p.m., mid-May through mid-Nov.

Glynwood Farm, 362 Glynwood Rd., Cold Spring, NY 10516;
(845) 265-3338; glynwood.org. Glynwood Farm is a working 225-acre
farm with a CSA and a farm store, but it's also a nonprofit foundation
working to empower communities to support farming and conserve
farmland. The foundation models and promotes environmentally
sustainable agriculture that farmers and landowners can use to take
advantage of new and emerging markets. It's a big mission that Glynwood handles with skill and imagination. Glynwood sponsors The Apple
Project, designed to not only preserve the Hudson Valley's historic role
as a center of apple production in the state but to revitalize it, taking
advantage of new laws allowing farm cider production and new interest in cider as an alcoholic beverage. Glynwood organizes **Cider Week**
each October—see p. 308 for details. The farm store offers seasonal
fare and prepared dishes, along with high-quality local products such
as Hudson Valley cheeses, locally milled flour and grains, and locally
grown fruit. See the recipe for **Glynwood Apple Soup** on p. 312. Store
hours during the CSA season are Tues, 3 p.m. to 6 p.m.; Fri, 3 p.m. to 6
p.m.; and Sat, 9 a.m. to 1 p.m.

Vera's Philipstown Fruit and Vegetable Market, 3091
**Rte. 9, Cold Spring, NY 10516; (845) 265-2151; facebook.com/philips
townmarket.** A local favorite for fresh fruits and vegetables, along with

Community-Supported Agriculture

Community-supported agriculture, or CSA, is a way for farmers and community members to come together and support local farms. At a CSA farm, members purchase a share of the harvest in the early spring. This helps the farmer get the money needed to buy seeds and equipment to begin planting for the season. In return for their share price, members get a steady portion of the harvest through a weekly distribution of whatever is ripe that week. Most CSAs provide produce to their members for about 22 weeks, from early in the spring when the first greens are available into the early fall, when the winter root crops are harvested. Some CSAs also offer fruit shares, egg shares, and winter vegetable shares. Some CSAs are CSAs only, with all the produce going to the members. Others are bigger farms that also sell their produce at farmers' markets and farm stands. In this book, the CSAs are listed under the heading Farm Bounty.

The beauty of CSA is that the members and the farmers share the risks and share the rewards. The farmers know from early on that they have a market for their produce and get a cash infusion when they need it in the early spring. Just as important is that the farmers and the members get to know and trust each other—that's the community-supported part of the arrangement. The members get abundant weekly shares of picked-that-day produce. On the other hand, if bad weather or some sort of farm catastrophe means

cheese, homemade doughnuts and other baked goods, fresh bread, freshly made mozzarella, cider, Italian ices, and a nice selection of imported pastas and other gourmet items. This is also a great place to that the harvest is slim for a few weeks, the members share in that as well. Generally speaking, CSA farmers plan for disaster by planting a wide range of crops. If some crops aren't doing well, others are bound to be flourishing. The share basket still gets filled, though perhaps not to the top and perhaps not with your favorite vegetables that week.

CSA farms encourage their members to visit the farm and volunteer to help out. Volunteering give members insight into the day-to-day operations of a working farm—and new appreciation of how hard their CSA farmers work and how dedicated they are. Many CSAs have potluck suppers, harvest dinners, workshops, cooking demos, and other events for members.

A full CSA share is a lot of produce—it's meant to feed a hungry family of four for a week. If you can't use that much produce, most CSA farms let you purchase a half share or split a share with someone. Policies vary if you can't make your scheduled pickup. Some CSAs let you designate someone else to take your share; others will donate it to a local food bank. Whatever the policy, you can be sure the food won't go to waste.

In the Hudson Valley, community-supported agriculture is increasingly popular—so popular that some farms have waiting lists. If you want to sign up, do it early in the season. Most CSAs have pickups at the farm once or twice a week; some also have pickups at a central location off the farm. A few offer delivery to members in New York City.

pick up annuals, perennials, and other garden supplies. Open daily, 8 a.m. to 6:30 p.m., from mid-Mar to the end of Dec.

Garrison

The Bird & Bottle Inn, 1123 Old Albany Post Rd. (Route 9), Garrison, New York 10524: (845) 424-2333; thebirdandbottleinn .com; New American: $$$$. The Bird & Bottle Inn has been serving guests since 1761, when it was a coach stop on the road between Albany and New York City. At this lovingly restored historic inn you can dine by the fireside in the Tap Room, bask in the romantic setting of the Map Room (excellent choice for a date), or enjoy your meal in the cozy Inn dining room. The inn may be historic and filled with antiques, but the food here is based on a contemporary seasonal menu that draws heavily from Hudson Valley producers. The dessert menu gets the seasonal treatment as well, meaning that in the fall, for instance, the flourless chocolate cake is served with pumpkin gelato. The Inn's famed Champagne brunch on Sunday features gourmet takes on the classics, such as Scotch eggs with smoked salmon served on crisp potato pancakes.

Tavern at Highlands Country Club, 955 Rte. 9D, Garrison NY 10524; (845) 424-3254; highlandscountryclub.net/tavern; New American; $$$$. The winter-season sister restaurant to **Valley at the Garrison** (see opposite page), Tavern features the same engaged approach to ingredients. Those that aren't grown on the 2-acre farm at Valley are sourced locally whenever possible; the beer and wine lists feature many Hudson Valley producers. Tavern Restaurant is open only from mid-December through March, so the menu tends to feature food that matches well with wintery weather, such as crispy pork belly with grits, roasted local beets, and confit garlic in an herb- and sherry-infused jus. The corn bread that arrives at the table soon after you're seated is simply wonderful. The atmosphere at Tavern is cozy and relaxed, with attentive service, a lovely hammered copper bar, and a fireplace; there's an outdoor terrace with fire pit for warmer weather. Reservations are suggested; at the start and end of the season, call ahead to be sure the restaurant is open. Tavern is located in the rugged Hudson Highlands, so check the weather first to avoid driving through a snowstorm on narrow, icy roads.

Valley at the Garrison, 2015 Rte. 9 (Snake Hill Road), Garrison, New York 10524; (845) 424-3604; thegarrison.com; New American; $$$$. The spectacularly beautiful golf course at the Garrison is matched by the spectacular food served at Valley, the restaurant at the clubhouse. Valley takes the farm-to-table concept to the max: Much of the produce served at the restaurant is grown in an adjoining 2-acre kitchen garden. The signature salad at Valley features nine different lettuces, all grown on the premises. Similarly, the ingredients for other dishes are locally sourced whenever possible. The main course polenta dish, for instance, is made with ramps, garlic confit, and smoked Toussaint cheese from **Sprout Creek Farm** in Poughkeepsie (see p. 99). Thursday night is Eat Local, offering a lounge menu that includes burgers and small plates. The elegant but relaxed dining room, designed by acclaimed architect Tony Chi, has a wall of windows that give stunning views out onto the Hudson Highlands, the Hudson River, and mighty Storm King Mountain on the far side of the river. Valley is open seasonally mid-Mar to mid-Dec; dinner is served Thurs through Sun. At the start and end of the season, call ahead to be sure the restaurant is open. Reservations strongly suggested.

Maple Syrup Madness

Only Vermont produces more maple syrup than New York State—and a fair amount of that syrup is produced in the Hudson Valley. Visiting a maple syrup farm is a lot of fun. The old-fashioned method of tapping a maple sugar tree and hanging a bucket from it have given way to high-tech production methods that involve miles of plastic tubing, reverse osmosis machines, and heat-exchanging evaporators. The process is fascinating to watch. Most of the maple farms listed here open their doors to visitors for the annual Maple Weekend every March (nysmaple.com), and are often open to visitors at other times of the year (check the websites or call ahead). Maple Weekend events includes demonstrations, pancake breakfasts, tastings, and lots of great stuff for the kids to do. March in the Hudson Valley can be chilly and wet—dress for the weather. The maple products, which go far beyond just syrup, can be purchased at the farm, online, and at many local farmers' markets and events.

Cronin's Maple Farm, 2109 Rte. 52, Hopewell Junction, NY 12533; (845) 226-3815; croninsmaplefarm.com; see listing description on p. 51.

Hummingbird Ranch, 18 Hummingbird Way, Staatsburg, NY 12580; (845) 266-0084; hummingbirdranch.biz; see listing description on p. 129.

Madava Farms, 47 McCourt Rd., Dover Plains, NY 12522; (845) 877-0640; crownmaple.com; see listing description on p. 44.

Niese's Maple Farm, 136 Wiccopee Rd., Putnam Valley, NY 10579; (845) 526-3748; niesesmaplefarm.com; see listing description on p. 23.

Platte Creek Maple Farm, 808 Glasco Tpke., Saugerties, NY; (845) 853-4240; facebook.com/plattecreekmaplefarm; see listing description on p. 280.

Remsburger Maple Farm and Apiary, 756 Traver Rd., Pleasant Valley, NY 12569; (845) 635-9168; remsburgermaple.com; see listing description on p. 79.

Farm Bounty

St. Christopher's Inn Farmers' Market, St. Christopher's Inn Thrift Shop, 21 Franciscan Way (Graymoor building), Garrison, NY 10524; (845) 335-1141. Fri, 10 a.m. to 2:30 p.m., mid-Apr to late Nov.

Putnam Valley

Farm Bounty

Niese's Maple Farm, 136 Wiccopee Rd., Putnam Valley, NY 10579; (845) 526-3748; niesesmaplefarm.com. Seven generations of the Niese family have been boiling maple syrup in the Hudson Valley since 1892, making them the oldest family producers in southern New York. Niese's participates every year in the New York Maple Weekend during the last two weekends of March. Glenn and Doreen Niese are also Certified Maple Educators who share their knowledge and history year-round with any group that's interested—the farm tour includes a hearty pancake breakfast. The farm is open Wed through Fri, 10 a.m. to 4 p.m.; weekends 9 a.m. to 4 p.m.; closed Mon and Tues.

Putnam Valley Farmers' Market, Grace United Methodist Church, 337 Peekskill Hollow Rd., Putnam Valley NY 10579. Fri from 3 p.m. to 7 p.m., June through Sept.

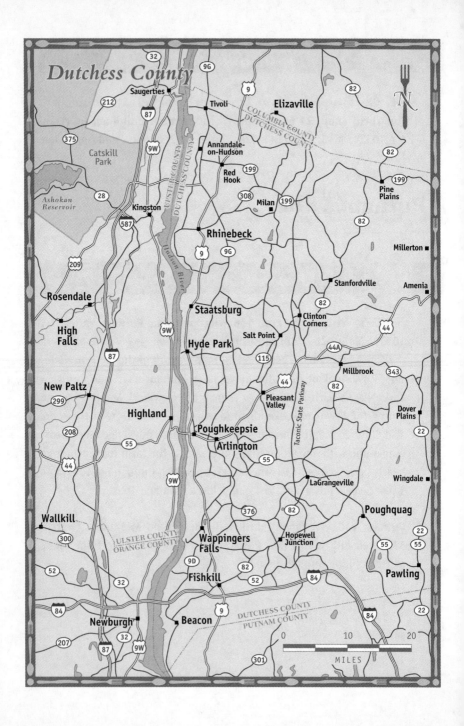

Dutchess County

The deep roots of Dutchess County date back to the earliest days of Dutch settlement in the early 1600s. In later years, the countryside became a major agricultural region full of dairy farms and lush orchards. The river towns and cities, however, became major manufacturing regions, shipping goods first by water down the Hudson and then by the railroads that ran along the river and crisscrossed the area. Much of the northern part of the county remains semirural and agricultural. In the southern portion, suburbanization and industry, such as IBM's major facility in Fishkill, have taken away some of the rural charm, but a surprising amount still remains along the back roads.

The decline of manufacturing over the decades left small cities such as Beacon and Poughkeepsie with shrinking populations and deserted downtowns. More recently, that situation has changed for the better— a lot. Less than a hundred miles from New York City and full of space begging to be renovated and repurposed, these places have become magnets for artists of all sorts. The opening in 2005 of the amazing Dia:Beacon art museum, in the factory building that once printed the cartons for Nabisco's animal cracker cookies, was a major catalyst for growth in arts tourism in the region. The many historic small towns in the county, such as Rhinebeck and Millbrook, are also magnets for tourism. At the same time, the influence of the Culinary Institute of America in Hyde Park has spread throughout the entire Hudson Valley. On top of that, the region is full of productive farms (more than 600 of them), orchards, and food artisans. In Dutchess County, talented chefs, farm abundance, and an appreciative audience have all come together to create a food lover's paradise.

Amenia

Foodie Faves

Serevan, 6 Autumn Ln. at Route 44, Amenia, NY 12501; (845) 373-9800; seravan.com; Mediterranean; $$$$. Soon after the doors of Serevan opened in 2005, this outstanding restaurant was acclaimed as one of the finest in the Hudson Valley. Over the years, Serevan has only improved, while Chef Serge Madikians has won award after award for his richly imaginative blending of Middle Eastern and Mediterranean cuisines. Well-known in the area for his innovative use of local produce and support of local farmers and purveyors, Chef Serge varies every aspect of his menu weekly, crafting the dishes from what is freshest and best and infusing them with multicultural flavors that lift them to another level. At Serevan, diver scallops, an appetizer found on many upscale menus, rise to an entirely different plane when served as a ceviche beside a citrus salad made with Osetra caviar and Persian saffron. Similarly, the very popular main course dish Chicken Bastillia is made with free-range chicken seasoned with cloves and cardamom, braised with golden raisins and romaine in an orange-curry broth, and served wrapped in layers of phyllo. The rich Middle Eastern tradition of delicately flavored desserts is honored here with choices such as honeydew soup with saffron, rose water, and yogurt sorbets. A carefully chosen wine list means that there is always a good pairing for the dishes. Serevan is in a comfortable house that dates back to the late 1800s. The uncrowded dining room has a lovely fireplace and offers views into the small open kitchen. In warm weather, enjoy outdoor dining on the patio, where Chef Serge also grows the herbs he uses in the kitchen. Serevan is open for dinner only, Thurs through Mon, 5 p.m. to 10 p.m. Reservations are very strongly suggested.

Troutbeck Inn and Conference Center, 515 Leedsville Rd., Amenia, NY 12501; (845) 373-9681; troutbeck.com; New American; $$$$. The Troutbeck Inn and Conference Center is located on 43 lush acres of gardens and woods. As the name suggests, it's primarily a place for corporate retreats, weddings, and similar events, but the public is welcome from Friday dinner through Sunday brunch. The restaurant is the historic stone manor of the original estate, which dates back to 1765. The food here is contemporary American cuisine with a hint of a French accent. The menu features beautifully prepared classics such as Black Angus strip steak, stuffed paupiettes of sole, and leg of lamb. The attentive service and English country house decor make dining here a pleasure, perfect for special occasions and celebrations. Reservations are strongly suggested.

Cafes & Quick Bites

Back in the Kitchen, 3312 Main St. (Route 343), Amenia, NY 12501; (845) 789-1444; Breakfast/Brunch; $$. Open only for breakfast and lunch, Back in the Kitchen offers an array of home-baked pastries (including real jelly doughnuts); gluten-free pastries are always available. The rich, creamy yogurt comes from nearby Hammond Dairy. The wonderful, fresh-brewed coffee comes from Intelligentsia. At lunchtime, there's always a good choice of sandwiches, salads, entrees, and a daily special or two. The soups here are particularly good. They're well-made and interesting, plus many are gluten-free. Open daily from 7 a.m. to 3 p.m.; on Sun from 8 a.m. to 1 p.m.

Specialty Stores & Producers

Andrea's Pasta di Casa, 3312 Main St. (Route 343), Amenia, NY 12501; (845) 789-1414. Andrea herself makes the fresh pasta, sauces, and Italian specialties to go here. Her ravioli are particularly good—plumply stuffed with a variety of fillings, including meat, spinach, Gorgonzola, and ricotta. The *ragù* and fresh pesto sauce are customer favorites. Special dishes, such as lasagna for 12, need to be ordered in advance. The store is upstairs, above the **Back in the Kitchen** cafe (see p. 27).

Cascade Mountain Winery, 835 Cascade Rd., Amenia, NY 12501; (845) 373-9021; cascademt.com. When the Wetmore family planted their vineyard on the slopes of Cascade Mountain in 1972, they were pioneers in producing wine on the east side of the Hudson River. The winery was built in 1977. Today, Cascade Mountain Winery produces a full line of award-winning table wines, including a dry white Seyval Blanc, Harvest Rosé, and a new release called Coeur de Lion, a Beaujolais-style red. The wine and tapas bar at Cascade Mountain is a popular weekend destination, open 11 a.m. to 5 p.m. on Sat, Sun, and Mon holidays. Picnic lunches to enjoy on the beautiful grounds are also available. On many weekends, Cascade Mountain offers special artisan tastings, pairing their wines with food from local producers.

Farm Bounty

Amenia Indoor Farmers' Market, Town Hall (4988 Rte. 22), Amenia, NY 12501; ameniafarmersmarket.com. First and third Sat, 10 a.m. to 2 p.m., Oct through Apr.

Amenia Outdoor Farmers' Market, Town Hall (4988 Rte. 22), Amenia, NY 12501; ameniafarmersmarket.com. Fri from 3 to 7 p.m., mid-May through Oct.

Beacon

Foodie Faves

Beacon Falls Cafe, 472 Main St., Beacon, NY 12508; (845) 765-0172; beaconfallscafe.com; New American; $$. The menu at Beacon Falls Cafe concentrates on well-prepared comfort food served in a relaxed bistro atmosphere. This is a good choice for a meal before an event at the nearby Howland Cultural Center. The focus is on generously sized burgers, but the menu also includes a good range of standard bistro entrees, such as *steak frites* and double-cut pork chops. The wine and beer lists at Beacon Falls Cafe are unusually interesting. The beer list is a carefully chosen selection of bottled micro-brew beers, from both local and international craft breweries; draft beers and beer flights are also available. Ditto for the wine list. It rotates with the seasons; the focus is California and local wines with a handful of unusual international bottles. A wine flight is a good way to sample the choices. Alternatively, visit on a Thursday night and enjoy special prices on wine by the glass. The cafe is closed Tues and Wed.

BJ's Restaurant, 213 Main St., Beacon, NY 12508; (845) 831-1221; facebook.com/bjsrestaurant; Soul Food; $$. With all the hoopla about new restaurants in the area, it's easy to overlook a stalwart such as BJ's Restaurant. This soul food storefront has been here for over 35 years, long before the foodies arrived. BJ's serves up Southern specialties that include fabulous fried chicken (served with the traditional waffles), oxtails (very hard to find anywhere else), and impeccably prepared collards, corn bread, mac and cheese, and other traditional sides. For dessert, try whatever homemade cake is on offer that day.

Brothers' Trattoria, 465 Main St., Beacon, NY 12508; (845) 838-3300; brotherstrattoria.com; Italian/Pizza; $$–$$$. Brothers' Trattoria has a bit of a split personality. One part of the trattoria is the informal pizza restaurant, offering pizza, hot and cold hero sandwiches, salads, and selected entrees. As the line out the door shows, the pizza is among the best in the area. The formal dining room is an elegant but still casual space, with northern Italian accents reminiscent of Tuscany. The extensive dinner menu at Brothers' focuses on classic northern Italian cuisine. It's well worth sampling, particularly the veal dishes. What's most fun about the dining room, however, is that personal-size specialty pizzas are on the menu. Pizza lovers don't often get to enjoy their favorite in white-tablecloth surroundings with friendly service and an extensive wine list.

Cafe Amarcord, 276 Main St., Beacon, NY 12508; (845) 440-0050; cafeamarcordbeacon.com; New American; $$$. Named in homage to the 1973 Fellini film about life in a small Italian village in the 1930s, the amber walls of Cafe Amarcord are decorated with vintage movie posters for the great director's movies. In keeping with the name, the menu here offers contemporary American dishes with a distinct touch of Italy. Appetizers such as the layered beet and goat cheese gâteau with crushed walnuts and pomegranate sauce and entrees such as grilled Berkshire pork chop served with sweet potato mash are definitely new American cuisine. The pasta dishes, however, are definitely Italian, including pappardelle with black pepper ricotta and gnocchi with oxtails. Somewhere in between are dishes such as the green bean tempura appetizer, topped with Parmesan and served with cognac herb mayonnaise. It's all served in a cozy dining room with friendly, unrushed service. The wine list offers a good choice of bottles and glasses.

Cup & Saucer Restaurant and Tea Room, 165 Main St., Beacon, NY 12508; (845) 831-6287; cupandsaucer.wix.com; Tearoom; $$. A British-style tearoom serving lunch and afternoon tea, the Cup & Saucer offers wraps, quiches, salads, crepes, and desserts, including traditional British dishes such as cottage pie. An alternative to the menu is the tea party for one, which includes finger sandwiches, the restaurant's famous scones, a mini dessert, and, of course, a pot of tea. The charming dining room is in a turn-of-the-20th-century building with a tin ceiling. The atmosphere here is upscale casual; reservations are suggested.

DimsumGoGo, 448 Main St., Beacon, NY 12508; (845) 831-8886; dimsumgogobeacon.com; Chinese; $$. If the restaurant scene in the Hudson Valley lacks something, it's authentic Chinese cuisine. Fortunately, DimsumGoGo is remedying that sad situation. The Beacon outpost of the well-known Chinatown dim sum restaurant is located in a former bank building (the 4-ton door to the bank vault is still visible by the bar) near the Beacon Theater and Howland Cultural Center. The restaurant offers two separate menus: a full menu of traditional Chinese dishes and a full menu of dim sum (individual small bites of dumplings, buns, and other traditional steamed dishes). If you're ordering dim sum, you'll be handed a menu and asked to check the boxes for the dishes you want. The check is calculated by adding up the plates on your table and multiplying by the flat price per dish. Eating at DimsumGoGo is relaxed and fun—and it opens your eyes to flavors, such as sticky rice in a lotus leaf and taro with pork, that are hard to find anywhere else.

Gerardo's Seafood Cafe, 244 Main St., Beacon, New York 12508; (845) 831-8500; facebook.com/GerardosSeafoodCafe; Seafood; $$–$$$. The only seafood restaurant in all of Beacon, Gerardo's is a small (it seats only 20 guests), casual, storefront restaurant with lots of exposed brick. The menu offers seafood selections carefully chosen to match the market and the season. The usual standards, including fish-and-chips and crab cakes, are prepared with as much care as the more ambitious offerings, such as the Caribbean seared sea scallops appetizer, served with pineapple coconut risotto and Scotch bonnet rum molasses, and the dinner entree of honey lemon thyme roasted salmon with pomegranate molasses, sautéed escarole, and parsnip puree. The presentations are lovely and the service is professional. Specials such as butternut squash and crabmeat soup enliven the menu further. Open for lunch and dinner.

Isamu, 240 Main St., Beacon, NY 12508; (845) 440-0002; isamu beacon.com; Japanese; $$. With a dinner menu that's seven pages long, Isamu sets a high standard for local Japanese food. The menu contains a number of standard Chinese items, but the focus is on Japanese food. Look for big bowls of noodles, a creative variety of hand rolls, and a standard set of sushi, sashimi, teriyaki, and tempura offerings. Bento boxes at lunch or dinner are well prepared and offer excellent value. The chef's specials here are more on the Chinese side. The Isamu duck wrap is a simplified but delicious version of Peking duck, made with crispy duck breast, scallions, and cucumber with hoisin sauce. The wine and beer list at Isamu is limited. If you want to bring your own, the restaurant charges a corkage fee.

Max's on Main, 246 Main St., Beacon, NY 12508; (845) 838-6297; maxsonmain.com; Traditional American; $$. Every town needs a local restaurant with reliably good food, a lively bar, capable staff, and an owner who greets every guest like an old friend. Max's on Main is that place in Beacon. The half-pound burgers here are always a good choice. Even better are the sandwiches, such as The Taking of Chicken 1-2-3, made with grilled chicken on a toasted ciabatta roll with melted swiss cheese, bacon, lettuce, tomato, red onion, and pesto mayonnaise. Max's is open 7 days a week. On weekend evenings, there's live music featuring local performers. Tuesday night is trivia night in the bar; Thursday is steak night.

Poppy's Burgers & Fries, 184 Main St., Beacon, NY 12508; (845) 765-2121; poppyburger.com; Traditional American/Burgers; **$$.** Poppy's opened in 2009 as a storefront farm-to-table restaurant featuring burgers made with grass-fed, humanely raised beef from Kiernan Farm in Gardiner, across the Hudson in Ulster County. These are burgers as they should be, with a rich beef flavor that is a revelation. Local farms provide the vegetables, and the fries are hand-cut. Poppy's got an extra boost when Chef Paul "Poppy" Yeaple won first place on the Food Network's chef competition show *Chopped* in 2010. In 2013, the restaurant went through a major renovation that added seats and expanded the menu offerings to include delicious desserts from the in-house pastry chef. Poppy's now has a bar featuring local craft beers and local wines. The nonalcoholic drinks list continues to offer a large selection of hard-to-find cane sugar sodas, including Mexican Coke. Closed Mon and Tues.

River Terrace Bar and Restaurant, 2 Beekman St., Beacon, NY 12508; (845) 831-5400; beaconriverterrace.com; Italian; **$$.** Located right on the Hudson, River Terrace Bar and Restaurant offers amazing views of the river, the Beacon–Newburgh Bridge, and the surrounding hilly terrain. If you can, time your visit for the warmer weather so you can eat outdoors on the terrace and enjoy the scenery.

The food here is fairly standard Italian and American regional fare, nicely prepared and served by a friendly staff. Check the seafood specials and ask your server about the unusual Egyptian dishes scattered here and there on the menu.

Sukhothai, 516 Main St., Beacon, NY 12508; (845) 790-5375; suk hotthainy.com; Thai; $$. Located at the far end of Beacon's bustling Main Street, Sukhothai is a spacious storefront in a brick building that is said to date back to 1818. Inside, the simple dining room has bare brick walls decorated with temple rubbings. The food at Sukhothai is traditional Thai, prepared precisely to your requested level of spiciness. The level of authenticity is high, with a wider range of dishes than usual. To confirm that, try the Thai curry sampler, which offers four kinds of curry—Panang, Massaman, green, and red with your choice of chicken, beef, pork, shrimp, tofu, or vegetables. Each variation is a distinctly different take on the curry theme. (Sadly, this option isn't available on Friday and Saturday.) There's also a wide selection of noodle dishes and some great desserts, including the restaurant's secret recipe fried ice cream.

Swift and the Roundhouse at Beacon Falls, 2 E. Main St., Beacon, NY 12508; (845) 765-8369; roundhousebeacon.com; New American; $$$. Beacon is an old industrial town that is now being revived by a lively arts and culinary scene centered on Main Street. At the far end of Main Street, overlooking Fishkill Creek and Beacon Falls, a cluster of derelict old mill buildings have been transformed into an architecturally stunning boutique hotel called the Roundhouse. Within the hotel are one fine dining restaurant (Swift), a sophisticated lounge serving artisanal cocktails and small plates (2EM), and a seasonal spot for casual alfresco dining (The Patio). Because the menus for all three locales are created by Executive Chef Brandon Collins (formerly of

Valley at the Garrison—see p. 21), the focus here will be on Swift. The restaurant's name honors Horatio Swift, who in the 19th century operated one of the mills here. The setting is spectacular—the spacious dining room seats 100 and has floor-to-ceiling windows looking out on Beacon Falls. The menu, austerely limited to only about 10 appetizers and 10 entrees at any given time, offers seasonally inspired dishes using local ingredients. The dishes are mostly sophisticated takes on the classics: the dry-aged strip steak comes with potatoes, but also sunchokes, pea greens, and black garlic. Some dishes are entirely original: The appetizer of octopus with white turnips, cipollini onions, and pink grapefruit won't be found anywhere else. Very unusually for restaurants in the area, the dessert menu includes a broad selection of dessert wines and after-dinner drinks. Reservations strongly suggested.

Cafes & Quick Bites

Bank Square Coffeehouse, 129 Main St., Beacon, NY 12508; (845) 440-7165; banksquarecoffeehouse.com; Coffeehouse; $. They take coffee seriously at the Bank Square Coffeehouse. This relaxing spot offers the best coffee drinks in Beacon, along with more than a dozen teas and a good range of bottled beers from local microbreweries. Try the Mt. Beacon roast, a dark-roasted Sumatran that Bank Square calls Beacon's official coffee. Pastries, salads, and lunch items are on hand, including gluten-free selections. The coffeehouse has a pleasant outdoor patio with river views and free Wi-Fi.

Beacon Bagel, 466 Main St., Beacon, NY 12508; (845) 440-6958; thebeaconbagel.com; Breakfast/Brunch; $. Bagels made on the premises are the foundation for the breakfast and lunch sandwiches served at Beacon Bagel. The variations on the basic breakfast egg sandwich here are amazing. The grilled sandwiches are also very good, even if a classic Cubano on a bagel takes a little getting used to. The house specialty is the Loaded Lox, made with locally prepared, nitrate-free lox and served with cream cheese, onions, capers, and a squeeze of lemon. Beacon Bagel offers vegetarian choices that are more than just afterthoughts, and also makes gluten-free bagels. Open 7 days a week, from 7 a.m. to 3 p.m. (4 p.m. on weekends).

Beacon Creamery, 134 Main St., Beacon, NY 12508; (845) 765-0444; facebook.com/beacon-creamery; Ice Cream; $. At Beacon Creamery's bright pink storefront, the menu is ice cream and nothing but. The store carries 24 flavors of **Jane's Ice Cream,** a popular local brand made in Kingston (see p. 21). The only options are the size and type of cone. Hours at the store are 1 to 9 p.m. Mon through Thurs; on weekends the store stays open until 10. Beacon Creamery also operates a cafe in the historic Beacon Theater down the road at 445 Main. The full cafe menu offers baked goods, soups, chili, light lunch items—and ice cream. The ice cream offerings here are a little different, however. Only eight of the most popular flavors from Jane's are available. To make up for this, however, the cafe offers Mercer's wine ice cream, made in Boonville, NY, near Utica. With flavors such as Cherry Merlot, Chocolate Cabernet, and Peach White Zinfandel, and with an alcohol content of 5 percent, this is ice cream for grown-ups only.

Carne, 512 Main St., Beacon, NY 12508; (845) 440-3699; facebook .com/carnebeacon; Sandwich Shop; $. Creative, hand-crafted sandwiches are the lure at this new addition to the Beacon food scene. The store opens early weekdays and serves breakfast choices, including made-to-order variations on egg sandwiches. From lunchtime until closing, Carne serves sandwiches, especially savory hot sandwiches, such as pulled pork with summer slaw on a kaiser roll and the Chorizo

Loco, a melted sandwich made with Cuban-style chorizo on a toasted ciabatta roll with *queso fresco* and black bean salsa. Other options here include great salads, such as the strawberry wheat berry salad with strawberry vinaigrette, and great homemade soups, including smoked chicken corn chowder. Open every weekday from 6 a.m. to 9 p.m.; Sat 9 a.m. to 9 p.m.; Sun 9 a.m. to 5:30 p.m.

Homespun Foods, 32 Main St., Beacon NY 12508; (845) 831-5096; homespunfoods.com; Sandwich Shop; $$. Eclectic and truly delicious sandwiches are the compelling reason for lunch at Homespun Foods. This is one of the very few places in the area to get an authentic *banh mi* (Vietnamese sandwich). An equally compelling reason for visiting Homespun Foods is the great selection of homemade cakes, cookies, bars, and tarts. The shop is very warm and welcoming; it has a lovely patio for eating outdoors. The shop also carries a wide selection of specialty foods, including a small but select cheese counter and high-end charcuterie offerings. Open 7 days a week, 11 a.m. to 5 p.m.; 8 a.m. to 5 p.m. on weekends. Homespun also operates the cafe at the Dia:Beacon museum, serving sandwiches, platters, soups, and desserts. The cafe is open during museum hours; there's no admission fee to eat here.

Seoul Kitchen, 469 Main St., Beacon NY 12508; (845) 765-8596; seoulkitchenbeacon.com; Korean; $$. Korean cuisine is a rarity in the Hudson Valley, making this tiny storefront restaurant very welcome to hungry diners looking for something a bit different. The food here, prepared by warmhearted chef-owner Heewon Marshall, is mostly vegetarian; the menu changes daily, depending on what's at the market that day. Seoul Kitchen is tiny, seating only about 10, and it's not exactly elegant—the food is served either buffet-style or in containers brought to the table. It's a good choice for a quick lunch or dinner or for takeout.

Tito Santana Taqueria, 142 Main St., Beacon, NY 12508; (845) 765-2350; tacosantana.com; Mexican/Tacos; $. Fast food, Mexican-style and reasonably priced, makes up the menu at Tito Santana Taqueria. Tacos (including vegan versions), quesadillas, and burritos are the main offerings. The fillings are all freshly prepared and seasoned exactly right. The combo pack plates are a great value and also a great way to sample the well-made sides of grilled corn on the cob, black beans, and guacamole with chips.

Zora Dora Paletaria, 201 Main St., Beacon, NY 12508; (646) 206-3982; zoradora.com; Ice Cream; $. A *paleta* is a Mexican popsicle, made with fresh fruit. *Paletas* at Zora Dora take the concept further by using only the very freshest local fruit and by making extremely imaginative combinations of fruit and other ingredients, such as pineapple, lime, chile, and sea salt. In all, the blackboard menu at Zora Dora lists 20 or more different variations on ice and ice cream pops; the offerings rotate with the seasons. A customer favorite is The Beacon, made with roasted peanut butter, chocolate chunks, and roasted bananas. Zora Dora is open seasonally in the warmer weather; in early spring and late fall, the shop may be open only on weekends. Check ahead.

Specialty Stores & Producers

All You Knead Bakery, 308 Main St., Beacon, NY 12508; (845) 440-8530; facebook.com/allyoukneadbakery. An artisan bakery producing outstanding breads using locally grown grains, All You Knead also sells great, freshly made sandwiches at lunchtime—on their own crusty bread, of course. The breads range from an olive loaf to a cranberry-raisin-walnut-currant loaf to a delicate challah. They also make ciabattas, baguettes, jalapeño cheddar bread, Irish soda bread, and cinnamon rolls. Their bialys, a delicacy hard to find in the region, are excellent; so are the bagels. If you can't get to the storefront shop, All You Knead sells at the Beacon and Cold Spring farmers' markets; the breads are also available at **Adams Fairacre** stores (see pp. 95, 138).

Alps Sweet Shop, 269 Main St., Beacon, NY 12508; (845) 831-8240; alpssweetshop.com.

In business as a chocolatier since 1922, Alps Sweet Shop offers more than a hundred different confections. In addition to classic chocolate delights such as glacé fruits, fudge, and truffles, Alps makes wonderful holiday specialties, including the cutest imaginable chocolate bunnies for Easter. The store is open 7 days a week, from 9 a.m. to 5 p.m.; Sun from 10 a.m. to 4 p.m. **Additional location:** 1054 Main St., Fishkill NY 12524; (845) 896-8080.

Artisan Wine Shop, 180 Main St., Beacon, NY 12508; (845) 440-6923; artisanwineshop.com.

Artisan Wine Shop specializes in natural, biodynamic, organic, and local wines, all hand-selected by the proprietors to be both ready to drink and affordable. Many are from lesser-known or small-production makers, meaning that they are unlikely to be found in the average wine store. Artisan arranges the wines by flavor profiles, going from light whites to full-bodied reds. The store holds lively, well-attended wine tastings, with food pairings prepared in the in-store kitchen, every Friday and Saturday.

Beacon Natural Market, 348 Main St., Beacon, NY 12508; (845) 838-1288; beaconnaturalmarket.com.

A community grocery store with a thorough selection of high-quality organic and natural products, including locally grown produce and local organic eggs, cheese, poultry, meat, and milk. The store has a juice bar and a good selection of gluten-free products.

Drink More Good, 259 Main St., Beacon, NY 12508; (845) 797-1838; drinkmoregood.com. This fun shop, a recent addition to the Main Street scene, sells 15 blends of organic and fair-trade loose tea, a huge selection of organic and fair-trade loose herbs and spices, and the fully flavored small-batch bitters, sodas, syrups, and tinctures that are Drink More Good's main products. The aroma alone makes the store worth a visit. Knowing that 10 percent of the profits go to Generosity Water, which works to make clean, safe water available to everyone, makes your purchase that much more satisfying.

Ella's Bellas, 418 Main St., Beacon, NY 12508; (845) 765-8502; facebook.com/ellasbellas. It's hard to believe, while enjoying an individual strawberry cheesecake or a slice of red velvet cake with raspberry filling and brown sugar butter cream at Ella's Bellas, that it's gluten-free, but it is! So is pretty much everything else at this storefront cafe. Ella's Bellas makes indulgent pastries and baked goods but also serves salads, soups, quiches, and even bread puddings. Open 8 a.m. to 4 p.m. Wed through Sat; 10 a.m. to 3 p.m. on Sun.

Gourmetibles, 494 Main St., Beacon, NY 12508; (845) 765-1165; gourmetible.com. A gourmetible isn't exactly a cookie, but it's not exactly a candy, either. As the owners of this fun store describe it, a gourmetible is a candy that thinks it's a cookie. Whatever it is, it's delicious and comes in eight different flavors, including Naked in the Dark, Peanut Butter Pretzel, and Pep'mint Power. The store also carries a good selection of candy and chocolates—you can buy gummi worms by the pound here.

The Hop, 458 Main St., Beacon, NY 12508; (845) 440-8676; the hopbeacon.com. A tasting room for craft beers and artisanal local food, The Hop offers over a hundred craft beers for purchase by the bottle and can. There's also a rotating list of nine different craft beers on tap available for tasting or to fill your growler. To go along with the beer, The Hop offers seasonal small plates, sandwiches, house-made sausages, terrines, and pâtés, local cheese plates, and gourmet sandwiches (including a vegan Reuben). The sausages and charcuterie products, all produced by Chef Matt Hutchins, are available for sale as well.

Pinoy Outlet, 301 Main St., Beacon, NY 12508; (845) 765-0227; pinoyoutlet.com. This storefront Filipino grocery has a large and interesting array of unfamiliar Asian food products. Seasonings, sauces, and condiments that are uncommon for the area, such as galingale powder, dried taro leaves, and papaya pickles, are on the shelves, along with dried seafood, canned goods, noodles, unusual rice varieties, and much more. The store does an extensive online business as well. Open Tues through Sun, 10 a.m. to 6 p.m.

Scarborough Fare, 257 Main St., Beacon, NY 12508; (845) 831-7247; scarboroughfarenp.com. See listing description on p. 263.

Utensil Kitchenware, 480 Main St., Beacon, NY 12508; (845) 202-7181; utensilkitchenware.com. Kitchenware stores tend to be very bare-bones and utilitarian. You get what you need, but the experience isn't particularly enjoyable. Not so at Utensil Kitchenware. Shopping here is fun. The store is airy and bright, with great window displays. The products are practical, stylish, and reasonably priced.

Farm Bounty

Beacon Farmers' Market, Beacon Sloop Club dock; Beacon, NY 12508; thebeaconfarmersmarket.com. Every Sun, 11 a.m. to 3 p.m.

Clinton Corners

Specialty Stores & Producers

Clinton Vineyards, 450 Schultzville Rd., Clinton Corners, NY 12514; (845) 266-5372; clintonvineyards.com. The 15 acres of Clinton Vineyards are devoted to cultivating Seyval Blanc vines to produce award-wining white wines, sparkling wine made in the classic *méthode champenoise,* and late-harvest dessert wines. In recent years, the offerings have expanded to include remarkable fruit dessert wines, including cassis, made from locally grown produce. Located in the rolling hills of northern Dutchess County, Clinton Vineyards is a beautiful place to visit. Guests can stroll through the vineyard, see the wine being made in a historic Dutch barn, visit the Champagne cellar, and sample the wines in a lovely tasting room. The property is open year-round, Thurs through Sun, from noon to 5:30 p.m. Hours vary a bit depending on the season and the weather; call ahead.

Farm Bounty

Knoll Krest Farm, 154 Old Bulls Head Rd., Clinton Corners, NY 12514; (845) 266-3845; knollkrestfarm.com. Knoll Krest raises

THE DUTCHESS WINE TRAIL

The official Dutchess Wine Trail (dutchesswinetrail.com) connects two wineries set among the rolling hills of eastern Dutchess County: **Clinton Vineyards** (see opposite page) and **Millbrook Vineyards & Winery** (see p. 62). Not part of the wine trail but still worth a visit are these other Dutchess County wineries:

Cascade Mountain Winery, 835 Cascade Rd., Amenia, NY 12501; (845) 373-9021; cascademt.com; see listing description on p. 28.

Oak Summit Vineyard, 372 Oak Summit Rd., Millbrook, NY 12545; (845) 677-9522; oaksummitvineyard.com; see listing description on p. 63.

free-range, organic chickens and eggs—it's one of the last egg farms in Dutchess County. The Messerich family has placed the farm into a conservation program that will protect it against development in the future. Knoll Krest products are sold at the Union Square Greenmarket in New York City all year round. In the warmer weather, look for them at local farmers' markets.

Meadowland Farm, 689 Schultzville Rd., Clinton Corners, NY 12514; (845) 554-6142; meadowlandfarmny.com. Historic Meadowland Farm has been in operation since 1790. Today, the farm sells its own grass-fed beef, pork, lamb, rabbits, poultry, and fresh eggs at their roadside stand and at local farmers' markets. The stand also carries home-grown vegetables in season. It's open most days from 9 a.m. to 6 p.m.; call ahead to check, especially in the winter. For larger cuts (quarters or more), call ahead to get on the waiting list.

Wild Hive Farm, 2411 Salt Point Tpke., Clinton Corners, NY 12514; (845) 266-0660; wildhivefarm.com. Longtime visitors to the region will remember with fondness the Wild Hive Cafe in Clinton Corners—it was a great place for breakfast or lunch, mostly because of the terrific baked goods. The cafe was closed in 2012 so that owner Don Lewis could concentrate on growing and milling grain at the Wild Hive Farm Community Grain Project. His goal is to reintroduce heritage wheats into the region and micromill them using stone-ground techniques. The richly flavorful grains and flours now produced by the project are available from the farm and at local farmers' markets and retailers.

Dover Plains

Farm Bounty

Madava Farms, 47 McCourt Rd., Dover Plains, NY 12522; (845) 877-0640; crownmaple.com. At President Obama's inaugural luncheon in 2013, Madava Farms' Crown maple syrup was featured in not one but two dishes: a butter squash puree and a Hudson Valley apple pie with Crown maple caramel sauce. There's a reason Crown maple syrup was selected to grace the presidential table: It's a superior product, produced organically from the 25,000 sugar and red maple trees that grow on the 800 acres of Madava Farms. A visit to Madava is an eye-opening look at what commitment to community and an intelligent approach to sustainable agriculture can achieve. On weekends, visitors can take a guided tour of the farm to see the maple syrup production process from tree to barrel. The Farm Stand Cafe, open on weekends, offers farm-to-table lunches made with seasonal ingredients from Madava's own garden and from local farm partners and craft breweries and wineries. The store offers Crown maple syrup and maple sugar, along with New York artisanal specialties. See the recipe for Madava Farms' **Crown Maple Blackberry Pork Chops** on p. 326.

Fishkill

Farm to Table Bistro, 1083 Rte. 9 (Lawrence Farms Market Square), Fishkill, NY 12524; (845) 297-1111; ftbistro.com; New American; $$$. As the name suggests, this restaurant strives to source as many of its ingredients as possible from local Hudson Valley farms, dairies, and other purveyors. In fact, they list all their local and regional providers on the menu and mention them by name in the dish names, such as the Taliaferro Farms organic beet salad, which uses fresh goat cheese from Sprout Creek Farm. The lunch and dinner menus here offer a good range of imaginatively prepared, seasonally based dishes. The dry-rubbed beer-braised short ribs are a popular favorite; ask your server about the butcher's cut for the day. The daily specials are a particularly good way to see what the restaurant is doing with whatever is freshest that day.

Hudson's Ribs and Fish, 1099 Rte. 9, Fishkill, NY 12524; (845) 297-5002; hudsonsribsandfish.com; Steak House; $$$. Ribs, steaks, and seafood are the main menu choices at this popular restaurant. Two things make Hudson's Ribs and Fish stand out beyond the usual high-end steak house. First, all dinners include Hudson's wonderful hot popovers, served with homemade strawberry butter. Second, the award-winning wine list here includes hundreds of well-chosen wines from American vineyards. The list includes many bottles from small or boutique vineyards that are hard to find anywhere else. The by-the-glass wine list is extensive as well, making this restaurant an excellent choice for wine lovers looking for a chance to sample new vintages.

Il Barilotto Enoteca, 1113 Main St., Fishkill, NY 12524; (845) 897-4300; ilbarilottorestaurant.com; Italian; $$$. Il Barilotto Enoteca is aptly named. In Italian, *barilotto* means wine barrel. An *enoteca* in Italy is a bistro-style restaurant with a good selection of local vintages. This is one of the finest Italian restaurants in the entire Hudson Valley—and it has an outstanding wine list that showcases Italian vineyards. The list focuses on lesser-known producers and lesser-known regions, giving Il Barilotto one of the most interesting cellars in the region. The food at this elegant but warm restaurant is beautifully prepared and served by a skilled and attentive staff. The dinner menu includes an outstanding selection of pasta dishes, such as the perfectly prepared *pappardelle al ragù d'anatra* (wide ribbon pasta with Tuscan duck *ragù*), that are rarely seen at other Italian restaurants. Even simple entrees, such as the roasted breast of chicken, are revelations when prepared here. The restaurant usually has at least two specials on any given evening. They're all worth trying, but if any have sausage in them, don't think twice—the sausage here is house-made and delectable. Il Barilotto is open for lunch and dinner; reservations for dinner only for groups of five or more.

Maya Cafe, 448 Rte. 9, Fishkill, NY 12524; (845) 896-4042; mayacafecantina.com; Mexican; $$. A popular local Mexican restaurant that's a big step up from the usual fare, Maya Cafe offers a good selection of standard dishes and combination platters. Unusually for a Mexican restaurant, the menu lists several very good vegetarian options that are serious efforts, not afterthoughts. It also takes fish tacos more seriously than most. What makes the menu here interesting, though, are the specials. Some, such as *poc-chuc* (pork filet marinated in Mayan spices, grilled, and served sizzling) have a genuine Mayan inflection. All are well prepared and flavorful. For the lunch crowd, Maya Cafe serves Mexican breakfast (a variety of really good egg dishes) from 11 a.m. to

3 p.m. Live mariachi music livens the restaurant up on weekends. A bit confusingly, Maya Cafe is the sister restaurant to **Cafe Maya** in Wappinger's Falls (see p. 137). The menus are the same.

Sapore Steakhouse, 1108 Main St., Fishkill, NY 12524; (845) 897-3300; saporesteakhouse.com; Steak House; $$$$. Sapore Steakhouse follows the classic chop house formula: dark wood decor with gilded mirrors, thick white linen on the table, gigantic menus, and comfy leather chairs and sofas in the lounge. The menu is classic as well, with all the usual appetizers, the usual dry-aged steak offerings, the usual range of non-steak entrees (including a token vegetarian paella), and the usual limited range of sides and desserts. What makes Sapore intriguing is the game section on the dinner menu. There aren't too many restaurants in the region where you can order elk, venison, buffalo, and game birds (even sometimes ostrich). More importantly, the kitchen knows what to do with these meats, as it does with all the other dishes. Lunch is served here only on weekdays; dinner every night.

Tanjore Cuisine of India, 992 Main St., Fishkill, NY 12524; (845) 896-6659; tanjoreindiancuisine.com; Indian; $$. Strip malls can contain surprisingly good restaurants, as Tanjore proves. This place is a bit of a hole-in-the-wall, and it won't win any awards for decor, but it offers a good range of authentic Indian dishes. The *dosas* (Indian crepes) on the dinner menu are particularly good. The wide selection of serious vegetarian dishes makes this restaurant a good choice for meat-avoiders and vegans. They do a particularly good version of *channa masala* (chickpeas Punjab-style). At lunchtime, Tanjore serves an all-you-can eat buffet that is an excellent value.

Toro, 1004 Main St., Fishkill, NY 12524; (845) 897-9691; toronew york.com; Korean; $$. Korean food is still a bit of a novelty in the Hudson Valley. Toro provides an excellent local introduction to this spicy cuisine. It's also one of the better places in the region for sushi and offers an extensive menu of over 20 different creative sushi rolls. The Korean dishes include some real standouts, such as *bibimbap* (the basic Korean rice bowl), *kimchi-chigae* (spicy kimchi soup with pork, tofu, mushrooms, and potato noodles), and *jae yook gui* (sautéed pork slices with spicy sauce). The menu also includes Korean barbecue dishes and sizzling stone bowl rice dishes. For the adventurous eater, there are some interesting specials, such as *bo-ssam* (steamed pork belly with spiced radish and Korean cabbage).

Cafes & Quick Bites

Frozenberry, 6 Broad St., Fishkill, NY 12524; (845) 897-0615; **frozenberry.net; Yogurt; $.** The Fishkill outlet for Frozenberry offers only self-serve frozen yogurt. See the listing description on p. 15.

Specialty Stores & Producers

Alps Sweet Shop, 1054 Main St., Fishkill, NY 12524; (845) 896-8080; **alpssweetshop.com.** See listing description on p. 39.

Joe's Italian Marketplace, 1083 Rte. 9 (Lawrence Farms); **Fishkill, NY 12524; (845) 297-1100; joesmarketplace.com.** The menu at this Italian deli offers a really good selection of hot and cold sandwiches and Italian specialties. The shelves are crammed with Italian imports, such as hard-to-find high-end olive oils and balsamic vinegars and an excellent cheese selection, including homemade fresh mozzarella. The butcher department offers premium organic meats, including game, goose, and rabbit, and a wide range of fresh sausages.

Farm Bounty

Fishkill Farmers' Market, Main Street Plaza, Fishkill, NY 12524; (845) 897-4430. Thurs from 9 a.m. to 4 p.m., late May to late Oct.

Obercreek Farm, 59 Marlorville Rd., Hughsonville, NY 12537; (845) 337-1906; obercreekfarm.com. Obercreek Farm took over the CSA operation of Common Ground Farm in Fishkill in 2013. For the first year, the produce for the members was brought in from **Hearty Roots Community Farm** in Clermont (see p. 159). Going forward, the produce comes from Obercreek's own 5 acres of outside land and four passive solar greenhouses (high tunnels).

Hopewell Junction

Foodie Faves

The Blue Fountain, 826 Rte. 376, Hopewell Junction, NY 12533; (845)226-3570; thebluefountain.com; Italian; $$. Family-owned and -operated since its opening in 1994, The Blue Fountain is a local favorite for reliably good Italian food. It's a good choice for a family meal. The menu offers a range of well-prepared Italian dishes, such as chicken *boscaiolo* (woodcutter's chicken, made with a grilled chicken breast topped with sautéed broccoli rabe, mushrooms, potatoes, and sun-dried tomatoes). The less adventurous can have individual pizzas from the brick oven. It's all served by a welcoming staff in very pleasant and spacious surroundings. There is indeed a blue fountain out front on the nicely landscaped lawn; in the warm weather, you can sit by it and enjoy a drink. Lunch is served Tues through Fri; dinner every night but Mon.

Le Chambord, 2737 Rte. 52, Hopewell Junction, NY 12533; (845) 221-1941; lechambord.com; French; $$–$$$. Le Chambord is beautiful inside and out. The romantic restaurant is in the main Inn house, an 1863 Georgian Colonial mansion with a remarkable pillared veranda. It's set in the midst of 10 acres of lawn and woods. Because Le Chambord is primarily a small, high-end country inn with an excellent kitchen, the main business here is corporate retreats, weddings, and similar events. The restaurant is open to the public, however. It's worth a visit, especially for a romantic date or special celebration. The restaurant offers a good prix-fixe menu that rotates with the seasons and the holidays. The dishes on the regular dinner menu are fairly standard French offerings, such as rainbow trout Grenobloise (trout with capers, white wine, lemon, and fresh herbs), always expertly prepared and served. The dessert menu includes soufflés for two in three different versions, including pistachio with chocolate sauce.

Farm Bounty

Barton Orchards, 63 Apple Tree Ln., Poughquag, New York 12570 (845) 227-2306; bartonorchards.com. This well-established pick-your-own operation is located in Poughquag, just to the east of Hopewell Junction. Barton Orchards offers a wide variety of apples to pick from early August to the end of October, PYO pumpkins for Halloween, and PYO veggies all summer long. Starting weekends after Labor Day and running through October, Barton also offers hayrides, a 5-acre corn maze, a haunted house, petting zoo, live entertainment, inflatable zone, family-fun theme park, and walking trails, all for a premium admission of $15 for adults, $10 for kids. This is one of the best values around for a fun day with the kids.

Cronin's Maple Farm, 2109 Rte. 52, Hopewell Junction, NY 12533; (845) 226-3815; croninsmaplefarm.com Maple syrup is made here using a wood-fired evaporator. In the woods around the sugar house, the sap is collected the traditional way, using taps and wooden buckets. Elsewhere, the sap is collected using a maze of plastic tubing incorporating the latest technology. Cronin's participates in Maple Weekend each March (see p. 22), with special pancake breakfasts and other activities. Visits to the sugar house in season are fun and educational— call ahead to schedule, especially for groups.

Fishkill Farms, 9 Fishkill Farm Rd., Hopewell Junction, NY 12533; (845) 897-4377; fishkillfarms.com. Few Hudson Valley farms have as much modern history to them as Fishkill Farms. Henry Morgenthau Jr. started Fishkill Farms in 1914; it soon became a major apple grower. Henry continued to own the farm while he went on to a long life of public service in New York and later in the Roosevelt administration as head of the Farm Credit Administration and eventually as secretary of the treasury. Franklin Roosevelt often traveled from his home in nearby Hyde Park to visit Henry on the farm. On one occasion, he brought Winston Churchill along. (The Roosevelt home in nearby Hyde Park is worth a visit: nps.gov/hofr.) After Henry passed away in 1967, the farm continued operations under his son, Robert Morgenthau (better known as the longtime district attorney for Manhattan). Today, Henry's grandson Josh is the farmer. Fishkill Farms is run on sustainable organic principles and offers a farm stand, a CSA, and a large pick-your-own fruit operation offering strawberries, cherries, berries, peaches, nectarines, and more than a dozen apple varieties. Pick-your-own begins in June with strawberries. July brings cherries and berries. The farm store offers fruits, vegetables, pasture-raised eggs, apple cider doughnuts, New York cheeses, and products from local food artisans. Fishkill Farms also has a community-supported agriculture (CSA) program for local residents. Unusually for a CSA, Fishkill Farms includes farm-grown fruits and berries as part of the weekly pickup.

Hyde Park

Foodie Faves

The Hyde Park Brewery and Restaurant, 4076 Rte. 9, **Hyde Park, NY 12538; (845) 229-8277; hydeparkbrewing.moonfruit .com; Pub Grub; $$.** The motto at Hyde Park Brewery and Restaurant is: Anytime is a good time for a beer. A lot of local beer lovers agree: Hyde Park Brewery has been brewing and serving their own ales and lagers here since 1995. The brewmaster serves up eight different homebrews in a range of styles from pale ales and light lagers to dark stout and porter. The menu here, not surprisingly, is designed to pair the beers with food—in fact, the suggestions are next to the dishes. The menu choices lean toward charcuterie, pizza, sandwiches, and burgers, but there's also a large (and good) selection of standard entrees, including a number of vegetarian choices. Live music is featured on weekends and some weeknights.

Joseph's Steakhouse, 728 Violet Ave., Hyde Park, NY 12538; **(845) 473-2333; josephs-steakhouse.com; Steak House; $$$.** This is a sleekly modern steak house, one of the best places in the region for perfectly cooked dry-aged Angus steaks, T-bones, New York strip, filet mignon, porterhouse, and rib eye. The other steak house standbys are also here: lobster tail, prime rib, grilled salmon, and some good pasta

CRAFT BREWERIES

Changes in the laws that govern beer brewing in New York State have led to big growth in craft breweries—small breweries that produce 1,500 barrels or less of beer each year (a beer barrel contains 31.5 gallons). In 2012, a new law created a farm brewery license that, among other changes, allows craft brewers to sell their products at farmers' markets, open restaurants that serve their products, and sell their products at the brewery. The law also says the breweries have to source at least half of their ingredients, including hops, from within the state. This has led to a big increase in hops farming in the region.

Craft breweries create jobs and help farmers, but most importantly, they create great beers with flavor and character. To sample the artisan brews in the region, check out these breweries:

Chatham Brewing, 59 Main St., Chatham, NY 12037; (518) 697-0202; chathambrewing.com. See listing description on p. 150.

Crossroads Brewing Company, 21 Second St., Athens, NY 12015; (518) 945-BEER (2337); crossroadsbrewingco.com. See listing description on p. 285.

The Gilded Otter, 3 Main St., New Paltz, NY 12561; (845) 256-1700; gildedotter.com. See listing description on p. 255.

Keegan Ales, 20 Saint James St., Kingston, NY 12401; (845) 331-BREW (2739); keeganales.com. See listing description on p. 245.

Mill Street Brewing Company, 289 Mill St., Poughkeepsie, NY 12601; (845) 485-2739; millstreetbrewing.com. See listing description on p. 87.

Newburgh Brewing Company, 88 S. Colden St., Newburgh, NY 12550; (845) 569-BEER (2337); newburghbrewing.com. See listing description on p. 212.

Sloop Brewing, Poughkeepsie, NY 12603; (917) 848-3865; sloopbrewing.com. See listing description on p. 98.

Restaurants of
The Culinary Institute of America

The Culinary Institute of America, 1946 Campus Dr. (Route 9 at St. Andrews Road), Hyde Park, NY 12538; (845) 452-9600; ciachef.edu. The Culinary Institute of America (CIA), located in Hyde Park on the Hudson River, is the top culinary college in America. As part of their education, future chefs at the CIA spend time working in both the front and back of the five student-staffed campus restaurants. The goal is for them to master the full scope of restaurant operations. Except for their youthful appearance, you would never know that students are practicing on you as they take your order and pour your wine.

The CIA restaurants are all located on the campus. Because they're run by students, all restaurants are closed on Sunday and major holidays. The restaurants are also closed at times during the school year to accommodate the academic schedule. Between their popularity and their schedule, dining at the CIA restaurants takes a bit more advance planning than usual. Except for the Apple Pie Bakery Cafe, reservations are a must. Weekday lunch and dinner reservations are often available the same day, but weekend reservations are harder to get. Call (845) 471-6608 or reserve online through OpenTable (opentable.com). The restaurants have a firm no-tipping policy. The 17 percent service fee added to your check goes toward student scholarships and activities.

American Bounty Restaurant; $$$. American Bounty serves award-winning, imaginative New American cuisine utilizing the wonderful diversity of regional ingredients. The wine list is drawn exclusively from the finest American vineyards. When classes are in session, American Bounty is open for lunch and dinner Tues through Sat.

Apple Pie Bakery Cafe; $. The Apple Pie Bakery Cafe is located just inside the main entrance of Roth Hall. This is the only CIA restaurant that doesn't need a reservation. Enjoy the sumptuous baked goods and cafe cuisine (salads, sandwiches, soups, and other goodies) made by students in the baking and pastry arts program. The menu items are available to take out or to enjoy in the relaxed dining area. When classes are in session, the cafe is open Mon through Fri from 7:30 a.m. to 5 p.m.

The Bocuse Restaurant; $$$$. The Escoffier Restaurant, once the flagship restaurant at the CIA, has been replaced by The Bocuse Restaurant. In other words, the CIA has replaced an outstanding if venerable French restaurant named for an iconic French chef with another outstanding flagship restaurant named for a more recent but equally iconic French chef. The change is most noticeable in the dining room decor, which has been updated and given a much sleeker, brighter look. In the spirit of Chef Bocuse, the menu has been updated as well to reflect modern techniques (*sous-vide*, for example) and creative new interpretations of classic French dishes. When classes are in session, The Bocuse is open for lunch and dinner Tues through Sat. Business casual attire is suggested.

Ristorante Caterina de' Medici; $$$. Located in the beautiful, villa-like Colavita Center for Italian Food and Wine, Ristorante Caterina de' Medici features Italian food in all its diversity. The restaurant has five different dining areas, ranging from the formal Joseph P. DeAlessandro main dining room, with Venetian chandeliers and brass sculptures, to the casual Al Forno dining room, with antipasto bar, wood-fired oven, and views of the kitchen. Al Forno serves a casual menu of pizza, paninis, desserts, and a range of coffees and teas. In the other dining rooms, classic Italian cuisine is served. When classes are in session, Ristorante Caterina de' Medici is open for lunch and dinner Mon through Fri; the Al Forno room is open Mon through Fri from 11:30 a.m. to 6 p.m. Business casual attire is suggested.

St. Andrew's Cafe; $$. Farm-to-table is the theme at the award-winning St. Andrew's Cafe. The menus here focus on sustainable and locally produced ingredients used in dishes drawn from American and European cuisine. The Green Restaurant Association has awarded the St. Andrew's Cafe two stars as a Certified Green Restaurant. When classes are in session, St. Andrew's Cafe is open for lunch and dinner Mon through Fri.

dishes and German specialties. Every dish, including the vegetables and other sides, is cooked with as much care as the steaks. Also, great bread pudding for dessert. The friendly and attentive service, the good bar, and the excellent food make Joseph's a really good choice for a special evening or celebration. The dress code is business casual. At lunch or in the tap room, the menu includes sandwiches and burgers; brunch is served on weekends. Joseph's Steakhouse is literally just down the road from Eleanor Roosevelt National Historic Site (nps.gov/elro), better known as Val-Kill, the name of the estate. This was Eleanor's hideaway during her marriage and her home after her White House years. It's well worth a visit, as is the nearby Franklin Roosevelt Home and National Historic Site (nps.gov/hofr). The building that houses Joseph's Steakhouse was once a tearoom on the estate, set up in the 1930s to provide employment for local workers. Today, Joseph's honors Eleanor Roosevelt's legacy with elegant three- and four-course afternoon teas, Thurs through Sat from noon to 2 p.m. Reservations are a must for teas; reservations are suggested for the restaurant.

2 Taste Food and Wine Bar, 4290 Albany Post Rd. (Route 9), Hyde Park, NY 12538; (845) 233-5647; 2tastefoodandwinebar.com; New American; $$$. Created and run by graduates of the nearby **Culinary Institute of America** (see p. 54), 2 Taste focuses on fresh food drawn from the Hudson Valley (suppliers are listed on the menu), matched with great wines. The fun of dining here is watching the chefs work in an open kitchen as they prepare dishes such as seared duck sliders with roasted fennel orange jam. The airy kitchen is visible from anywhere in the dining room, but true foodies ask to be seated at the chef's bar around the perimeter. A good choice of appetizers and small plates encourages sampling and sharing. The entrees on the menu are all imaginative and beautifully plated, but pay careful attention to the daily specials before making your choice. The very professional staff helps diners choose exactly the right wine pairing or wine flight from the selective international wine list. Open for dinner only.

Cafes & Quick Bites

Mr. Grumpy's, corner Route 9 and E. Market Street (in the auction hall parking lot across from Town Hall), Hyde Park, NY 12538; (845) 702-3376; facebook.com/Mr-Grumpys; Food Truck; $. Sweet potato fries, pulled pork, meatball subs, and classic hot dogs are on the menu at this mobile quick stop, along with specials. Don't let the name fool you. The chef-owner isn't grumpy at all; in fact, he's very friendly. The truck is there at lunchtime almost year-round.

Farm Bounty

Hyde Park Farmers' Market, Town Hall parking lot, Route 9, Hyde Park, NY 12538; (845) 229-9336; hydeparkchamber.org. Sat from 9 a.m. to 2 p.m., beginning of June to mid-Oct.

LaGrangeville

Farm Bounty

LaGrangeville Farmers' Market, M&T Bank plaza (1100 Rte. 55), LaGrangeville, NY 12540. Fri from 3 p.m. to 7 p.m., early June to end Oct.

Milan

Another Fork in the Road, 1215 Rte. 199, Milan, NY 12571; **(845) 758-6676; New American; $$.** This small restaurant with basic decor is a showcase for the imaginative use of local ingredients. The Fork, as it's affectionately known to locals, serves excellent breakfast choices on its early menu, including homemade corned beef hash and braised pork belly with grits and greens topped with a sunny-side-up egg. The later menus for lunch and dinner include basics, such as the Fork Burger (served with shallots, caramelized onions, swiss cheese, and arugula on a toasted baguette), and surprises, such as the duck tacos with cabbage, cilantro, and spicy ginger carrots. Check the daily specials on the big blackboard behind the counter—they are always interesting. The unusual name of this restaurant comes from the literal-minded gigantic fork sculpture found about half a mile to the west at the Y intersection of Routes 199 and 308. Another Fork in the Road is open Fri through Mon only, from 9 a.m. to 9 p.m.

Specialty Stores & Producers

Letti's Ice Cream, 6 Hidden Hollow Trail, Milan, NY 12571; **(845) 464-0724.** Letti is one of the cows; Stephanie is the owner and chief ice cream maker. This is ice cream made with really fresh, really creamy milk. It's available in eight flavors, including banana cream. Letti's is sold at the Milan and Red Hook farmers' market; special orders are also taken for pickup at the market or at the farm. All proceeds from the ice cream support the therapeutic riding program at Hidden Hollow Farms in Milan.

Farm Bounty

Great Song Farm, 475 Milan Hill Rd., Milan, NY 12571; (845) 758-1572; greatsongfarm.com. Sunny and Kate, Suffolk Punch draft horses, provide the power at Great Song Farm CSA. Located on 90 rolling acres, Great Song Farm grows 5 acres of a wide range of vegetables for its members. See their recipes for **Magic Soup** and **Basil Pesto** on pp. 314 and 318.

Milan Farmers' Market, Wilcox Memorial Town Hall parking lot, Rte. 199, Milan, NY 12571; facebook.com/MilanFarmersMarket. Fri from 3 p.m. to 7 p.m., mid-May to mid-Oct.

Second Chance Farm, 116 Lamoree Rd., Milan, NY 12572; (845) 876-7702. Pastured, sustainably raised beef, lamb, poultry, and heritage-breed pork. The meat is sold at the Milan Farmers' Market and by appointment at the farm.

Millbrook

Foodie Faves

Aurelia, 3299 Franklin Ave., Millbrook, NY 12545; (845) 677-4720; aureliarestaurant.com; Mediterranean; $$–$$$. Aurelia is a charming, informal place to eat for breakfast, lunch, or dinner. The lovely outdoor garden seating is a delight in warmer weather; indoors, the dining room is spacious and bright. The food here has a Mediterranean flair. The raw kale salad, made with toasted pine nuts, Zante currants, and aged ricotta, is locally famous. The menu at lunch and dinner is small but varied. At lunch, try the paninis; at dinner, the New York strip steak is always a great choice.

Cafe les Baux, 152 Church St., Millbrook, NY 12545; (845) 677-8166; cafelesbaux.com; French; $$–$$$. Cafe les Baux serves French bistro fare with a Provençal accent in an unpretentious setting. The menu has few surprises, but that's not the point. Diners have lunch or dinner here to enjoy the well-prepared French classics, such as the frisée salad with poached egg and bacon, or the *steak frites,* or the *moules marinière,* or any of the daily specials. The desserts include tarte tatin, not found on many menus. The wine list is surprisingly large for a small restaurant and is entirely French, with the exception of Millbrook reserve Cabernet from nearby **Millbrook Winery** (see p. 62).

Charlotte's, 4258 Rte., 44, Millbrook, NY 12545; (845) 677-5888; charlottesny.com; Continental; $$$. Situated in the beautiful rolling horse country of rural Dutchess County, Charlotte's is one of the more elegant restaurants in the area. The building was originally a church built in 1834. Today, the restaurant has lovely gardens for outdoor dining and four attractively decorated indoor dining areas, all with fireplaces. The menu at Charlotte's changes daily, depending on what's fresh at the local markets. In general, the food here is European in style, with some interesting twists. *Skagen,* for example, is regularly on the menu as an appetizer. This dish is a sort of Scandinavian shrimp salad, made with chopped shrimp, green apple, dill, and mayonnaise. In addition to standard, well-prepared entrees such as roasted pork tenderloin with mushrooms and Calvados sauce, dishes such as duck cassoulet with andouille and osso buco make regular appearances. The wine list is excellent here; a bit unexpectedly for a Continental restaurant, the beer list is good as well. In the winter, Charlotte's is open on weekends only. Call ahead to be sure of open days and hours. Reservations are strongly suggested.

La Puerta Azul, 2510 Rte. 44, Millbrook, NY 12545; (845) 677-2985; lapuertazul.com; Mexican; $$–$$$. The blue door of La Puerta Azul opens onto an award-winning interior design that evokes both old and new Mexico. The iron chandeliers, railings, and lamps were handmade for the restaurant at nearby Arrowsmith Forge; the austere iron is set off by colorful fabrics, exposed wooden beams, and a flowing waterfall at the entry. Mexican tiles and copper decorate the truly beautiful bar. Matching the menu to the interior is a self-imposed challenge this restaurant meets beautifully. This is polished, upscale Mexican, prepared with care and served by an attentive staff. The sweet corn soup, for instance, is made with corn, poblano cream, mushrooms, and truffle oil. The guacamole, made tableside, is a standout. So are the chicken mole, fish tacos, and tuna ceviche. The bar has a large selection of tequilas and Mexican beers; the margaritas have consistently been voted best in the Hudson Valley. Live music on weekends can make this restaurant a bit noisy. Open for lunch weekdays; brunch Sat and Sun; dinner every night.

Cafes & Quick Bites

Babette's Kitchen, 3293 Franklin Ave., Millbrook, NY 12545; (845) 677-8602; babetteskitchen.com; Sandwich Shop; $$. This small food market offers seasonal prepared food to go—it's all made on the spot, even the mayonnaise, using fresh local ingredients. The lunchtime menu is mostly sandwiches and salads; the dinner menu is more varied. The meat loaf is a perennial favorite. Other popular choices include seasonal salads, tomato tart, oven-fried chicken, and beef and butternut chili. The buttermilk biscuits, made from a secret recipe, are outstanding. Excellent pastries, pies, and cakes are available all day long. The store also sells a variety of gourmet local products, including cheese, syrups and honeys, and chocolates.

Rusty Tomato Snack Bar, 134 Church St., Millbrook, NY 12545; (845) 264-2991; facebook.com/TheRustyTomato; Sandwich Shop; $. This storefront sandwich shop, tucked away on a side street, is a great choice for a quick, inexpensive breakfast or lunch. The short menu includes freshly made sandwiches, great grilled cheese, and tacos.

Slammin' Salmon, 3267 Franklin Ave., Millbrook, NY 12545; (845) 677-5400; gourmettogony.com; Gourmet/Sandwich Shop; $$. Slammin' Salmon is well known as one of the finest gourmet stores in the Hudson Valley. This is the place above all others for artisan cheeses and the freshest, best fish. The shop carries local dairy products and eggs along with a full line of gourmet groceries. The take-out menu offers freshly prepared entrees and full dinners, along with homemade soups and salads. At lunchtime, Slammin' Salmon has cafe seating and a seasonal menu of sandwiches, salads, paninis, and specials. Lunch service is Tues through Sat, 10:30 a.m. to 3 p.m.

Specialty Stores & Producers

Millbrook Vineyards and Winery, 26 Wing Rd., Millbrook, NY 12545; (845) 677-8383; millbrookwine.com. Millbrook Vineyards had its first commercial vintage in 1985. Since then, it has become the flagship winery of the Hudson Valley, winning numerous awards for its outstanding products. More importantly, the pioneering work of owner John Dyson in supporting local wine and local agriculture has been an inspiration to many others in the region. Today the offerings include outstanding Pinots, Cabernets, and Chardonnays. Hunt Country Red, a Bordeaux blend, is a wonderful table wine. The estate-grown and -bottled Tocai Friulano is Millbrook specialty; this aromatic white wine isn't made anywhere else in the region. The winery and tasting room are in renovated Dutch dairy barn with magnificent views of the vineyards and distant Catskill Mountains. This is one of the most beautiful spots in rural Dutchess County. Millbrook Vineyards is open every day year-round from noon to 5 p.m. On weekends between Memorial Day and October, the Vineyard Grille & Cafe offers simple grilled food, sandwiches, salads, and desserts, all catered by **Slammin' Salmon** (see opposite page). Wine is offered by the glass, of course. Guided tours of the vineyard, winery, and tasting room are available; check with the winery in advance for hours and reservations. Frequent special events, such as a summer solstice lobster bake and the annual harvest party luncheon in October, are a great way to sample the winery's offerings while enjoying great food and beautiful scenery. The winery also has a lovely gallery featuring work from local artists. The retail store sells a good selection of wine books, cookbooks, wine accessories, and gourmet foods. Millbrook Vineyards is a stop on the **Dutchess Wine Trail** (see p. 43 for details).

Oak Summit Vineyard, 372 Oak Summit Rd., Millbrook, NY 12545; (845) 677-9522; oaksummitvineyard.com. This small vineyard—only 6 acres—produces exceptional Pinot Noir and Chardonnay. The estate-bottled wines have won numerous awards since becoming available in 2005. On the third Sunday of each month, Oak Summit offers a Best of the Hudson Grand Wine Luncheon. The five-course meal features local foods prepared on site and paired with Oak Summit wines and French and Italian Grand Crus. Seating is by reservation only; call the vineyard for details. Tours of the vineyard and winery are by appointment only; call for details.

Farm Bounty

Arch River Farm, 515 Woodstock Rd., Millbrook, NY 12545; (845) 677-4991; archriverfarm.com. A family-owned farm offering pastured beef, pork, and poultry. Products can be purchased at the farm year-round Sat, 1 p.m. to 5 p.m. and Sun, 10 a.m. to noon; call to schedule a visit during the week. Arch River Farm meat is also sold at the Millbrook Farmers' Market (see below) and other local markets.

Millbrook Farmers' Market, Tribute Garden parking lot, Front Street and Franklin Avenue, Millbrook, NY 12545; millbrook nyfarmersmarket.com. Sat from 9 a.m. to 1 p.m., mid-May to mid-Oct.

Millbrook Venison Products, 499 Verbank Rd., Millbrook, NY 12545; (845) 677-8457. Pastured venison is grown and harvested on this farm. The meat is primarily sold to high-end restaurants nationwide, but Millbrook Venison also sells at local farmers' markets.

Rockerbox Garlic, Millbrook, NY 12545; (631) 764-9418; rocker boxgarlic.wix.com. Handcrafted dehydrated garlic flakes, garlic dust, onion dust, and a sweet corn rub are the main products from Rockerbox. All the products are additive and preservative free. They're also free of the bitterness and gritty texture of commercial garlic powders. The garlic products are made from intensely flavored heirloom varieties grown locally. Rockerbox products are sold at local farmers' markets and are also carried by some local retailers, including **Olde Hudson** (see p. 181) and **Walbridge Farm Market** in Millbook (see below).

Shunpike Dairy, 1348 Shunpike Rd., Millbrook, NY 12545; (845) 702-6224; shunpikedairy.com. Shunpike Dairy has been certified to sell raw milk since 2010 by New York State. The milk comes from their mixed herd of stress-free Holsteins, Ayshire, Brown Swiss, Jersey, and Linebacker cows. The cows never get any hormones or antibiotics, and they're pastured on the farm's rolling hills. The milk is sold strictly on the honor system right at the farm. Bring your own container or purchase a jar from the farm. Shunpike Dairy doesn't have regular store hours; just stop by. If you get there at 5 p.m., you can watch the cows being milked.

Temple Farm, 339 N. Mabbettsville Rd., Millbrook, NY 12545; (845) 677-8757. Free-range, grass-fed Devon cattle are raised here. The meat from this heritage breed is sold in cuts, quarters, or halves at the farm. Call in advance to place your order.

Walbridge Farm Market, 538 Rte. 343, Millbrook, NY 12545; (845) 677-6221; facebook.com/WalbridgeFarmMarket. Locally raised, pastured Angus beef and poultry are sold at this farm stand, along with farm-fresh fruits and vegetables and a good range of local and homemade products, including pickles, cheese, honey, maple syrup, and gourmet items. The annual farm festival in early July is a local don't-miss event for the kids: hay rides, face painting, bounce house, music, and lots of local vendors—plus hot dogs. Summer hours are Thurs 10 a.m. to 4 p.m.; Fri 10 a.m. to 5 p.m.; Sat 9 a.m. to 5 p.m.; Sun noon to 4 p.m.; and Mon 10 a.m. to 2 p.m. Closed Tues and Wed. In the winter, the hours are Fri noon to 5 p.m.; Sat 9 a.m. to 5 p.m.; and Sun 10 a.m. to 2 p.m.

Millerton

52 Main, 52 Main St., Millerton, NY 12546; (518) 787-0252; 52main.com; Tapas; $$. Tapas, those Spanish-inspired small plates, are the featured offering at 52 Main. The tapas here range from the simple—house-marinated olives—to the more ambitious, such as the duck confit quesadilla or the truffle fries. The restaurant also offers a handful of nicely done entrees, including braised short ribs. For a true taste of Spain, however, try the paella. This generous dish serves at least two and takes about 40 minutes to prepare, but it's worth waiting for, not least because it gives you more time for the excellent cocktails served up at the bar. The wine menu offers a good selection of wines by the glass. There's live music every Saturday night.

Manna Dew Cafe, 54 Main St., Millerton, NY 12546; mannadew .com; Traditional American; $$. Located close to the Millerton movie theater, Manna Dew is a popular spot for a pre-movie dinner or post-movie drink. The food here is American bistro, meaning the usual excellent burgers, strip steak, seared salmon, and free-range chicken are on the menu. In season, Manna Dew uses its own home-grown herbs and vegetables—the garden is behind the restaurant. In the warmer weather, diners get a good view of it as they eat outdoors on the terrace. The bar at Manna Dew is cozy and welcoming, but serves only beer and wine. Most diners don't care, because the restaurant's wine and beer menus are both large and varied. On weekends, Manna Dew features live music. Open for dinner only.

No. 9, 53 Main St., Millerton, NY 12546; (518) 592-1299; number9 millerton.com; New American; $$$. No. 9 is located in the luxurious

Simmons' Way Village Inn, a restored Victorian mansion from the late 1800s. The expansive lawn and front porch welcome guests to one of the finest restaurants in the area. The menu here is contemporary American with French and Austrian accents. This is a restaurant that takes wiener schnitzel seriously. It takes the farm-to-table concept even more seriously. The ever-changing menu relies heavily on local producers, such as beef from **Herondale Farm** (see p. 146) and pork from **Black Sheep Hill Farm** (see p. 78). Chef Tim Cocheo puts it all together with skill and panache in dishes such as grilled halibut, peas, bacon, hedgehog mushrooms, and carrot-ginger emulsion. For a dessert change of pace, try the cheese plate, made up entirely of local offerings. The midweek prix-fixe dinner is an excellent value. The attentive staff and attractive contemporary decor make dining here even more pleasurable. Open for dinner only, Tues through Sat; brunch on Sun. Reservations strongly recommended, especially in the summer tourist season.

Cafes & Quick Bites

Irving Farm Coffee House, 44 Main St., Millerton, NY 12546; (518) 789-2020; irvingfarm.com/locations/millerton-coffee-house; **Coffeehouse; $.** This relaxed coffeehouse is the Hudson Valley outpost of Irving Farm Coffee Roasters (three other shops are in Manhattan). Irving Farm roasts all its coffee just a few miles away in historic Coleman Station. The many single-origin and blended coffees available here are, needless to say, expertly prepared and very fresh. A good selection of pastries, sandwiches, soups, and salads make this a good spot for a break or lunch. On Fri and Sat, it's open for a quick dinner before a film at the Millerton movie house. Free Wi-Fi.

Salsa Fresca Mexican Grill, 5916 N. Elm St., Millerton, NY 12546; (518) 789-6900; salsafrescagrill.com; **Mexican; $.** Salsa Fresca is a great place for quick, high-quality, very fresh Mexican food. The shop offers all the usual Mexican-American basics, but it also has some well-done variations on the basic themes. Try the Red-Hot Acapulco burrito—it's made with pork, Mexican rice, beans, cheese, red onion, jalapeños, and Salsa Fresca's special sweet chipotle salsa. Salsa Fresca in Millerton is the original shop; since then, the local owners have opened branches in Bedford Hills and Yorktown Heights.

Terni's Store, 42 Main St., Millerton, NY 12546; (518) 789-3474; facebook.com/ternis; Soda Fountain; $. For nearly a century, the Terni family has operated a sort of general store on Millerton's main drag, selling everything from fishing tackle and Pendleton outdoor clothing to candy and lottery tickets. Much more importantly, Terni's still has the original marble soda fountain. This is one of the rare places in the Hudson Valley where you can get a real banana split served at a real soda fountain. (The other is **McKinney & Doyle** in Pawling at the southern end of Dutchess County—see p. 72.)

Specialty Stores & Producers

Harney & Sons Fine Teas, 13 Main St., Millerton, NY 12546; (518) 789-2121; harney.com. Harney & Sons has been selling fine teas, both wholesale and retail, since 1983. The main factory and offices are on the outskirts of Millerton. The retail shop, tasting room, and lunch tea bar are located in the heart of Millerton (there's another tasting room in Manhattan's SoHo). Few shops are as much fun to visit—you can enjoy a very nice lunch or tea break here, browse the extensive inventory of tea and tea paraphernalia, and participate in a tea tasting (on weekends). The tea bar is open every day, 11 a.m. to 4 p.m., noon to 3 p.m. on Sun.

Farm Bounty

McEnroe Organic Farm Market, 5409 Rte. 22, Millerton, NY 12546; (518) 789-4191; mcenroeorganicfarm.com. One of the largest organic operations in the area, McEnroe Farms has some 800 acres under cultivation or in pasture. The farming here is strictly organic and sustainable. The farm's own certified-organic meats, vegetables, and fruits can be purchased at the market, along with regional dairy products and artisan products. Homemade baked goods, prepared foods, and great sandwiches and burgers are also available. The Discovery Garden and quarter-mile farm walk next to the market are fun to explore, even if you don't have kids along. Family Farm Days at McEnroe offer a range of activities and crafts, along with farm tours. They're on Sat from 10 a.m. to 5 p.m. between May and Oct.

Millerton Farmers' Market, Railroad Plaza (off Main Street), Millerton NY 12546; millertonfarmersmarket.org. Sat from 9 a.m. to 1 p.m., end of May to last week of Oct.

Silamar Farm, 5744 Rte. 22, Millerton, NY 12546; (518) 789-3067. This popular roadside stand offers a full range of home-grown vegetables, along with blueberries, strawberries, and raspberries; you can pick your own strawberries if you prefer. Lamb from nearby Dashing Star Farm is available here. Open every day from 8:30 a.m. to 6 p.m.

Sol Flower Farm, 41 Kaye Rd., Millerton, NY 12546; (518) 567-1951; solflowerfarm.com. In addition to CSA shares, Sol Flower Farm sells produce at the Millbrook and Millerton farmers' markets and at the **Herondale Farm** store in Ancramdale (see p. 146). About 10 acres of the farm are in flower and vegetable production.

Dutchess County Diners

The Daily Planet, 1202 Rte. 55, LaGrangeville, NY 12540; daily planetdiner; Diner; $. Superman of the 1940s and TV shows of the 1950s rules the decor at this small but popular diner. Standard diner fare with a bit of a Superman twist: The menu lists items such as kryptonite sticks (OK, they're really fried mozzarella sticks). Open from 5 a.m. to midnight every day.

Eveready Diner, Route 9 N., Hyde Park, NY 12538; (845) 229-8100; theevereadydiner.com; Diner; $$. The Eveready Diner, with its giant statue of a busboy with a coffee mug, is a Hyde Park fixture, a sort of counterweight to the serious restaurants of the nearby Culinary Institute of America. It's such a classic example of the genre that it's been featured on the Food Network's *Diners Drive-Ins & Dives*. The food here is standard diner fare, expertly and quickly prepared and served by an efficient crew of ever-cheerful waitresses. Eveready bakes its own pies, cakes, cookies, and bread and has a genuine soda fountain. Open 7 days a week, 24 hours a day.

Eveready Diner, 6595 Route 9 (across from the fairgrounds), Rhinebeck, NY 12572; (845) 876-1900; theevereadydiner.com; Diner; $$. The Rhinebeck branch of Eveready in Hyde Park has the same menu but not quite as much chrome. Open daily from 6 a.m. to 1 a.m. See listing description above.

"Historic" Village Diner, 7550 N. Broadway, Red Hook, NY 12571; (845) 758-6232; historic-village-diner.com; Diner; $. An unusually well-preserved Silk City dining car from the 1920s is what makes this diner in Red Hook historic—so historic that it's on the National Register of Historic Places. The food here consists of well-prepared standard diner fare and excellent specials. Open every day from 6 a.m. to 9 p.m.

I-84 Diner, 853 Rte. 52 at I-84 (I-84 exit 12), Fishkill, NY 12524; (845) 896-6537; thei84diner.com; Diner; $. More truck stop (in a good way) than family diner, the I-84 diner has a vaster than usual menu, efficient service, and good food. The chrome and glass block construction, topped with a clock tower, is hard to miss when exiting I-84. The Sunday buffet is very popular. Open 24 hours.

Oakhurst Diner, 19 Main St., Millerton, NY 12546; (518) 592-1313; facebook.com/oakhurstdiner; Diner; $$. Diner classics such as eggs Benedict, meat loaf, and roast chicken are on the menu at the Oakhurst Diner, but they're joined here by organic burgers using beef from **Herondale Farms** (see p.

146), venison chili, cheese fries, frisée salads, and the macro plate, a big bowl with brown rice, black beans, acorn squash, and other veggies in tahini dressing with seaweed salad on the side. The traditional diner breakfast foods are served until 5 p.m.; the eggs are farm-fresh and free-range. The focus in on local produce and meats, along with homemade desserts, **Harney & Sons** (see p. 68) juices and teas, and really good coffee. The food is good, reasonably priced, and served efficiently. Oakhurst has a big neon sign, a classic chrome diner exterior, and a retro diner interior. It's cozy, with only 7 booths and 16 counter stools; an outdoor patio has a few more tables when the weather is nice. This is popular spot for people starting off or coming in from the Harlem Valley Rail Trail (hvrt.org); the Millerton entrance to the trail is right across the street. Open daily 7 a.m. to 9 p.m.

Palace Diner, 194 Washington St., Poughkeepsie, NY 12601; (845) 473-1576; thepalacediner.com; Diner; $$. Plenty of chrome, neon, and good food at this popular spot in Poughkeepsie. Very convenient to Marist College and St. Francis Hospital. Open 24/7. Free Wi-Fi.

Red Line Diner, 588 Rte. 9, Fishkill, NY 12524; (845) 765-8401; dineatredline.com; Diner; $$. The classic neon sign welcomes the hungry to classic diner food all day and night, every day.

Yankee Clipper Diner, 397 Main St., Beacon, NY 12508; (845) 440-0021; beaconyankeeclipper.com; Diner; $. In 1994, some scenes for the movie *Nobody's Fool,* with Paul Newman, Bruce Willis, Jessica Tandy, and Melanie Griffith, were filmed at the Yankee Clipper Diner. Celebrity didn't rub off on the Yankee Clipper—the diner is still the same local eatery it's been since 1946. The food here is good, the portions are generous, the coffee is excellent, and the service is friendly. Open from 6 a.m. to 10 p.m. Sun through Thurs; until 11 p.m. Fri and Sat.

Pawling

McKinney & Doyle Fine Foods, 10 Charles Colman Blvd., Pawling, NY 12564; (845) 855-3875; mckinneyandodyle.com; cafe and bakery; $$$. McKinney & Doyle began as an old-fashioned bakery back in 1986. The owners were graduates of the Culinary Institute of America and believed strongly in using only the finest ingredients, and the bakery was an immediate success. Soon they were serving soups and entrees; by 1991, it was time to move the bakery down the street to a beautiful old brick building and open the Fine Foods Cafe alongside. The cafe was an immediate success as well, helped along by an award-winning wine list. Another expansion in 2011 added a lovely bar, a bigger dining room, and a restored soda fountain. The bakery continues to turn out delicious breads, rolls, brownies, cookies, turnovers, scones, cakes, pies, and tarts. At dinner, the café menu offers a great selection of outstanding small and large plates, such as smoked deviled eggs, warm chickpea flatbread, and pan-roasted duck breast with kumquat sherry sauce and bacon marmalade. The lunch menu offers excellent sandwiches and burgers and an extensive array of interesting and well-prepared entrees. The dessert menu features a wonderful range of after-dinner drinks as well as home-made sweets. The soda fountain offers the traditional milkshakes, egg creams, sodas, and malts, along with a good choice of freshly made coffee drinks. McKinney & Doyle is open for lunch Tues through Fri; dinner Wed through Sun; brunch on the weekends.

Pine Plains

Lia's Mountain View Restaurant, 7685 Route 82, Pine Plains, New York 12567; (518) 398-7311; liasmountainview.com; Italian; $$. Lia's Mountain View is a local favorite for well-prepared Italian cuisine. The large menu is fairly standard, but it includes some original surprises, such as the Italian nachos appetizer: fried pasta chips topped with ground sausage, tomatoes, pepperoncini, olives, marinara, and mozzarella. The *arancini* (rice balls) here are very nicely done, but are available only on the weekend and only by special order. The menu offers a good selection of baked and specialty pasta dishes. Among Lia's specialty dishes, the Chicken Vivace is a standout—chicken sautéed with artichokes, tomatoes, and mushrooms in a sherry cream sauce. The specials are where the kitchen gets creative, with appetizers like fried sausage ravioli and smoked tomato soup with clams and entrees like herb-crusted pork loin served with port-cranberry demi-glace and sweet potato puree. The Mountain View part of the restaurant name is literal—the views from the dining room are spectacular. Pasta night on Wed and the prix-fixe dinner on Thurs are very good values. Open for lunch and dinner every day except Mon; dinner only on Sun.

Stissing House, 7801 S. Main St. (Route 199 and Route 82), Pine Plains, NY 12567; (518) 398-8800; stissinghouse.com; French; $$$. The historic Stissing House restaurant dates back to 1782, when it was a tavern. Food has been served at the building almost continuously ever since, making Stissing House one of America's oldest and longest-operating restaurants (see the **Beekman Arms** in Rhinebeck on p. 111 for the oldest inn in America). Stissing House features a wood-burning oven that turns out really good pizza (and also roasted clams with chorizo and *sofrito*), but the reason to eat here is Chef Michel Jean's Provençal-inflected French country cooking. The dishes he creates, especially from the wood-burning grill, are seasonal and fresh, drawing heavily on regional producers. A typical dinner entree is a simply prepared organic poussin, made only with garlic, lemon, and the bird's natural juices. Fondue Savoyarde for two is available for lunch, definitely a rarity in the area. The decor at Stissing House preserves the building's long history. The vintage tavern room is the casual main dining room, but intimate dining nooks with fireplaces are available; they're great for small groups. Stissing House is open for lunch on weekends; it's open for dinner Thurs through Sun. Dinner reservations suggested.

Cafes & Quick Bites

Pine Plains Platter, 2987 Church St., Pine Plains, NY 12567; (518) 398-0500; pineplainsplatter.com; Breakfast/Sandwich Shop; $. Breakfast all day, great sandwiches and soups at lunchtime, and a good choice of take-home dinners make this small shop a standout. They also serve outstandingly good coffee. At breakfast, check out the 7-inch waffles. At lunch, try the shrimp po' boy. Not too many places in the Hudson Valley offer po' boy sandwiches, let alone po' boys made with such a deep understanding. The other lunchtime sandwiches, such as the curried chicken hoagie, are also very good. Check the blackboard for the specials of the day. Open 7 days a week for breakfast and lunch.

Specialty Stores & Producers

Amazing Real Live Food Co., Chaseholm Farm Creamery, 100 Chase Rd., Pine Plains, NY 12567; (518) 398-0368;

amazingreallive.com. The real live part of Amazing Real Live Food Co. refers to the live probiotic bacteria and natural enzymes that are found in naturally produced cheese. The artisanal cheese from ARL is indeed amazing—flavorful, rich, and aromatic. The primary products are herbed farmer cheese, a semi-firm *queso blanco,* Stella Vallis (a raw-milk tomme-style cheese), and two signature cheeses: Chaseholm Camembert and Chaseholm Moonlight (a bloomy rind cheese). The milk for the cheese comes from the farm's own herd of 50 registered Holsteins. The farm has been placed into permanent conservation easement to help make sure agriculture remains viable in this part of the Hudson Valley. ARL products are served at many fine restaurants in the area and are widely available throughout the region at farmers' markets and many retail outlets, such as **Adams Fairacre Farm** (see pp. 95, 138). See ARL's recipe for **Hudson Valley Raclette** on p. 324.

Coach Farm, 105 Mill Hill Rd., Gallatinville, NY 12523; (518) 398-5325; coachfarm.com. That goat cheese is now routinely found in most good supermarkets has a lot to do with the pioneering work of Miles and Lillian Cahn, who founded Coach Farm in 1985. They made delicious, fresh goat cheese and used the marketing expertise they had acquired as the owners of Coach Leather to introduce them to the public. Today, Coach Farm offers award-winning fresh and aged goat cheeses (including a raw-milk variety), goat milk yogurt, and goat milk. Their products are found in upscale food shops and are served by name in many fine restaurants. The milk comes from their happy herd of over 900 French Alpine dairy goats. Scheduled tours of the farm aren't available, but visitors are welcome to come see the goats and watch them being milked at 3 p.m. every day.

Dutch's Spirits, 98 Ryan Rd., Pine Plains, NY 12523; (212) 729-5649; dutchsspirits.com. Back in the days of Prohibition, gangster

New York State Farm Distilleries

For many decades, antiquated laws dating back to the Prohibition era prohibited small-scale distilleries from operating in New York State. That lingering relic of a failed experiment was finally lifted in 2002 when the Farm Distillery Law was passed. The new law allowed small-scale producers of distilled spirits to make up to 35,000 proof-gallons of liquor each, give tours of the distillery, and operate tasting rooms where their products could be sold. The law required the new distillers to source at least 50 percent of their ingredients within New York State—not really a hardship given the state's abundant agricultural resources. Legalizing small distilleries led to a rebirth of what had once been a vibrant business. In the Hudson Valley region, several small distilleries opened and quickly became successes.

In 2012, a new law was passed, allowing licensed farm distilleries to sell their products at the annual New York State Fair in Syracuse, at county fairs, and at local not-for-profit farmers' markets. The law puts farm distilleries on a par with farm wineries and farm breweries, which were already able to sell their products in these settings. The new law means that it is now easier than ever to sample and purchase the products of the growing number of Hudson Valley farm distilleries.

Within the geographic area of this book are these farm distilleries:

Coppersea Distillery, West Park, NY 12493; (845) 444-1044; coppersea.com; see listing description on p. 282.

Dutch's Spirits, 98 Ryan Rd., Pine Plains, NY 12523; (212) 729-5649; dutchsspirits.com; see listing description on p. 75.

Harvest Spirits Farm Distillery, 3074 Rte. 9, Valatie, NY 12184; (518) 253-5917; harvestspirits.com; see listing description on p. 192.

Hillrock Estate Distillery, 408 Pooles Hill Rd., Ancram, NY 12502; (518) 329-1023; hillrockdistillery.com; see listing description on p. 145.

Stoutridge Vineyard, 10 Ann Kaley Ln., Marlboro, NY 12542; (845) 236-7620; stoutridge.com; see listing description on p. 249.

Tuthilltown Spirits, 14 Grist Mill Ln., Gardiner, NY 12525; (845) 255-1527; tuthilltown.com.

Not officially within the geography of this book but still worth a visit, especially for those following the **Shawangunk Hudson Valley Wine Trail** (see p. 208), **Tuthilltown Spirits** is a small-batch distiller that was one of the first to open in New York after the law was changed in 2002. Tuthilltown Spirits made the first legally distilled and aged grain spirits in New York since Prohibition. The distillery's flagship product is Hudson Baby Bourbon, 100 percent distilled from New York corn. Other products include Half Moon Orchard gin, Hudson Manhattan rye, and Basement Bitters. The landmark building, once a water-powered grain mill, dates back to 1788 and is listed on the National Register of Historic Places. The tasting room is open Thurs through Mon; tours of the distillery are offered on Sat and Sun.

Dutch Schultz built a sizeable bootlegging operation in underground bunkers on a farm in rural Pine Plains. On the surface, the property was a turkey farm; underground, it produced forbidden booze on an industrial scale. The site was raided in 1932; 10,000 pounds of sugar were confiscated and the operation was shut down. Soon after, Prohibition ended and Dutch Schultz moved into the numbers racket instead. The farm passed through different owners and uses, and eventually ended up as 400-acre Harvest Homestead Farm, owned by co-founder Alex Adams's family. The crumbling remnants of the bootlegging operation remained untouched. In 2012, Alex Adams and partner Ariel Schlein decided to rebuild a craft distillery on the original foundations of Dutch's underground empire. The site was added to the New York State Archaeological Inventory as a "Bootleg-Era Bunker Complex," and the New York State Historic Preservation office deemed the site eligible for inclusion in the State and National Register of Historic Places. Today, Dutch's Spirits produces three hand-crafted, small-batch products: Dutch's Spirits Sugar Wash Moonshine, Dutch's Spirits Peach Brandy, and Dutch's Colonial Cocktail Bitters, made from an 18th-century recipe featuring American spicebush and kinnikinnick leaf. The products are served at many regional restaurants; bottles are available from a growing number of New York liquor stores (check the website for an updated list). Bottles can also be purchased in the tasting room. See Dutch's Spirits' recipe for **Bootlegger's Swizzle** on p. 319.

Farm Bounty

Black Sheep Hill Farm, **1891 County Rte. 83, Pine Plains, NY 12567; (518) 771-3067; blacksheephill.com.** Black Welsh Mountain sheep, a heritage breed, are raised at this family-owned farm for their fleece as well as their meat. Tamworth and Tamworth/Hereford cross heritage pigs are raised for their meat. The farm also has a hundred laying hens (including Araucanas, which lay eggs with beautiful blue shells) and several acres of garden vegetables. The farm stand on the property is open from June through Sept. Black Sheep Hill Farm products are also served at many restaurants in the area.

Pleasant Valley

Specialty Stores & Producers

Quattro's Game Farm and Farm Store, Route 44 at Tinkertown Road, Pleasant Valley, NY 12569; (845) 635-2018; facebook .com/QuattrosFarm. In business since 1942 and still run by members of the founding Quattrociocchi family, Quattro's raises, butchers, and sells its own chickens, pheasants, ducks, geese, domestic, wild and heritage turkeys, and venison. Also available are eggs from chickens, pheasants, wild turkeys, and duck and geese eggs. All the animals are free-range and raised without hormones, chemicals, or antibiotics. The meats here are famous well beyond the Hudson Valley for their quality. Quattro's is also a retail outlet for products from Hudson Valley Foie Gras (hudsonvalleyfoiegras.com). Open Mon through Sat 8 a.m. to 7 p.m.; Sun 8 a.m. to 1 p.m. Quattro's also sells at the **Rhinebeck Farmers' Market** (see p. 196).

Farm Bounty

Remsburger Maple Farm and Apiary, 756 Traver Rd., Pleasant Valley, NY 12569; (845) 635-9168; remsburgermaple.com. On the maple side, Remsburger makes maple syrup, maple sugar, maple cream, maple candy, maple popcorn—if you can make it with maple, Dennis and Juliette Remsburger do. On the honey side, they produce honey, cream honey, honey candy, and more, along with pure beeswax candles. The Remsburgers mostly sell by mail through their website, but they also sell their products in person at many fairs, festivals, and events throughout the region. You can also buy their products at **Adams Fairacre**'s Poughkeepsie location (see p. 95).

Wigsten's Farm Market, 1096 Salt Point Tpke., Pleasant Valley, NY 12569; (845) 235-7469. Home-grown organic fruits and vegetables, including apples, berries, pumpkins, and seasonal vegetables from asparagus in the spring to potatoes in the fall. Open daily 9 a.m. to 6 p.m. in season.

Poughkeepsie

Foodie Faves

Akari Sushi and Japanese Food, 35 Main St., Poughkeepsie, NY 12601; (845) 471-1773; akarisushi.com; Japanese; $$. The menu at Akari Sushi has plenty of very fresh, carefully prepared sushi and sashimi, along with a good selection of standard teriyaki, tempura, and noodle dishes. They all make Akari very much worth a visit, but what makes Akari fun is the extensive and inventive selection of rolls. The Crazy Roll, made with tuna, shrimp, cucumbers, avocado, scallions, and the chef's special sauce, is a customer favorite. The other signature rolls are equally imaginative and equally well prepared with very fresh ingredients. All are attractively presented and served in generous portions. Akari is very small and doesn't accept reservations, so be prepared for a bit of wait on a busy night.

Andy's Place, 45 Dutchess Ave., Poughkeepsie, NY 12601; (845) 452-2525; Traditional American; $$. Andy's has been a neighborhood favorite ever since it opened in 1948. In those days, the railroad bridge above it was in active service. Today, the bridge is the famed Walkway Over the Hudson (walkway.org), making Andy's a good spot for lunch or dinner after an invigorating stroll across the Hudson and back. The menu here is heavy on burgers, sandwiches, and pastas, along with specials that often have a Polish accent. It's hard to find pierogies on a menu in the Hudson Valley, let alone pierogies this good. But the real reason to visit Andy's is the award-winning chili. Like all good chili, it's made from a secret family recipe. Andy's version is rich and thick and served with plenty of American cheese and chopped onions. The atmosphere here is very friendly and relaxed, even during the lunchtime rush. Enjoy the outdoor terrace in the warmer weather.

The Artist's Palate, 307 Main St., Poughkeepsie, NY 12601; (845) 483-8074; theartistspalate.biz; New American; $$$. The Artist's Palate is one of the restaurants that have led to Poughkeepsie's revival as a foodie destination. When it opened in 2005, it sparked a restaurant renaissance in the tired downtown district that continues to this day. The restaurant is in the ground floor of an opulent former department store that had sat vacant and decaying for years. The space has been renovated to include a sleek, contemporary dining room (while preserving the original wooden joists and the ornate tin ceiling), an open kitchen, and gallery space featuring local artists. The menu here is straightforward and leans toward comfort foods, such as the lobster mac and cheese appetizer. The emphasis is on dishes made with local seasonal products, simply but expertly prepared to emphasize their natural flavor—pan-roasted chicken with escarole, currants, and pine nuts is a representative dinner entree. The wine list here offers a very good range of wines by the glass. Reservations strongly suggested.

Babycakes Cafe, 1–3 **Collegeview Ave., Poughkeepsie, NY 12603; (845) 485-8411; babycakescafe.com; Traditional American; $$$.** A popular spot for the Vassar crowd, Babycakes Cafe serves breakfast, lunch, and dinner in a relaxed atmosphere. The food is good all day long and into the evening. The American bistro menu is varied and well prepared, with interesting daily specials, such as the quinoa hush puppies appetizer and the grilled Italian sausage with polenta fries, arugula, and smoked provolone at dinner. The lunch menu offers a good variety of interesting sandwiches. Babycakes began as small cafe serving just breakfast, lunch, and pastries. Even after the cafe was expanded into a much bigger restaurant in 2007, the pastries part of the equation remained important—save room for dessert. Babycakes has gallery space featuring local artists and offers live music on some evenings.

The Beechtree Grill, 1–3 **Collegeview Ave., Poughkeepsie, NY 12603; (845) 471-7279; facebook.com/beechtreegrill; Traditional American; $$.** This small, friendly restaurant is a longtime standby in the Vassar College area. The food here is standard American, ably prepared. The restaurant offers some popular starters, including a very large order of fried calamari and a baked double crème brie. The entrees include very good burgers and sandwiches. More substantial dishes on the menu run to pulled pork, hanger steak, and grilled fish, all with interesting sides such as vegetable couscous. The nightly specials are where the kitchen gets a bit more imaginative, with choices such as pistachio-coated cod filet with pureed root vegetables. Brunch and lunch at the Beechtree are much like dinner—dependably good food but never any surprises. The lively bar at the Beechtree has a very good selection of beers on tap. The bar and restaurant can get crowded, especially on live music nights or when something is happening across the street at Vassar or at the Powerhouse Theater on the campus.

Billy Bob's BBQ, 35 Fairmont Ave., Poughkeepsie, NY 12603; (845) 471-7870; billybobsbbq.biz; Barbecue; $$. It's hard to believe, but not everybody loves barbecue. That's what make Billy Bob's BBQ special. Barbecue is indeed a high art here, but the menu has more variety than the typical barbecue place—and the barbecue itself is served in some imaginative and very tasty ways. Try the Armadillo Eggs appetizer: jalapeño peppers stuffed with pulled pork, breaded and fried and served with Billy Bob's own dipping sauce. There's also the Piggy Mac, Billy Bob's take on a traditional side dish served at barbecue restaurants: the creamy mac and cheese here are on top of a bed of pulled pork, topped with bread crumbs and baked. Hamburgers get more than the usual cursory treatment here. You can build your own single, double, or even triple burger and add a range of toppings. A bit surprisingly, the menu also includes a number of quesadillas. Barbecue is the real reason to come to Billy Bob's, however. The standard offerings of beef brisket, chicken, pulled pork, and ribs are all here, carefully prepared to just the right level of smoky goodness. The combination plates are excellent value. Billy Bob's sampler, which includes all the meats and three sides, is more than ample for two.

Brasserie 292, 292 Main St., Poughkeepsie, NY 12603; (845) 473-0292; brasserie292.com; French; $$$. Another restaurant that is part of the exciting rebirth of downtown Poughkeepsie, Brasserie 292 is located in the former Elting building, once home to a children's clothier. The ground floor has been renovated into a classic bistro setting. The dining room seats 80 and has a traditional black-and-white checkerboard linoleum floor, cozy red leather booths, brass lamps, and the original tin ceiling The overall impact is a sense of being transported back in time and place, a century and a continent away. The outstanding food matches the setting. The cooking here is very well-prepared traditional French bistro fare. The menu is primarily bistro classics, such as duck breast with confit, *steak frites,* and short ribs, along with daily special plates such as cassoulet and bouillabaisse. The excellent desserts here are also in the bistro tradition, including profiteroles, apple tart tatin, and milk chocolate *pot de crème.* A lively bar and an excellent, mostly French, wine list round out the bistro experience. Open for lunch and dinner every day; dinner reservations suggested.

Cafe Bocca, 4 Mt. Carmel Pl., Poughkeepsie, NY 12601; (845) 483-7300; cafebocca.net; Italian; $$. After a brisk stroll on the Walkway Over the Hudson (walkway.org), walk just few blocks farther west on Parker Avenue to Cafe Bocca for lunch, dinner, or just a refreshing hot doppio cappuccino. This small, informal, very friendly cafe is a local favorite; it's also very popular with people enjoying the Walkway and the Dutchess Rail Trail (dutchessrailtrail.com). The menu here offers a good selection of flavorful paninis and individual pizzas. The paninis are really good here—they're made with freshly baked ciabatta rolls. The entrees are limited to a handful of cafe favorites such as spaghetti *amatriciana* and chicken parmigiana. The weekend brunch, available from 10 a.m. to 2:30 p.m., is very popular. Look for the weekend frittata, made with local seasonal vegetables, farm eggs, and local cheese and served with home fries.

Cinnamon Indian Bistro, 260 North Rd., Poughkeepsie, NY 12601; (845) 232-5430; Indian; $$. The Poughkeepsie branch of **Cinnamon** in Rhinebeck; see listing description on p. 113.

Cosimo's Trattoria, 120 Delafield St., Poughkeepsie, NY 12601; (845) 485-7172; cosimospoughkeepsie.com; Italian; $$. Cosimo's Trattoria has a large, wood-fired brick oven ideal for turning out great pizzas. The menu lists over a dozen variations, plus you can create your own. The rest of the menu is fairly standard Italian. The restaurant takes these classics, such as veal scaloppine, seriously—these dishes are consistently well prepared. Cosimo's has an unusually broad and tasty gluten-free menu, making this restaurant one of the best choices in the region if this dietary restriction is an issue. The restaurant also has several beautifully decorated private dining areas that are ideal for group meals such as family celebrations or business get-togethers.

Coyote Grill, 2629 South Rd., Poughkeepsie, NY 12601; (845) 471-3900; coyotegrillny.com; New American; $$$. As much a bar as a restaurant—the martini lounge alone offers 15 varieties—Coyote Grill has an eclectic American menu that focuses mainly on a range of interesting and well-prepared burgers, pastas, sandwiches, and salads. Coyote Grill is one of the very few non-diner restaurants in the area that keeps the kitchen open late. You can order until midnight on weeknights and until 1 a.m. on weekends. Open for lunch and dinner starting at 11 a.m. on weekdays; on weekends, open for brunch and dinner starting at 10 a.m.

Crave, 129 Washington St., Poughkeepsie, NY 12601; (845) 452-3501; craverestaurantandlounge.com; New American; $$$. The Walkway Over the Hudson (walkway.org) has led to the birth of several excellent restaurants within easy reach of the entrance (see **Cafe Bocca** on opposite page and **Lola's Cafe** on p. 92). Crave is yet another addition to the mix. It's located at the foot of the stairway entrance to the Walkway on Washington Street. The food at Crave is outstanding—this is one of the best restaurants in the whole Poughkeepsie area. The appetizers are particularly inventive. Duck scrapple, served with a polenta cake and a sunny-side-up egg on frisée with a mustard vinaigrette, is a good example. The vegetables that accompany the entrees, such as the pork chop served with bacon chili jam and smoked pork belly, vary with the season and are all from local producers. The dessert menu is worth waiting for: Goat cheesecake isn't found at most restaurants, and the peanut butter bomb, made with peanut butter mousse and chocolate ganache, is an unusual and unusually delicious treat. The carefully chosen wine list offers a good selection of by-the-glass choices. The great food, attentive staff, and cozy dining room at Crave make eating here a real pleasure. Open for dinner every night except Mon; Sun brunch 11:30 a.m. to 3 p.m. Reservations strongly suggested.

Crew Restaurant and Bar, 2290 South Rd., Poughkeepsie, NY 12601; (845) 462-8900; crewrestaurant.com; New American; $$$. Crew frankly doesn't look like much from the outside—it's in an undistinguished strip mall with a view across the highway into a car dealership. On the inside, however, Crew is a sleekly modern restaurant; the open kitchen, bar and dining room are all one space. The menu here is focused on fresh, regional food, cooked to perfection, beautifully plated, and very professionally served. A typical entree is organic chicken breast, pan roasted with truffled potato croquettes, seasonal vegetables, and a mushroom Marsala sauce. Crew is very good about offering seasonally based specials, such as spring ratatouille, made with roasted eggplant, zucchini, yellow squash, red peppers, and onions and served over a goat cheese polenta. At Crew, even the desserts are seasonally inspired: The cheesecake, crème brulèe, and bread pudding all vary daily. The beer selection here is outstanding. In addition to an interesting selection of bottle brews, several drafts, including local offerings, are always in rotation. The award-winning wine list has an extensive collection of international bottlers. If you'd rather have something stronger, the martinis here are excellent. Open for lunch and dinner; reservations suggested for dinner.

Ice House on the Hudson, 1 Main St. (Waryas Park), Poughkeepsie, NY 12601; (845) 232-5783; poughkeepsieicehouse.com; New American; $$$. Well over a century ago, ice harvesting was a big business along the Hudson. The advent of refrigeration ended the business, leaving large ice houses dotting the waterfront. Ice House on the Hudson began life as such a structure—the 25-foot ceiling is a clue to the building's former use, as are the exposed brick walls. The wonderful views of the Hudson from every window make eating here a lot of fun. The menu leans toward seafood, with entrees such as pan-roasted trout with smoked pistachio cream and a wild rice cake. The menu also offers a very good burger, strip steak, and even vegetarian tacos. Wine pairings for the dinner entrees are suggested on the menu. The service and atmosphere here are fun and upbeat. Ice House on the Hudson is within easy walking distance of the Metro-North train station and the Walkway Over the Hudson (walkway.org). Open every day for lunch and dinner.

Mill Street Brewing Company, 289 Mill St., Poughkeepsie, NY 12601; (845) 485-2739; millstreetbrewing.com. Pub Grub; $$$. The craft brewing scene in the Hudson Valley is richer by another brewpub with the addition of Mill Street Brewing Company in 2013. Encompassing 5,000 square feet, including a brew house, the restaurant has mellow exposed brick, antique windows, and raftered high ceilings. A bar with six taps and seating on both sides and an outdoor patio give a casual but upscale feel. The food here is well-crafted pub fare with emphasis on local ingredients, but the beer is the real focus.

Nic L Inn Wine Cellar on the Hudson, 135 N. Water St., Poughkeepsie, NY 12601; (845) 452-5649; nliwinecellar.com; New American; $$. Located just below the Walkway Over the Hudson (walkway.org), Nic L Inn Wine Cellar offers seasonal bistro cuisine combined with an outstanding wine list. The cleanly modern restaurant features an unusual wine-dispensing machine that lets a patron select a taste, half glass, or full glass, directly. It's an approach that encourages sampling from a wide range of interesting wines chosen from around the world. The menu has something of an Italian slant appropriate for the neighborhood, which is Poughkeepsie's version of Little Italy. It's oriented toward local producers, including local cheese and charcuterie boards. Excellent pasta dishes and farm to table blackboard specials make up the main courses; at least one hand-crafted soup is always available. Open Wed through Sun for lunch and dinner; brunch on weekends.

River Station, 1 N. Water St., Poughkeepsie, NY 12601; (845) 452-9207; riverstationrest.com; Traditional American; $$. Back in the 1860s, the building that's now River Station was a waterfront saloon. During the Prohibition years, it was a speakeasy known as Myers Clam Tavern. So it remained until 1958, when the owner died. In the meantime, the flourishing riverfront area, once the dock for visitors enjoying a day trip on the Hudson line, fell on hard times. Many vicissitudes later, the original tavern building became today's River Station restaurant. The long history makes River Station the oldest continually operated food establishment in Poughkeepsie. Today, the 350-seat restaurant anchors a revitalized waterfront district and boasts an outdoor terrace with magnificent views overlooking the Hudson. The food here is consistently good, with the standard offerings of burgers, sandwiches, steaks, and pub food. A special feature that makes River Station worth a visit is the chowder bar. The restaurant offers five different homemade chowders every day; all are outstanding.

Hudson Valley Fresh

Over the decades, economic pressures have forced many dairy farmers in the Hudson Valley and elsewhere to give up their cows and sell their land. In 2005, a group of dairy farmers in Columbia, Dutchess, and Ulster counties came together and formed Hudson Valley Fresh, a not-for-profit dairy cooperative dedicated to preserving the agricultural heritage of the Hudson River Valley. Today, 10 HVF dairy farmers milk contented, pastured cows that are humanely treated and never given any hormones. Because the cows are very healthy, their milk is very clean, containing far fewer white blood cells than even the strictest organic limits. Milk this clean doesn't need to be ultra pasteurized; instead, the milk is lightly pasteurized and retains its full flavor. The milk from Hudson Valley Fresh cows is processed at Boice Brothers Dairy in Kingston, a family-run business since 1914. It meets the strict standards for kosher law and is certified kosher. Hudson Valley Fresh products include whole, skim, low-fat, and chocolate milk along with half-and-half, heavy cream, yogurt, and sour cream.

The milk reaches store shelves within 36 hours of leaving the farm—conventional milk often takes a week. In the region, HVF milk is carried by many retailers, including some supermarkets, and is served exclusively at many regional restaurants. The economics of Hudson Valley Fresh are impressive. In all, the co-op farmers milk about 2,000 cows. Each milking cow generates some $15,000 per year in economic activity to the local community, which translates into $30 million for the region. The economic multiplier effect is much larger. HVF also has an impact on regional employment. Boice Brothers employs about 45 people; each farm employs anywhere from 3 to 10 people.

A half gallon of Hudson Valley Fresh milk costs about a dollar more than the conventional product. It's a small price to pay for helping to maintain a way of life, support the local economy, preserve more than 8,000 acres of beautiful farmland in the region, and bring home a local food. See HVF's recipes for **Sour Cream Onion Dip** and **Sour Cream Pancakes** on pp. 316 and 317.

47 S. Hamilton St., Poughkeepsie, NY 12601; (845) 264-2372; hudsonvalleyfresh.com.

Schatzi's Pub and Bier Garden, 202 Main St., Poughkeepsie, NY 12601; (845) 454-1179; facebook.com/SchatzisPubBier Garden; German; $$. With fifteen rotating craft beers on tap, a menu that features modern takes on classic brauhaus dishes, and a large outdoor patio in the back, Schatzi's is an authentic German-style beer garden. The indoor pub part is very nice as well, with a large and lively bar and a small dining area. The food here is simple and very good—the wursts come from **Elia's** in nearby Highland (see p. 227), so even a frankfurter on a pretzel roll at Schatzi's is a special experience. Also on the menu are some original creations, including the duck confit grilled cheese sandwich and the tater tots appetizer, stuffed with braised pork belly, cheddar, and scallions. In true beer garden spirit, Schatzi's is for late owls—on weekdays the restaurant opens at 3 p.m. and stays open until 4 a.m.; on weekends, the hours are 11:30 a.m. to 4 a.m. The hours make Schatzi's just about the only restaurant and bar in the region to be open that late.

Shadows on the Hudson, 176 Rinaldi Blvd.; Poughkeepsie, NY 12601; (845) 486-9500; shadowsonthehudson.com; Traditional American; $$–$$$. Perched on a cliff 40 feet above the Hudson River, Shadows on the Hudson is beautifully designed. Five different dining areas, each with its own decor, let guests choose an ambience ranging from the casual Sunset Room to the modern Winter Room. The menu at Shadows on the Hudson is fairly standard American steaks, burgers, and seafood; it's all well-prepared and surprisingly reasonable. The best reason to go to Shadows on the Hudson is to enjoy the sophisticated nightlife scene here. On Stereo Saturday, Shadows offers a high-energy club experience with a resident DJ and dancers. Be aware that an upscale dress code is strictly enforced for the club.

The Crafted Kup, 44 Raymond Ave., Poughkeepsie, NY 12603; (845) 483-7070; craftedkup.com; Coffeehouse; $. A spacious, relaxed cafe just next door to Vassar College, The Crafted Kup offers one of the best cups of coffee in town. The beans for the extensive list of coffee drinks come from local roasters, including **J.B. Peel** (see p. 106); teas come from **Harney & Son** (see p. 68). Also available are a good array of coffee snacks, including scones from **Bread Alone** and cupcakes from **Moxie's** (see p. 262). The cafe offers free Wi-Fi and that rare amenity, a bike rack.

Debra T's Ice Cream Cafe, 141 Overlook Rd. (Route 43), Poughkeepsie, NY 12601; (845) 471-3357; facebook.com/DebraTs IceCreamCafe; Ice Cream; $. The distinctive turquoise and pink paint job at Debra T's roadside cottage tips you off right away that this is a place that takes ice cream seriously—but not too seriously. The frozen treats here come in an almost bewildering range of flavors and types, including hard serve, soft serve, and frozen yogurt. The milk shakes and banana splits are wonderful, but what seems to draw customers most of all are the generously sized and very creative sundaes. The raspberry truffle sundae, for instance, is made with your choice of ice cream topped with homemade raspberry fudge, mini raspberry truffles, and raspberry sauce, finished off with a raspberry cookie. Kids love this place not only for the ice cream but for the fun, kid-friendly atmosphere. In season, open daily from 11:30 a.m. to 9 p.m. Closed from mid-Nov to early Apr.

Kavos Gyros, 4 N. Clover St., Poughkeepsie, NY 12601; (845) 473-4976; kavosgyros.com; Greek Sandwich Shop; $. The standard gyro sandwich is nowhere in sight at Kavos Gyros—you won't see a brownish hunk of indeterminate meat rotating under the grill. Instead, the basic gyros here are made with freshly grilled chicken or pork (no lamb), stuffed into a pita and topped with homemade tzatziki sauce, lettuce, tomato, onions, and french fries. Variations on the gyros theme here include the vegetarian Village, made with smoked tofu and topped with feta, tomato, cucumber, red onion, and green peppers. The Red Pepper gyro is made with pork or chicken and topped with roasted red pepper, fresh basil, fresh mozzarella, and balsamic vinegar; the fabulous Gyro #9 is topped with hummus, lettuce, cabbage-carrot slaw, and tabouli. A range of other well-made Greek dishes, such as spanokopita, stuffed grape leaves, and *kalamaki* (grilled chicken skewers) are also available. The location on Clover St. is conveniently close to the Metro-North train station and the Walkway Over the Hudson (walkway.org), making this a good place for a fortifying or reviving meal. Kavos Gyro is a small restaurant and it can get crowded during the lunchtime rush.

Lola's Cafe and Gourmet Take Out, 131 Washington St., Poughkeepsie, NY 12601; (845) 471-8555; lolascafeandcatering .com; Sandwich Shop; $. Located just next door to its elegant sister restaurant **Crave** (see p. 85), Lola's Cafe is a great lunch choice for a quick, made-to-order sandwich, panini, wrap, or salad, perhaps accompanied by a bowl of soup or chili. The food here is inventively simple—

a typical offering might be the poblano turkey panini, made with roasted turkey breast, swiss cheese, pickled red onions, and baby greens, topped with jalapeño poblano aioli. The casual atmosphere and pleasant surroundings make Lola a popular stop-off for walkers and bikers enjoying the Walkway Over the Hudson (walkway.org). Gluten-free bread is available. The store is open only on weekdays from 10 a.m. to 5 p.m.

Rosticceria Rossi and Sons, 45 S. Clover St., Poughkeepsie, NY 12601; (845) 471-0654; rossideli.com; Sandwich Shop; $–$$. This long-established, no-frills Italian deli and sandwich shop is a favorite lunchtime stop in the downtown Poughkeepsie area. The sandwiches and paninis here are made with only the finest Italian charcuterie and artisan cheeses, and they're served on fantastic, fresh-baked focaccia or ciabatta. Hot entrees such as baked ziti, eggplant parmigiana, and other Italian favorites are also available, but it's paninis like rosemary grilled chicken with fresh mozzarella, pesto, and sun-dried tomatoes and sandwiches like the traditional meatball parmigiana that keep people coming back. Be warned: Portions are generous here and even the small panini is a lot to eat. There's always a line at lunchtime, but it moves quickly. Plan to take your sandwich with you to eat somewhere else—seating is very limited. Closed Sun.

Savana's Gourmet Hot Dogs and Sausages, 50 Raymond Ave., Poughkeepsie, NY 12603; (845) 337-3400; savanashotdogs .com; Hot Dogs; $. The super-good dogs and sausages at Savana's are served with a range of unusual toppings, including Savana's own two special hot sauces: Grim Reaper and 666. The most popular topping here is the addictively good sweet and tangy homemade papaya salsa; others toppings include Savana's homemade neon green relish, homemade chili, and Thai peanut sauce. This might also be the only place to ever put pastrami on a hot dog. The sausages here come in a range of flavors, including beef and bacon stuffed Monterey jack cheese and chicken apple with Vermont maple syrup. Sausages and hot dogs are served on sturdy Italian bastone rolls, the better to support the toppings. Those who dare can sign a liability waiver and try the Savana hot sauce challenge. Winners get their picture on the Wall of Flame.

Soul Dog Restaurant, 107 Main St., Poughkeepsie, NY 12601; (845) 454-3254; souldog.biz; Hot Dogs; $. The owners of Soul Dog Restaurant say they are dedicated to redefining the hot dog experience.

Do they ever! It's amazing how a basic Sabrett all-beef hot dog (or an Applegate chicken dog or a veggie dog) is transformed when it's topped with Soul Dog's secret Soul sauce, or with chipotle cream, or spicy peanut sauce, especially if guacamole, sour cream, turkey chili, fresh jalapeños, or even classic onions in sauce are added to the mix. Add in a side order of hand-cut fries or quinoa salad, and a fast, cheap lunch turns into a gourmet treat. The rare individual who doesn't like hot dogs can opt instead for one of Soul Dog's hot sandwiches, such as the Poughkeepsie cheese steak. Soul Dog offers gluten-free options, including a gluten-free bun for the dogs and gluten-free individual pizzas. They also bake gluten-free and vegan pastry treats on the premises. Their gluten-free bread is now so popular that it's sold in many local retail outlets, including **Adams Fairacre** (see pp. 95, 138) and **Rhinebeck Health Foods** (see p. 124).

Twisted Soul Food Concepts, 47 Raymond Ave., Poughkeepsie, NY 12603; (845) 454-2770; twistedsoulconcepts.com; Fusion Cuisine; $. The food at Twisted Soul is so hard to describe that it can leave even an experienced writer groping for words. Chef-Owner Ira Lee brings together street food concepts from around the world and gives them his own special twist. He doesn't seem to believe in boundaries, so the menu is full of dumplings, empanadas, steamed buns, rice bowls, and other variants on international fast foods. As just one example, the dumpling menu ranges from traditional Chinese steamed dumplings with pork and ginger to Chef Lee's interpretation of the traditional Chinese steamed dumpling, made with lamb and portobello mushrooms. This is one of the few places in the entire region where you have a very good chance of eating something—maybe several things—you've never eaten before, like chickpea fries, Malaysian coconut curry grilled tofu, or, to take an especially twisted concept, an Ethiopian grilled tofu arepa, served with fried plantains, peanuts, and green onions. To drink, choose from an equally eclectic list of bubble teas, smoothies, and Twisted's signature beverages, such as lavender lemonade with basil seeds. For dessert, have one of Chef Lee's remarkable cupcakes. Ambience isn't the point at Twisted Soul—the restaurant is small, narrow, and often crowded. Much of the business here is takeout. Open for lunch and dinner every day except Tues and Sun.

Specialty Stores & Producers

Adams Fairacre Farms, 765 Dutchess Tpke., Poughkeepsie, NY 12603; (845) 454-4330; adamsfarms.com. Back in 1919, Ralph A. Adams and his family ran a farm stand in Poughkeepsie, selling fresh produce from their own 50-acre farm. The stand gradually got bigger and bigger, and around 1960 it was replaced by a small retail store. The retail store gradually got bigger and bigger and in 1977 started offering cheese, meats, baked goods, seafood, and gourmet deli items. In 1981, a second store was added in Kingston; a third store was added in Newburgh in 1998, and in 2011 a new store opened in Wappingers Falls. Times have changed since 1919, but Adams family members still run the stores and are still committed to great food and great service. The Adams stores are also very committed to local farmers and producers—they carry a huge range of local products. The Adams stores are often the only retail outlet for local farmers and producers who otherwise sell only or mostly through farmers' markets. If you can't visit the region on a market day, visit an Adams store instead for the freshest and best local products. See the recipes for **Simple Fresh Garden Pasta Sauce** and **Adams's Own Tattooed Rosemary Potatoes** on p. 326 and p. 327.

Arlington Wine and Liquor, 718 Dutchess Tpke., Poughkeepsie, NY, 12603; (866) 729-9463; arlingtonwine.net. One of the best-stocked and most spacious stores in the area, Arlington Wine and

Liquor carries a very broad wine selection, including many local vintages. The store holds wine tastings almost every Saturday from noon to 5 p.m. The knowledgeable staff are very friendly and helpful.

Caffe Aurora Pasticceria, 145 Mill St., Poughkeepsie NY 12601; (845) 454-1900; caffeaurora.com. An old-fashioned Italian pastry shop dating back to 1941, Caffe Aurora is a reminder that the Mt. Carmel neighborhood of Poughkeepsie was once called Little Italy. The shop specializes in perfect miniature Italian pastries, such as petits fours, cannoli, napoleons, cream puffs, and sfogliatelle. The amaretti and biscotti here are classic perfection, available in 14 flavors. Caffe Aurora also makes hard-to-find Italian seasonal specialties, including *mostaccioli* (a Christmas treat) and the unusual *biscotti ossi di morti* (literally, bones of the dead), offered from November 2 (All Souls' Day) through Christmas. Adding to the lost-in-time feeling is the authentic soda fountain. The shop has a comfortable seating area that's a great place to relax and enjoy a pastry along with an espresso made by a very large and shiny machine.

Half Time Beverage, 2290 South Rd., Poughkeepsie, NY 12601; (845) 462-5400; halftimebeverage.com. Opened in 2002, Half Time Beverage quickly achieved a reputation among aficionados for having the world's largest selection of beer. It's now widely regarded as the best source in the world for craft beers. Local and regional brews are thoroughly represented here. The cavernous store is crammed with beer in cans and bottles; the store also has a dozen draft beer taps for filling growlers. Half Time frequently holds beer tastings and meet-the-brewmaster events—check the website for details.

Hudson Chocolates, 211 Cottage St., Poughkeepsie, NY 12601; (845) 853-5544; hudsonchocolates.com. Francisco Migoya, the owner of Hudson Chocolates, is also a professor at the nearby Culinary Institute of America, teaching future chefs all about pastry. His goal with his chocolate workshop, opened in 2013, is to create new chocolate experiences and present them beautifully. He balances flavors, textures, and the very finest ingredients (sourced locally whenever possible) to create chocolates that are truly remarkable. An example of Chef Migoya's sensibility and skill is the Hudson Valley Terroir Bar. Inspired by the flavors of autumn, the bar contains candied apples, cinnamon, toasted pecans, cranberries, and pumpkin seeds. The bar is surrounded by a creamy cinnamon ganache, coated in dark chocolate, and finished with miniature leaves to resemble the topsoil of the Hudson Valley forest floor. The bar is astonishing, both visually and to the palate. All creations from Hudson Chocolate are presented in a beautifully designed signature box, each numbered and signed by Chef Migoya. The primary sales outlet for Hudson Chocolates is its online store, but the workshop is open to the public on Sat from 1 p.m. to 6 p.m. and by appointment.

Krishna Grocery, 2300 South Rd., Poughkeepsie, NY 12601; (845) 463-4330; krishnagrocery.com. This large, well-stocked store offers Indian groceries and produce and a good selection of freshly made takeout food. It also has a large library of Indian films in four languages for sale and for rent.

La Deliziosa Italian Pastry Shoppe, 10 Mt. Carmel Pl., Poughkeepsie, NY 12601; (845) 471-3636; ladeliziosany.com. La Deliziosa is justly famous for its cannoli and for its invention of the cannoli chip: chips of cannoli shell served with filling on the side for dipping. Other old-school house specialties here are rainbow cookies, amaretti, and biscotti. They also make great *taralli,* an Italian snack food sort of like a pretzel or breadstick, but round. Like bagels, *taralli* are briefly boiled before being baked. At La Deliziosa, they come in a range of shapes and flavors, from savory to sweet, all very addictive. Sfogliatelle at La Deliziosa are a weekend-only specialty; get there early.

Mother Earth's Storehouse, 1955 South Rd., Poughkeepsie NY, 12601; (845) 296-1069; motherearthstorehouse.com. See listing description on p. 247.

Phil-Asian Foods, 794 Dutchess Tpke., Poughkeepsie, NY 12603; (845) 363-6633. Specializing in Filipino products, Phil-Asian Foods also has a thorough selection of Asian food items. This is a good place to purchase hard-to-find foods such as dried squid, rice flour, Asian snack foods, Asian produce, and unusual instant noodle brands. The store also sells a wide array of homemade Filipino dishes, such as *ginataang kalabasa* (squash cooked in coconut milk) and beef mechado (beef stew in a tomato sauce) that are very hard to find anyplace else in the region.

Sloop Brewing, Poughkeepsie, NY 12603; (917) 848-3865; sloop brewing.com. Sloop Brewing is a licensed nano-brewery, meaning that each beer is produced in amounts of three barrels or less. A beer barrel contains only 31.5 gallons, or about 50 cases of bottled beer, so Sloop Brewing beers are a bit hard to find. It's not just that they're brewed in tiny amounts—it's because they're locally very popular. The beers are sold in bottles at a number of local farmers' markets and at local retailers. They're also available on tap, usually on a rotating basis, at local bars and beer specialists, such as **Grand Cru** in Rhinebeck (see p. 123) and **The Hop** in Beacon (see p. 41). Two of the brews are a bit unusual: The Black C and The Sauer Peach are bottle-conditioned, meaning that they contain active yeast cultures and continue to mature in the bottle.

Welcome Oriental Grocery, 1820 New Hackensack Rd., Poughkeepsie, NY 12603; (845) 462-6433. With only two aisles, this small grocery is surprisingly well-stocked with hard-to-find (at least locally) Asian ingredients such as frozen dumplings and miso paste.

The friendly staff is good at answering questions and helping befuddled shoppers locate and identify items.

Farm Bounty

Arlington Farmers' Market, Alumnae House Lawn (Raymond Avenue at Fulton Avenue), Poughkeepsie, NY 12601; (845) 559-0023. Mon and Thurs, 3 p.m. to 7 p.m., June through Oct.

Poughkeepsie Farm Project, Raymond Avenue at Hooker Avenue, Poughkeepsie, NY 12603; (845) 516-1100; farmproject.org. Founded in 1999, the Poughkeepsie Farm Project (PFP) is a nonprofit organization that works toward a just and sustainable food system in the mid-Hudson Valley. One way they do this is with a very popular member-supported farm, a great example of how the urban agriculture movement can be a success. Going beyond community-sponsored agriculture, however, the PFP also sponsors community education programs, workshops and classes at the farm, and the Farming for the City training program for future farmers. PFP also sponsors a food-share program that donates about 25 percent of the produce harvested on the farm to local food banks, emergency food providers, and individuals through subsidized CSA shares.

Sprout Creek Farm, 34 Lauer Rd., Poughkeepsie, NY 12603; (845) 485-9885; sproutcreekfarm.org. Nonprofit Sprout Creek Farm does three things at once: It's a working farm producing free-range beef, pork, chicken, and eggs, along with produce. It's a market, selling farm products, especially their award-winning artisan cheeses. Sprout Creek is internationally famous for their cheeses, particularly for their raw cow's milk Ouray and Toussaint varieties. Finally, Sprout Creek Farm is also an educational center, offering numerous programs and classes designed to help connect young people with the land. The farm market is open 7 days a week, 10 a.m. to 5 p.m., from Memorial Day through Labor Day. Sprout Creek cheeses can also be purchased online year-round.

Red Hook

Foodie Faves

Bread and Bottle, 7496 S. Broadway, Red Hook, NY 12571; (845) 758-3499; breadandbottle.net; Traditional American; $$. This enjoyable cafe with an airy, very modern design focuses on home-baked and very good bread, beer, and wine. The focus on bread expands to include foccacia, flatbread pizza, paninis, sandwiches, and more, plus daily special soups. There's also a great selection of homemade charcuterie and cheese. The beer list includes many local brews on tap; the wine list has a local focus as well. In the evening, the focus is more on the bottle end, with a steady roster of live performers. Tuesday is all-you-can-eat pizza night. Closed Sun. Bread and Bottle also sells their breads at the Milan and Red Hook farmers' markets.

Flatiron, 7488 S. Broadway, Red Hook, NY 12571; (845) 758-8260; flatironsteakhouse.com; Steak House; $$$. A casual restaurant with a very good bar, Flatiron is a high-end steak house serving steaks, seafood, and an interesting selection of burgers—the merguez-spiced local ground lamb burger is great, and the ground duck topped with a fried egg and duck cracklins is eye-opening. Appetizers include excellent oysters and well-crafted homemade charcuterie. All the baking is done in-house. The specials, especially if they include game, are always worth trying. (The restaurant offers prix-fixe wild game dinners on a regular basis.) The vegetables at Flatiron, however, are what take this restaurant beyond the usual steak house. No massive baked potatoes are served, and while creamed spinach is on the menu, it's alongside a good variety of other vegetable choices. The vegetables here are fresh, seasonal, locally sourced whenever possible, and carefully prepared. Very unusually for a steak house, the menu at Flatiron has vegetarian options, such as chickpea-flour gnocchi, that are serious dishes, not afterthoughts. Reservations suggested. Closed Mon and Tues.

Max's Memphis BBQ, 736 S. Broadway, Red Hook, NY 12571; (845) 758-6297; maxsbbq.com; Barbecue; $$. Max's Memphis BBQ is consistently named one of the best barbecue places in the Hudson Valley. It's not just that the food is very good—guests love the lively central bar (with a great beer list), cozy dining spaces, and friendly service, to say nothing of the very popular wing nights. The barbecue here is hickory-smoked for up to 16 hours out back. In addition to the usual ribs, brisket, pulled pork, and chicken, Max's offers house-smoked local spicy sausages that are outstanding. The traditional dinner platters, served with two sides, are very generous—count on leftovers. Max's doesn't take reservations for groups smaller than six, so there may be a wait on a busy weekend night. Open for dinner only; closed Mon.

Mercato Osteria and Enoteca, 61 E. Market St., Red Hook, NY 12571; (845) 758-5879; mercatoredhook.com; Italian; $$$. The chef-owner at Mercato is Francesco Buitoni, a seventh-generation descendant of the Buitoni pasta family. His small, cozy restaurant is modeled after an Italian osteria, a place serving wine and a short menu of simple, seasonal dishes. Chef Buitoni's menu fits that description nicely. It varies daily, depending on what's local and fresh. Typical dishes are grilled branzino fillets with herb-roasted potatoes and sautéed lacinata kale and penne *arrabiata* with smoked pancetta in a spicy tomato sauce made with cream from nearby **Ronnybrook**

Dairy (see p. 146). The *enoteca* part of the name means wine shop, and here too Chef Buitoni hits the mark exactly. The extensive wine list at Mercato is exclusively Italian and well worth exploring. Open for lunch Thurs through Sun and for dinner Wed through Sun. Reservations suggested on the weekend.

Cafes & Quick Bites

Bubby's Burritos (food truck), **Route 199 near Route 9G, Red Hook, NY 12571; facebook.com/TheBurritoStand; Food Truck; $.** This tiny roadside burrito trailer is perched off the road a bit, next to the **Hardeman Orchards** farm market (see p. 108). It's open seasonally, from about mid-May into Oct; during the open season the trailer is sometimes closed for rain or for reasons known only to the proprietor. The menu is as tiny as the trailer. It's limited to just four or five varieties of delicious, freshly made vegetarian burritos and quesadillas. The portion is substantial and the price is very reasonable. Enjoy your meal sitting at a picnic table or on a bench overlooking the orchard.

Holy Cow, **7270 S. Broadway, Red Hook, NY 12571; (845) 758-5959; Ice Cream; $.** When an ice cream shop has lines out the door in the middle of winter, you know it's doing something right. Holy Cow offers excellent homemade ice cream, sundaes, milk shakes, ice cream cakes, and other ice cream concoctions at very reasonable prices. The family-owned store prides itself on the quality of its hard and soft ice cream and doesn't worry too much about having a lot of flavors. Compared to some other places, the choices are limited, and for some reason there's no chocolate hard serve. Those are quibbles, however, because the existing flavors, such as black raspberry, blueberry pie, and pistachio, are outstanding. The chocolate banana and coffee milk shakes are perfection, as are the ice cream sandwiches made with homemade chocolate chip cookies. Holy Cow is no-frills—there's no inside seating and only a few picnic tables outside. That doesn't stop the crowds, especially on a hot summer night. Open 11 a.m. to 10 p.m. every day year-round. No credit cards.

Me-Oh-My Cafe and Pie Shop, 7466 S. Broadway (Firehouse Plaza), Red Hook, NY 12571; (845) 835-8340; meohmypieshop .com; Traditional American; $. Without question, Me-Oh-My makes the best chocolate chip cookies in the entire region. Opinion is divided on the pies; some say they are the best in the region; others say they are the best, period. All the fruit pies are handmade using only fresh, seasonal produce; the cream and savory pies are made with equal attention to quality ingredients. They come in the standard 10-inch size, but are also available as 6-inch pies and small hand pies—and by the slice in the cafe. You can also buy Me-Oh-My pies and baked goods at local farmers' markets. The baked goods star at Me-Oh-My, but the cafe food is just as good. The individual pot-pies alone are worth a trip. The bites—small slices of fresh baguette topped with house roasted meat and grilled fresh vegetables—are the perfect midafternoon snack, especially if dinner will be late. This is a favorite place for a delicious and very fairly priced lunch. Thursday through Saturday nights, it's also a place for an equally delicious and very fairly price dinner. The dinner menu offers $10 meals that feature satisfying, simple dishes, such as house-made meat loaf with two sides. Order them to take out or eat them on the spot. The cafe is small and can get crowded at lunchtime; if you don't want to wait for a table, take your order to go. Closed Mon.

Rusty's Farm Fresh Eatery, 5 Old Farm Rd., Red Hook, NY 12571; (845) 758-8000; rustysfarmfresheatery.com; Traditional

American; $. The farm-to-table concept at Rusty's works exceptionally well. This small, informal restaurant, almost hidden among other shops on the site, serves excellent, locally sourced food at very reasonable prices. The menu consists mostly of salads, wraps, paninis, burgers, and subs; there's also a choice of two daily soups, plus really good fresh-cut french fries. Order one of Rusty's special smoothies or fresh juices to go with your meal. The specials for the day are based on what's fresh and local—they're always worth trying. Rusty's offers the option of gluten-free bread for all the sandwiches. It also offers vegetarian options, including a flavorful veggie burger, making this little restaurant a good choice for people with dietary restrictions.

Taste Budd's Chocolate and Coffee Cafe, 40 W. Market St., Red Hook, NY 12571; (845) 758-6500; tastebudds.com; Coffeehouse; $. At this cozy, very popular local cafe, the coffee and tea drinks are just an excuse for sampling the wide array of creative home-baked cookies, cakes, pies, pastries, and chocolates. (More substantial food, including freshly made paninis, sandwiches, and quesadillas, is also available.) This is a good spot for breakfast, a quick lunch, or a coffee break. You can linger as long as you like, enjoying the comfy couches, using the free Wi-Fi, and perhaps playing a board game. Live music is offered every Sat from 2 p.m. to 4 p.m. and every Sun from noon to 2 p.m. Taste Budd's is open every day from 7 a.m. (8 a.m. on Sun) to 10 p.m.

Two Boots, 4604 Rte. 9G, Red Hook, NY 12571; (845) 758-0010; bard.twoboots.com; Pizza; $$. The Hudson Valley outpost of the famed Two Boots pizza chain is located directly across the street from the main entrance to Bard College. The pizza here is as good as it is at any of the other stores, which means very good indeed. Two Boots pizzas have names, such as the Night Tripper, made with sun-dried tomatoes, roasted garlic, and jalapeño pesto on a white pie with a whole-wheat crust. The Red Hook restaurant offers them all, along with a local variant: the St. Tula, made with **Fleisher's** sausage of the day (see p. 245), roasted garlic and peppers, sweet red pepper pesto, ricotta, and mozzarella. The Two Boots blend of Cajun and Italian cuisines means that the menu also offers wings, po' boy sandwiches, and other alternatives to pizza. The staff here is very friendly.

Specialty Stores & Producers

Annandale Cidery, **8 Davis Way (Route 9 and Route 9G), Red Hook, NY 12571; (845) 758-6338; mporchards.com.** Part of the **Montgomery Place Orchards** operation (see p. 107), Annandale Cidery began producing hard ciders from over 60 apple varieties, antique and modern, grown in the historic Montgomery Place orchards. The signature cider is Annandale Atomic, made from a blend of at least six varieties. It's semidry and comes in at 7 percent alcohol by volume. The ciders are available at the farm market.

Gigi Market and Cafe, **227 Pitcher Ln., Red Hook, NY 12571; (845) 758-1999; gigimarket.com.** Located on the historic, 500-acre Greig Farm, Gigi Market is a year-round, daily farm market with a very pleasant cafe. The market, in a renovated barn, is stocked with seasonal produce, local and imported cheese, natural meats and poultry, baked goods, and a very broad range of regionally crafted pickles, relishes, sauces, honeys, and much more. The cafe area serves Gigi's special farm breakfast sandwiches all day. At lunchtime, you can order a salad, panini, sandwich, or skizza (thin-crust pizza), made fresh with local ingredients, of course. On weekends from June to Oct, Gigi Market hosts weekly prix-fixe *agriturismo* dinners, where the four-course menu is entirely seasonal, local, and delicious. Reserve well in advance. Owner Laura Pensiero is also the proprietor of **Gigi Trattoria** in Rhinebeck (see p. 114). Open Wed through Sun, 8 a.m. to 6 p.m.

J.B. Peel Inc., 7582 N. Broadway (Red Hook Commons), Red Hook, NY 12571; (800) 231-7372; jbpeelcoffee.com. J.B. Peel is primarily a roaster and distributor of fine coffee to restaurants and inns, but the store is open to the public. This is an excellent place to purchase the freshest and finest roasted Arabica beans from Colombia. All the beans are roasted and ground the same day they arrive. The store offers a number of single and blended coffees, along with a wide range of loose teas. J.B. Peel isn't a coffee shop by any means, but you can sip a fresh cup while you inhale the heady aroma of roasting beans and try to decide what to take home.

Farm Bounty

Fraleigh's Rose Hill Farm, 19 Rose Hill Farm Rd., Red Hook, NY 12571; (845) 758-4215; pickrosehillfarm.com. Family owned since 1798, Fraleigh's Rose Hill Farm offers pick-your-own apples, cherries, raspberries, peaches, apricots, and pumpkins at Rose Hill Farm or buy them at the farm stand. Open 9 a.m. to 6 p.m. weekends only in summer and fall; call ahead to find out what's ready to pick.

Greig Farm, 223 Pitcher Ln., Red Hook, New York 12571; (845) 758-1234; greigfarm.com. Historic Greig Farm is one of the best pick-your-own spots in the region, starting with fresh asparagus in May and continuing over the summer with peas, strawberries, blueberries, raspberries, followed by apples and pumpkins in September and October. If you don't want to pick you own, sign up for a fresh-fruit membership and pick up a brimming weekly basket every Friday in season. Greig Farm produce is also available at **Gigi Market** (see page 105).

CONSERVING THE FOODSHED

The six counties of the mid-Hudson Valley region covered in this book have, in total, nearly 3,000 working farms covering some 407,000 acres. These farms are all within 150 miles of New York City—the distance from farm to table is actually fairly short. Regional farms already supply many greenmarkets, restaurants, and groceries in the city. The demand for regional farm goods far exceeds the supply, yet farmland in the Hudson Valley is disappearing into subdivisions, strip malls, and suburban sprawl at an alarming rate.

Conserving the farmlands of the region is a top priority for Scenic Hudson, a nonprofit organization that works to protect and restore the Hudson River region. The organization combines land acquisition, support for agriculture, and citizen-based advocacy to preserve the valley's inspiring beauty and natural resources. To date, Scenic Hudson has created or enhanced more than 50 parks, preserves, and historic sites and conserved nearly 30,000 acres.

When farms continue to be part of the landscape, they preserve not only a rural way of life but the scenic beauty of the area—an attraction that drives a multibillion-dollar tourism industry. Conserving farms also means conserving wildlife habitat and sensitive environmental areas; Conserved farmland protects aquifers and drinking water supplies.

Today, regional efforts to conserve farmland through conservation easements, purchase of development rights, land trusts, and other economic incentives are a patchwork of various, sometimes conflicting, programs at the federal, state, regional, and nonprofit level. Scenic Hudson alone has helped conserve 11,500 agricultural acres in recent years.

Much more needs to be done, and quickly, to save farmland that is in peril of being lost forever. In 2013, Scenic Hudson released its Foodshed Conservation Plan for the region. The plan is a bold, forward-looking proposal for a new public-private partnership of farmers, land trusts, and government, all working together to maintain a sustainable regional food system. It's an idea whose time has very much come. The plan is worth reading—download it at scenic hudson.org/foodshedplan.

Hardeman Orchards, 194 W. Market St., Red Hook, NY 12571; **(845) 758-5154.** Apples from Hardeman's own orchard out back are for sale here, along with local produce and fresh cider in season. Open daily from mid-May to Nov.

Hudson Valley Farmers' Market at Greig Farm, 229 **Pitcher Ln., Red Hook, NY 12571; greigfarm.com.** Every Sat from 10 a.m. to 3 p.m.

Migliorelli Farm Stand, 7357 S. **Broadway, Red Hook, NY 12571; (845) 758-3273; migliorelli.com.** Migliorelli Farm is a family-run farm based in Tivoli. One of the largest operations in the area, Migliorelli sells its own 130 varieties of vegetables and fruit at some  30 farmers' markets, mostly in New York City. Locally, their produce is available at the Rhinebeck farmers' market and at two farm stands. The Red Hook stand is open in season (mid-May into Nov) daily from 9 a.m. to 6 p.m. In 1998, the Migliorelli Farm sold all development rights and protected the land through a Scenic Hudson conservation easement (see p. 107). This means the property will remain farmland forever.

Montgomery Place Orchards, 8 Davis Way **(Route 9 and Route 9G), Red Hook, NY 12571; (845) 758-6338; mporchards.com.** The Hudson Valley is full of historic old farms, but the orchards at Montgomery Place are perhaps the most historic of all. The property dates back to 1802, when Janet Montgomery, widow of the Revolutionary War hero Richard Montgomery, bought a large, prosperous farm along the Hudson. The farm remained in the hands of the prominent Montgomery/Livingston clan until 1998, when it was passed to the preservation organization Historic Hudson Valley and was opened to the public (hudsonvalley.org). Today, the extensive orchards at Montgomery Place are still productive; some 70 different apple varieties, many of them antique, are grown. Not all are meant to be eaten (see **Annandale Cidery,** p. 105), but many of the varieties are sold at Montgomery Place Orchards farm stand, along with fresh produce from local farms and a great selection of jams and preserves made from Montgomery Place fruit. From mid-June through Thanksgiving, the stand is open every day but Mon from 9 a.m. to 6 p.m.

Oriole Orchards, 134 Feller-Newmark Rd., Red Hook, NY 12571; (845) 758-9355. Pick your own berries, apples, cherries, peaches and other tree fruit, and pumpkins. Apple varieties include McIntosh, Ida Red, Red Delicious, Mutsu, Rome, Winesap, Greening, Cortland, Macoun, Golden Delicious, Spy-Gold, and Paula Red. Open every day in season; call ahead to find out what's ready to pick and how the weather is.

Red Hook Outdoors Farmers' Market, 7467 S. Broadway (municipal parking lot), Red Hook, NY 12571; (845) 464-3598; face book.com/RedHookOutdoorsFarmersMarket. The outdoor market is every Sat, June through Nov, 10 a.m. to 2 p.m.

Red Hook Winter Farmers Market, 7562 N. Broadway, Red Hook, NY 12571; (845) 943-8699; heartyroots.com. The indoor market is held the second Sat of the month, Dec through Feb, from 10 a.m. to 2 p.m. at the historic Elmendorph Inn. The market is organized by **Hearty Roots Farm** (see p. 159).

Shoving Leopard Farm, 845 River Rd., Barry-town, NY 12507; (845) 758-9961; superiorconcept .org/shovingleopard. This small CSA is located at Rokeby, a historic Hudson River mansion in Barrytown (a hamlet of Red Hook). The farm grows over 100 varieties of more than 50 vegetables.

Rhinebeck

Arielle, 51 E. Market St., Rhinebeck, NY 12572; (845) 876-5666; ariellerhinebeck.com; Mediterranean; $$–$$$. A cozy storefront restaurant with a classic brasserie decor, Arielle offers a classic French brasserie menu of well-prepared cassoulet, chicken paillard, and the like, enlivened by outstanding pasta dishes, some Mediterranean touches (try the chicken tagine), and daily specials. For the less adventurous, Arielle also has a traditional and very good steak menu. Round out your meal with a classic brasserie dessert, such as *pot du chocolat* or cardamom crème brûlée. The drinks here are perfectly mixed and generously sized. The servers are attentive and very knowledgeable. Their suggested wine pairings, drawn from a mostly French wine list, are always on the mark. The three-course prix-fixe lunch here is a fabulous value and a great way to sample the Arielle menu. Sunday brunch from noon to 4 p.m. Closed Mon. Dinner reservations suggested.

Aroi Thai, 55 E. Market St., Rhinebeck, NY 12572; (845) 875-1114; aroirestaurant.com; Thai; $$. Located in a converted house, Aroi offers authentic Thai food in a relaxed atmosphere with friendly service. Customer favorites include the *tom yum* soup, all the *pad* (noodle) dishes, and the various curries. Aroi also has very good dinner specials based on fresh, local ingredients. Try the homemade ice cream in Thai flavors, such as ginger, for dessert. The prix-fixe lunch special here is an excellent value—on a Sunday in season, this a good way to fortify yourself for a stroll through the Rhinebeck Farmers' Market right next door. Beer and wine only. Lunch every day but Tues and Wed; dinner every night.

Art Bar, 6367 Mill St., Rhinebeck, NY 12571; (845) 417-8990; the-artbar.com; Black Sea; $$–$$$. The cuisine of the Black Sea region doesn't get much attention in the Hudson Valley, which makes the menu at Art Bar more interesting than you would expect from a place that is primarily a music venue and art gallery. Art Bar offers *zakuski,* small plates much like tapas or mezze, featuring choices such as stuffed grape leaves, olives, and assorted charcuterie. The menu also features fresh fish, littleneck clams, and salads made with fresh, locally sourced vegetables. Art Bar offers 20 different house-infused vodkas. The restaurant features a large collection of original artwork for sale; the walls are also home to a large private collection of original signed works on paper, including pieces by Marc Chagall, Salvador Dalí, and Pablo Picasso. Enjoy it all indoors in four different lounges or outdoors on the large patio. Live music some weeknights and on the weekends. Art Bar is one of the few places in Rhinebeck that are open late—until 1 a.m. on Wed and Thurs and until 2 a.m. on Fri and Sat. Lunch on the weekend only. Closed Mon and Tues.

Beekman Arms and Delamater Inn, 6387 Mill St., Rhinebeck, NY 12572; (845) 876 7077; beekmandelamaterinn.com; New American; $$$. The Beekman Arms is the oldest inn in America—it's been serving food to guests continuously since 1766. The restaurant at the Beek (as it's affectionately called by locals) is the Tavern. The oldest part of the restaurant is the historic Tap Room, which dates back to colonial times and has the original beamed ceiling (watch your head) and open-hearth fireplace. The other restaurant areas include the greenhouse, which looks out onto the lawn where Continental Army troops once drilled, and two elegant dining rooms. When you dine at the Beek, you're eating where George Washington and Franklin D. Roosevelt, among other famed Americans, also dined. The menu offers well-prepared American classics, such as chicken potpie, braised short ribs, and the Tavern burger, made with pepper jack cheese, smoked bacon, and horseradish cream sauce. The lunch menu is a bit simpler but just as good; it offers that genuine rarity, a well-prepared turkey club sandwich. Brunch here is special, with an unusually long menu that incorporates the usual omelets, quiche, and other breakfast dishes with heartier fare drawn from the lunch and dinner menus. The Beekman Arms is a favorite spot for family celebrations and wedding meals—reservations are strongly recommended.

Calico Restaurant and Patisserie, 6384 Mill St., Rhinebeck, NY 12572; (845) 876-2749; calicorhinebeck .com; Continental; $$$. The smallest restaurant in Rhinebeck (just seven small tables) is also one of the finest. Chef Anthony Balassone creates amazing dishes for bistro-style lunches and sophisticated, romantic dinners; pastry chef Leslie Balassone crafts delectable pastries, cakes, and desserts that are sold at the patisserie counter and appear on the menus. This husband-and-wife team together have created a place that is an important regional dining destination. The dinner menu at Calico sticks mostly to perfectly prepared classics with a French accent, such as roasted garlic soup with crème fraîche, bouillabaisse, and flatiron steak with hunter sauce. The simplest dishes, such as the vegetarian penne pasta tossed with wild mushrooms, baby spinach, roasted red peppers, shallots, and oven-roasted garlic, are prepared with all the care that goes into more complex choices. The menu changes with the seasons—Calico offers a special winter dining series that is in very heavy demand (call or check the website for details). The lunch menu at Calico is a bit simpler and smaller, with some sandwich choices; the brunch menu offers some entrees from the main menu along with quiches and the panini of the day. Dessert at Calico comes from the heavenly patisserie offerings.

Try the macaroons, the fruit tarts, the cakes, or the gluten-free Sarah Bernhardt cookie, made with almond paste and chocolate ganache. Reservations are a must at Calico. Dinner and lunch are served Wed through Sat; brunch on Sun from 11 a.m. to 2 p.m. Closed Mon and Tues. Because Calico is up three steps from the street and is very small, it is not easily accessible for people with mobility problems.

China Rose, 1 Shatzell Ave., Rhinecliff, NY 12574; (845) 876-7442; chinaroserestaurant.com; Chinese; $$. China Rose is located on the waterfront near the Amtrak station in Rhinecliff, a hamlet just next to Rhinebeck. The river view from the patio is lovely—it's fun to watch the river traffic and see the trains go by. The food here is authentic and well prepared, with good daily specials. The fried wontons, made with **Coach Farms** goat cheese (see p. 75) and crabmeat, are a bit out of the ordinary for a Chinese restaurant. Frozen sake margaritas, a house specialty, are a major draw. China Rose is almost always crowded; the live music on weekends adds to the decibel level. The take-out business here is very active. No reservations, so be prepared for a bit of a wait. Open for dinner only; closed Tues.

Cinnamon, 5856 Rte. 9, Rhinebeck, NY 12572; (845) 876-7510; facebook.com/CinnamonIndianCuisine; Indian; $$. The menu at Cinnamon hits all the expected high notes for a quality Indian restaurant, including excellent tandoori dishes, and adds a few extra notes with dishes emphasizing the spicy cuisine of southern India and Sri Lanka. The careful spicing and good service, combined with the intriguing menu, make this one of the best Indian restaurants in the region. Out of the ordinary dishes here include *lasuni gobi* (battered fried cauliflower florets), *meen malabar* (halibut curry made with coconut milk and southern Indian spices), and *eral varuval,* a Sri Lankan shrimp dish. Try the *garam halwa,* or carrot pudding, for dessert—it will change forever how you think about carrots. The menu also offers a good choice of vegetarian dishes. It's well worth driving 10 minutes south from the center of Rhinebeck to try Cinnamon. The varied and well-prepared lunch buffet here is an excellent way to sample the menu. Open daily for lunch and dinner; dinner buffet on Sun nights.

Gaby's Cafe, 6423 Montgomery St., Rhinebeck, NY 12572; (845) 516-4363; gabyscafe.com; Mexican; $$$. A relaxed, informal cafe with a great selection of tequilas at the bar, Gaby's offers well-prepared if unsurprising Mexican cuisine. The menu has the usual selection of appetizers and platters, along with chimichangas, tacos, burritos, and quesadillas. The fajitas here are more varied than ordinary, including good seafood and vegetarian versions. Also of interest on the menu is the good selection of seafood choices, including Gaby's special seafood paella. The lunch menu is more limited, with burgers and wraps taking the place of fajitas and entrees. The portions are generous here. Open from 11 a.m. to 10 p.m., making this a good choice for a late supper or drink. Live mariachi music on Thurs evenings.

Gigi Trattoria, 6422 Montgomery St., Rhinebeck, NY 12572; (845) 876-1007; gigihudsonvalley.com; Mediterranean; $$$. A pioneer in the use of fresh, locally sourced ingredients, Gigi Trattoria has been a hit restaurant since it opened in 2001, quickly garnering regional honors and national fame. The food here is aptly described by owner Laura Pensiero as Hudson Valley Mediterranean. The dishes are mostly Italian, but the ingredients are almost exclusively from nearby farms and producers. Gigi's trademark (literally) dish is the skizza, a crispy flatbread topped with fresh ingredients. The Bianca skizza, for instance, is topped with Coach Farm goat cheese, Gigi's own fig jam, pear, arugula, and truffle oil. Gluten-free skizzas are available. Skizzas are very light and flavorful, making them a great alternative to the antipasti as a starter. Aside from the skizzas, the dinner menu follows the traditional Italian structure of salads, antipasti, first-course pasta dishes and second-course entrees, plus specials, all centered on what's fresh and local that day. All are imaginative, expertly prepared, and beautifully presented. The menu descriptions detail the source of the ingredients, giving a real sense of how closely Gigi's is involved with the local producers. Gigi's famous burger, for instance, uses Meiller Farms ground beef topped with Mountain Smokehouse nitrate-free bacon, smoked tomato jam, bread and butter pickles, and Adirondack cheddar on a Gigi-made onion-seed brioche bun, served with Tuscan fries. Open for lunch and dinner every day. Gigi's is extremely popular, but reservations are taken only for groups of six or more. On a busy weekend, be prepared for a wait. Alternatively, try **Gigi Market and Cafe** in nearby Red Hook—skizzas are on the menu there (see p. 105).

Le Petit Bistro, 8 E. Market St., Rhinebeck, NY 12572; (845) 876-7400; lepetitbistro.com; French; $$$. Le Petit Bistro is aptly named—it's cozy in this small restaurant, a Rhinebeck favorite ever since it opened more than 25 years ago. The food here is classic French bistro, perfectly prepared from the freshest ingredients. Le Petit Bistro is so good because it sticks to the basics. The appetizers, for example, include escargots, French onion soup, and clams casino. The entrees feature coquilles St. Jacques au poivre, half roast duckling with sauce du jour, and veal Française. No surprises here, but that's the point: beautifully prepared, classically simple bistro dishes, served by an attentive staff. Even so, check the handwritten specials list on the blackboard for the chef's creations of the day. It's often worth departing from the menu to try them. The seafood offerings, which sometimes extend as far as fish tacos, are always good choices. The mostly French wine list is excellent. Open for dinner only; closed Tues and Wed. Reservations recommended.

Liberty of Rhinebeck, 6417 Montgomery St., Rhinebeck, NY 12571; (845) 876-1760; libertyrhinebeck.com; New American; $$$.

Rhinebeck is a very historic town, founded in 1686 by refugees fleeing religious persecution in the Palatine area of Germany. It's full of historic buildings such as the one that houses Liberty of Rhinebeck, which dates back to 1860. The building was originally the Starr Institute, a library and social center for the town until 1974. Today, this upscale pub captures the historic spirit of the building beautifully in the decor, especially in the remarkable Flag Room (the main dining room), the tavern area, with historic FDR memorabilia, the Boat Bar (adorned with a 23-foot sailboat), and the basement nightclub area. The food here at lunch and dinner is based on a small, seasonally rotating menu, sourced as locally as possible. The dishes are sophisticated pub fare, including fish-and-chips, truffle mac and cheese, hanger steak, and meat loaf. Try the house-made ravioli in whatever version is being offered that week. The beer and wine menus are relatively short but carefully chosen. Liberty of Rhinebeck is one of the few places in town to stay open late: until 11 p.m. on weeknights and Sun, and until 2 a.m. on Fri and Sat.

The Local Restaurant and Bar, 38 W. Market St., Rhinebeck, NY 12572; (845) 876-2214; thelocalrestaurantandbar; New American; $$$. The Local is a fun restaurant with a relaxed atmosphere. The two-story interior features a cozy dining balcony that overlooks the first-floor dining room and open galley kitchen. Diners can enjoy watching Chef Wesley Dier in action as he crafts great food from local ingredients. The food here is contemporary American, with signature dishes such as phyllo-wrapped Coach Farm goat cheese and roasted sweet potato ravioli. Chef Dier's beef sliders, made with Black Angus from nearby Meiller's Farm, are served on a soft brioche with roasted garlic, herb mayo, and pickled red onion, and are locally famous. Thursday is meat loaf night, a good motivation to try The Local. The outstanding bar at The Local serves up modern takes on classic cocktails, including the

Hudson Mule, a takeoff on the Moscow Mule that first became popular in the 1940s. At The Local, it's made with Core apple vodka from **Harvest Spirits Farm Distillery** in Columbia County (see p. 192) and served in a chilled copper mug. There's also a good selection of craft beers and a small but select wine list. Open for dinner only; closed Sun and Mon.

Market Street, 19 W. Market St., Rhinebeck, NY 12572; (845) 876-7200; marketstrhinebeck.com; Italian; $$$. Famed chef Gianni Scappin brings his signature Italian cooking to this elegant restaurant. The rustic-chic decor features comfy upholstered booths and pleasantly soft lighting. The centerpiece of the restaurant is the wood-burning oven in the open kitchen. Guests can opt to sit at the communal counter and enjoy nine different varieties of fabulous pizza straight from the oven. The menu has much more than just pizza, however. The small plates offer an intriguing range of flavors, such as roasted asparagus with Parmesan shavings and delectable little beef meatballs in tomato sauce with polenta. The appetizers, pastas, and entrees are all equally well prepared contemporary versions of Italian classics such as *fusilli anitra* (duck *ragù* with sage, pine nuts, and currants). Unusually for restaurants in the area, braised rabbit with baby carrots, turnips, and polenta is on the menu. The prix-fixe dinners, offered on some weeknights and on special days, offer a good range of dishes not on the regular menu. Open every night for dinner; lunch on Fri only; brunch from 11 a.m. on Sat and Sun.

Momiji, 43 E. Market St., Rhinebeck, NY 12572; (845) 876-5555; momijius.com; Japanese; $$. Tucked into the courtyard area off East Market Street, Momiji offers hibachi tableside cooking along with a solid menu of very fresh sushi and sashimi. For those who don't like raw fish, well-prepared standard Japanese dishes such as tempura and teriyaki are good choices. The long and varied roll list at Momiji is fun—the rolls and hand rolls have a creative Asian-fusion approach. There's even a kids' menu. The service at Momiji is very good and the food is reasonably priced, making this a good choice for family meals. Open every day for lunch and dinner.

Osaka, 22 Garden St., Rhinebeck, NY 12572; (845) 876-7338; osakasushi .net; Japanese; $$–$$$. Located in the Garden Street shops complex off West Market Street, Osaka is a regional destination spot for sushi lovers. The elegant wraparound sushi bar is the focus of this small restaurant; the handful of tables in the dining room are almost afterthoughts. The menu includes a good range of very good standard Japanese dishes, such as tempura, teriyaki, and udon dishes. Fish-loving regulars here stick to the very fresh, expertly prepared sushi, sashimi, rolls, and hand rolls. The service at Osaka is very hospitable and helpful—ask your server to recommend a sake pairing. Open for lunch and dinner every day but Tues. A sister restaurant is in nearby Tivoli—see p. 133.

Puccini Ristorante, 22 Garden St., Rhinebeck, NY 12572; (845) 876-3055; puccinirhinebeck.com; Italian; $$$. If it's time for a special night out in Rhinebeck, Puccini Ristorante is an excellent choice. Tucked away in the Garden Street shops of West Market Street and right next to **Osaka** (see above), family-owned Puccini Ristorante serves upscale Italian cuisine in a romantic setting. The opera theme is carried through with posters from La Scala and a soundtrack of works by the master of verismo opera himself. The food here runs to classics such as fettuccine carbonara, saltimbocca, and veal Marsala, all beautifully prepared and presented. Puccini is a good reminder that while contemporary reimaginings of classic dishes have an important role in moving cuisine forward, there's also still a lot to be said for keeping the classics classic. In the warm weather, guests can dine on the outdoor patio. Open for dinner only; closed Mon. Reservations suggested.

The Rhinecliff, 4 Grinnell St., Rhinecliff, NY 12574; (845) 876-0590; therhinecliff.com; Pub Grub; $$. The Rhinecliff is a boutique hotel located just next to the Amtrak station in Rhinecliff, a hamlet of Rhinebeck. The historic hotel is a truly elegant place to stay and is much in demand for weddings and other celebrations. The restaurant part of the hotel is known as The Bar and features historic touches such as the restored original bar from the original hotel, now over 150 years old. The food at The Bar is high-end gastropub with a faint British accent—the menu features a ploughman's board appetizer and a sticky toffee pudding dessert—along with other favorites such as *steak frites,* burgers, and roasted half chicken. In season, enjoy dining on the outdoor patio, with a great view of the Hudson River. The Rhinecliff serves dinner daily and a very enjoyable brunch on the weekends; on Sun, brunch is enlivened by live jazz. Tues night at The Rhinecliff is showcase night for local musicians.

Terrapin, 6426 Montgomery St., Rhinebeck, NY 12572; (845) 876-3330; terrapinrestaurant.com; New American; $$$. One of the top dining destinations in the Hudson Valley, Terrapin offers two ways to experience its outstanding food. The setting alone makes Terrapin worth a visit—the soaring ceilings are a legacy of the building's original purpose as a Baptist church dating back to the 1820s. Dine in the lovely, very calm formal dining room, or eat in the more relaxed and livelier (also much noisier) Red Bistro. The menus are a bit different but the food is equally excellent on either side of the restaurant. One of the most enjoyable aspects of eating at Terrapin is trying inventive dishes not found on menus elsewhere. In the dining room, start with an appetizer such as the macadamia nut tempura calamari with a pineapple dipping sauce. From there, move on to a soup, such as the asparagus and sweet pea soup with Parmesan crust, or a salad made with tart cherries, almonds, mesclun, and pomelo, served with white balsamic vinaigrette and shaved Asiago cheese. Entrees such as the maple syrup–brined, double pork chop with a Calvados-apple demi-glace topped with crushed maple- and bacon-flavored almonds, or the vegetarian farmers' market buckwheat crepes with a raclette cheese Mornay sauce, really show off just how good Terrapin is. Save room for dessert—the triple chocolate mousse cake shouldn't be missed. The bistro menu includes many of the dining room choices along with many pub food options, including chicken wings, quesadillas, nachos, excellent sandwiches, and what may very well be the best burgers in the Hudson Valley. In the summer season, Terrapin celebrates the bounty of the Hudson Valley with special farm dinners on some week-nights. Call the restaurant or check the website for details; reservations are a must. The dining room is open for dinner only; reservations are strongly recommended. Dressy casual attire is suggested. The bistro is open for lunch and dinner daily; no reservations are accepted and you may have to wait for a table on busy days. The bistro is open until midnight Sun through Thurs and later on Fri and Sat.

Cafes & Quick Bites

Artigiani del Gelato, 41 E. Market St., Rhinebeck, NY 12572; (845) 876-2338; facebook.com/artigianidelgelato; Ice Cream; $. Gelato is Italian for ice cream, but with a difference. Like ice cream, gelato is made with milk and cream, but unlike ice cream, which must have at least 10 percent fat, gelato usually contains only about 5 to 7 percent fat. That means gelato flavors are more intense, because they're not covered up by the fat. Gelato is also served a bit warmer and softer than ice cream, which makes the flavors easier to taste. At Artigiani del Gelato, the gelato is made on the spot, using local milk and fresh fruit in season. The flavors are remarkable. In addition to standard flavors such as vanilla, chocolate, and strawberry, the shop offers surprisingly delicious flavors such as wasabi, ramp, rosemary, and lychee, and also puts together amazing combinations, such as goat cheese and honey. In addition to the gelato in cups, the shop offers gelato burgers: two flavors on a brioche. Also available are gelato shakes, granitas, pastries, and fresh-brewed coffee. The shop has a few small tables and some very popular chairs outside the door. On a hot summer day, expect a short line.

Pizzeria Posto, 43 E. Market St., Rhinebeck, NY 12572; (845) 876-3500; postopizzeria.com; Pizza; $$. This cozy restaurant, tucked away in the courtyard off Market Street, is dominated by the huge, wood-burning pizza oven—it's fun to watch your artisan pizza being prepared and cooked right in front of you. The menu at Pizzeria Posto is classically simple, almost austere: a couple of antipasti, a handful of interesting salads (arugula, goat cheese, and apples in a sherry vinaigrette, for instance) and just six perfectly prepared pizza choices, starting with the basic Margherita (tomatoes, fresh mozzarella, basil) and ending with the sophisticated Morandi (Grana Padano, red onions, pistachios, rosemary). Lunch and dinner every day except Tues.

Samuel's of Rhinebeck, 42 E. Market St., Rhinebeck, NY 12572; (845) 876-5312; shopsamuels.com; Coffeehouse; $. Samuel's is a popular Rhinebeck stop for a cup of really good coffee and a locally baked pastry or Moxie cupcake (see p. 262) to go with it. In addition to being a great little place for a relaxing coffee break, Samuel's also sells fair-trade organic coffee beans. Also for sale here are handmade chocolates from a local artisan, including choices such as dark chocolate sea salt caramels and dark chocolate, cranberry, and mixed nut bark. In contrast to the sophisticated chocolates, Samuel's also carries a good line of nostalgic candy treats, including Chuckles and Teaberry chewing gum.

Tavola Rustica, 51 E. Market St., Rhinebeck, NY 12572; (845) 876-6555; Italian/Deli; $. Located in the cobblestoned courtyard area off Market Street, Tavola Rustica is a combination Italian cafe and gourmet market. The food here is quick but sophisticated. The antipasto menu, for instance, includes grilled polenta with truffle oil, and porchetta is one of the entrees. Tavola Rustica also makes great paninis (try the brie with pear and arugula) and offers both savory and sweet crepes. Check the whiteboard for the day's specials. Order at the counter and your meal gets delivered to your table soon after. Tavola Rustica is also a good place for Italian gourmet specialty items. Open for lunch from 11:30 a.m. to 2:30 p.m.; dinner from 5 p.m. to 10 p.m.; closed Tues.

Specialty Stores & Producers

Blue Cashew Kitchen Pharmacy, 6423 Montgomery St., Rhinebeck, NY 12572; (845) 876-1117; bluecashewkitchen.com. Quality gear for the home kitchen—all kinds—are for sale at Blue Cashew Kitchen Pharmacy. This amazing store stocks everything a sophisticated home chef could want, from bakeware to serving pieces. All the products are carefully chosen to combine form, function, and style. Among the brands represented here are Royal Copenhagen, MUD Australia, Chantal, and Mauviel. The store is great for browsing; if you don't want to carry your choices home, order them through the website instead.

Bread Alone, 45 E. Market St., Rhinebeck, NY 12572; (845) 876-310; breadalone.com. The Rhinebeck outlet and cafe for the famed Bread Alone bakery in Woodstock has a very popular front counter area that sells bread, baked goods, coffee, and sandwiches. There's some seating here. For restaurant service, head to the back area. The counter is open every day from 7 a.m. to 5 p.m.; the back dining room hours are 8 a.m. to 3 p.m. weekdays and 8 a.m. to 4 p.m. weekends.

Bumble & Hive, 43 E. Market St., Rhinebeck, NY 12572; (845) 876-2625; facebook.com/Bumble&Hive. This charming gift shop specializes in honey and things made by bees, such as beeswax candles, along with **Harney & Sons** teas (see p. 68) and lots of fun gift items. The selection of jarred honey is extensive. Just as wine shops offer tastings, Bumble & Hive has a honey tasting bar offering honeys from all over the country and the world, including tupelo honey, palmetto honey, and manuka honey from New Zealand. Stop by the bar for some sampling and be astonished at the vast range of flavors high-quality honey can have. Among the brands stocked is honey from **Hummingbird Ranch** in nearby Staatsburg (see page 129).

Grand Cru Beer and Cheese Market, 6384 Mill St., Rhinebeck, NY 12572; (845) 876-6992; grandcrurhinebeck.com. Craft beers from the region, New York State, and around the world are the focus at Grand Cru—they even offer gluten-free beer. The emphasis is on New York State beers and regional artisan food products, including cheese and charcuterie. Grand Cru regularly rotates craft beers among six taps; buy a growler or bring in your own for a fill-up. The small cafe area is a good spot to sample a glass of beer and some cheese. Grand Cru features regular tap takeovers by brewmasters and offers live music—check the website for details.

Oliver Kita Chocolates, 18 W. Market St., Rhinebeck, NY 12572; (845) 876-2665; oliverkita.com. Oliver Kita has been making amazing chocolate in Rhinebeck since 2007. His products are made using only the finest organic and fair-trade chocolate, flavored with the aromas of flowers, herbs, citrus, exotic fruits, berries, nuts, and spices. These chocolates are jewel-like works of art, delighting all the senses. Oliver Kita is highly regarded for his special collections of themed chocolates, including charming holiday collections. Of special interest is the Great Estates collection, Oliver's tribute to the many historic mansions that line the Hudson Valley. Using flavors from Hudson Valley artisans and farms, this collection is a taste tour of the region. It comes in beautiful box decorated with a photo of the Hudson and includes a tour map of the mansions.

Pure Mountain Olive Oil, **23 E. Market St., Rhinebeck, NY 12572; (845) 876-4645; puremountainoliveoil .com.** The finest and freshest olive oils, vinegars, sea salts, and other gourmet kitchen essentials are the primary stock at Pure Mountain Olive Oil. This little shop will open your taste buds to the variety of flavors that high-end olive oil can have—over 30 varieties are in stock, to say nothing of the other flavorful oils, such as unrefined toasted sesame oil. The store is fun to visit, especially when a tasting is being held. Check the website for events.

Rhinebeck Health Foods, **24 Garden St., Rhinebeck, NY 12572; (845) 876-2555; rhinebeckhealthfoods.com.** This well-stocked store carries a great assortment of health foods, dietary supplements, and the like. It's well known to locals as a great place to find fresh, organic produce, local cheese and milk, and local pastured meat, along with organic treats such as vegan chocolate bars and Treeline vegan cheese (it's made from nuts). The mostly vegetarian Garden Street Cafe within the store is a great spot for a quick, healthy lunch. The cafe serves great sandwiches and wraps, house-made soups, salads, and organic smoothies and juices.

Spacey Tracy's Pickles, **PO Box 488, Rhinebeck, NY 12572; (845) 876-8083; spaceytracys.com.** Pickles of all sorts are Spacey

Tracy's specialty. She makes crispy, flavorful pickles, including addictive sweet and spicy sunshine pickles and mouth-warming hot and spicy garlicky dill pickles, using only the freshest and best local ingredients. Spacey Tracy's products are sold at many farmers' markets and retailers, including **Adams Fairacre** (see pp. 95, 138). Watch for the colorful Spacey Tracy's food truck at farmers' markets and many regional outdoor events. The very popular truck offers dill pickles coated in a tempura batter, deep-fried on the spot, and served with a choice of homemade dipping sauces.

Warren Kitchen and Cutlery, 6934 Rte. 9, Rhinebeck, NY 12572; (845) 876-620; kitchen-class.com. Warren Kitchen and Cutlery is where serious cooks in the area go to shop for professional-grade cookware, kitchen tools, serving pieces, bakeware, glassware, and most important of all, knives. In fact, quality knives are the specialty at Warren Kitchen—more than 1,500 different sizes and styles are in stock. The store offers in-store professional knife sharpening. They'll even engrave your name on your knives.

Farm Bounty

Brittany Hollow Farm, 7115 Albany Post Rd., Rhinebeck, NY 12572; (845) 758-3276; brittanyhollowfarm.blogspot.com. One of the founding vendors of the Rhinebeck farmers' market, Brittany Hollow Farm is a family-owned, pesticide-free vegetable grower. The produce is sold only at the market, but Brittany Hollow also has a u-pick flower operation open from July through Sept that is a lot of fun. Pick your own cut flowers, including cosmos, celosia, zinnias, black-eyed Susans, strawflowers, snapdragons, and others.

Cedar Heights Orchard, Crosby Ln., Rhinebeck NY 12572; (845) 876-3231; rhinebeckapples.com. In addition to the many heirloom apple trees at Cedar Heights Orchard, popular varieties such as Galas, Cortlands, Jonamacs, Empires, Macouns, and Red Delicious are all available to be picked. Cedar Heights is aptly named: The views from this hilltop orchard are spectacular. The orchard has been family-owned for more than 150 years. The u-pick season runs from Aug into late Oct, 9 a.m. to dusk. Call ahead to find out about the weather and what's ready to pick. Also check out the new cider operation.

Migliorelli Farm Stand, Route 199 at River Road, Rhinebeck, NY, 12572; (845) 758-3273; migliorelli.com. This is the Rhinebeck stand for Migliorelli Farm. See listing description on p. 108.

Rhinebeck Farmers' Market, 61 E. Market St. (municipal parking lot), Rhinebeck, NY 12572; rhinebeckfarmersmarket.com. Founded in 1994, this is the market that began the farmers' market movement in the region. It's still the best. The outdoor market is open every Sunday from 10 a.m. to 2 p.m. from Mother's Day to Thanksgiving. The winter market is held every other Sun from 10 a.m. to 2 p.m. from Dec through Apr at the Rhinebeck Town Hall, 80 E. Market St.

Wonderland Florist, Nursery, and Farm Market, 199 Rte. 308, Rhinebeck, NY 12572; (845) 876-4981; facebook.com/ wonderlandfloristnursery. Now owned and operated by the third generation of the Lobotsky family, the farm market at Wonderland offers a wide array of pesticide-free fruits and vegetables from the nearby family farm. The nursery section has an excellent selection of annuals and perennials. The farm itself, located on 91 White Schoolhouse Rd., is a great spot for pick-your-own pumpkins in the fall; call (845) 876-6760 for picking dates and availability.

Salt Point

Copperfield's, 2571 Rte. 44, Salt Point, NY 12578; (845) 677-8188; copperfieldrestaurant.com; Traditional American; $$–$$$. The food at Copperfield's is standard American fare, relying heavily on well-prepared steak, seafood, and pasta. The quality is high and the portions are more than ample. Copperfield's has a nice, relaxed atmosphere, with friendly service and a good bar. The very popular Turkey Tuesday at Copperfield's is an excellent value—a full turkey dinner with all the fixings at a very reasonable price. Sunday brunch is very popular here for the same reason: great food at very fair prices. Live music every Fri night.

Fireside Barbecue & Grill, 1920 Salt Point Tpke., Salt Point, NY 12578; (845) 266-3440; facebook.com/firesidebbq; Barbecue; $$$. More grill than barbecue, Fireside serves a good mix of traditional American fare and a good range of excellent barbecue dishes, including their famous hog wings and tri-tip beef. On the grill side, the well-prepared dishes tend toward the familiar, such as chicken parmigiana with linguine, fried shrimp basket with fries, sole stuffed with crabmeat, and prime rib. The food here is consistently good, with generous portions and good service. The restaurant is in an old carriage house—it's cozy but the noise level can be high. Kids eat free on Tues; live music or karaoke on weekends.

Hahn Farm, 1697 Salt Point Tpke., Salt Point, NY 12578; (845) 266-5042; hahnfarm.com. The seventh generation of Hahns work this farm, founded in 1798. They raise organic meat, including Angus beef (Hahn Farm is the biggest direct-to-the-consumer producer in Dutchess County), pork, chicken, and lamb. They also grow a wide range of vegetables. The roadside farm stand sells the farm's vegetables and a good range of products from local producers. It's open year-round, but hours vary with the season. In the colder weather, the stand is open Fri 2 p.m. to 6 p.m. and Sat 10 a.m. to 2 p.m. In the summer, the stand is open all day every day. Call ahead for pricing on meat orders. From mid-Sept through the end of Oct, Hahn Farm has Fall Festival weekends—bring the kids and pick your own pumpkin, get lost in the corn maze, take a hayride, pet an animal, and more.

Terhune Orchards, 761 North Ave., Salt Point, NY 12578; (845) 266-5382; terhuneorchardsny.com. Terhune Orchards is a popular pick-your-own spot for apples, peaches, apricots, plums, cherries, nectarines, pears, berries, and other fruits. The farm also has a retail stand selling its own fruit and local produce, including sweet corn, pumpkins, and gourds, along with baked goods. The farm and the farm stand are open from 10 a.m. to 6 p.m. daily from mid-July through the end of Oct. If you want to pick your own, call ahead to learn what's ripe and what the weather is likely to be.

Staatsburg

Foodie Faves

Portofino Ristorante, 57 Old Post Rd., Staatsburg, NY 12580; (845) 889-4711; portofinorest.com; Italian; $$. Portofino is a local favorite for fresh, well-prepared, traditional Italian food in an unpretentious, friendly atmosphere. The portions are generous here—expect to take home leftovers. Wednesday and Thursday nights, Portofino offers Flight Nights: a four-course pasta dinner with a flight of three red or white wines. The price is very reasonable, adding to Portofino's popularity. Open for dinner only; closed Mon and Tues.

Farm Bounty

Breezy Hill Orchard and Cider Mill, 828 Centre Rd., Staatsburg, NY 12580; (845) 266-3979; hudsonvalleycider.com. Breezy Hill Orchard grows over a hundred varieties of heirloom apples and other fruit. The apples and other fruits are sold at farmers' markets in the region and in New York City Greenmarkets. Owner Elizabeth Ryan also makes several varieties of hard cider, sold at markets under the name Hudson Valley Farmhouse Cider. The farm isn't open to the public, but special events, such as the annual wassail party in May, are held fairly often. Check the website for details.

Hummingbird Ranch, 18 Hummingbird Way, Staatsburg, NY 12580; (845) 266-0084; hummingbirdranch.biz. The products from Hummingbird Ranch go beyond basic honey and maple syrup to include maple candy, beeswax candles, soap, creamed honey (very luscious), and more. The products are sold online from the farm, at area farmers' markets and events, and in some retail shops.

Stanfordville

Foodie Faves

Bangall Whaling Company, 97 Hunns Lake Rd., Stanfordville, NY 12581; (845) 868-3349; bangallwhalingcompany.com; Traditional American; $$. The historic hamlet of Bangall in Stanfordville is the home to this cozy, family-friendly restaurant serving hearty American cuisine. The traditional menu of steaks, seafood, burgers, and salads is complemented by the interesting blackboard specials, such as beer-marinated pork cutlets and shrimp and salmon Florentine with scampi sauce over linguine. The welcoming bar has a good selection of draft beers. The lounge area at the front of the restaurant is a good place for a drink while checking e-mail using the free Wi-Fi. Closed Mon and Tues.

Red Devon Market, Cafe, Bar and Restaurant, 108 Hunns Lake Rd., Stanfordville, NY 12506; (845) 868-3175; reddevon restaurant.com; New American; $$$. A farm-to-table destination dining spot, Red Devon is in Bangall, a historic hamlet in Stanfordville. (Old-timers in the area will remember the building as the Stage Stop Steakhouse, owned for many years by actor Jimmy Cagney.) The building is state-of-the-art green, with a green roof, solar electric and hot water, and native species plantings in the landscaping. Inside, the Red Devon has two parts. On one side is the market/cafe, which serves breakfast and lunch dishes and sells prepared foods and homemade baked goods, along with products from local farms, such as honey, jam, and maple syrup. The other side is the rustic but elegant restaurant and the historic bar from the Stage Stop. Owners Julia and Nigel Widdowson are deeply committed to supporting local sustainable agriculture. At Red Devon, just about everything is locally sourced (OK, the fair-trade coffee and olive oil are imports) and house-made, including the fabulous charcuterie. The menu varies seasonally, of course. In the spring, a typical appetizer is buttermilk ramp salad with Old Chatham ewe's blue cheese, buttery croutons, buttermilk ramp dressing, sun-dried tomatoes, and mesclun greens. Entrees include buttermilk fried chicken with bacon-braised collard greens, mashed potatoes, and black pepper 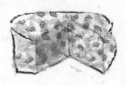 honey. The food on both sides of Red Devon is consistently wonderful. The ingredients are fresh and beautifully handled—every dish is imaginative and prepared with care. Every house product, from the bread to the ketchup, is expertly made and richly flavorful. Red Devon is that rare restaurant that sincerely believes in the principles behind farm-to-table dining and does everything possible to uphold them. The market is open for breakfast and lunch Thurs from 8 a.m. to 12:30 p.m., Fri through Sun from 8 a.m. to 4 p.m. and Mon from 8 a.m. to 3 p.m. The restaurant is open for dinner only Fri, Sat, and Sun. Reservations suggested. Hours for the market and restaurant vary a bit seasonally; call ahead or check the website.

Farm Bounty

Sisters Hill Farm, 127 Sisters Hill Rd., Stanfordville, NY 12581; (845) 868-7048; sistershillfarm.org. The CSA at Sisters Hill Farm is sponsored by the Sisters of Charity of Saint Vincent de Paul of New York. One of the farm's main goals is to share a portion of the harvest with those in need in the local community by donating produce directly to families and to local food pantries and soup kitchens. An active CSA since 1999, Sisters Hill Farm has 5 acres under cultivation, feeding more than 200 families and harvesting some 60,000 pounds of produce each year.

Thunder Hill Farm, 5908 Rte. 82, Stanfordville, NY 12581; (845) 868-1306. This small, grass-based farm raises free-range cattle, sheep, pigs, chickens, and turkey. The meat is sold at the farm stand, along with fresh eggs and vegetables. The stand is open daily, 8 a.m. to 8 p.m. Call ahead for special orders.

Tivoli

Foodie Faves

Luna 61, 55 Broadway, Tivoli, NY 12583; (845) 757-0061; luna61 .com; Vegetarian; $$. Luna 61 serves only organic vegetarian food, but even the most confirmed meat eater will find something delicious on the menu. The food here is very creative. Dishes such as the Machismo starter—tofu, black beans, avocado, and roasted red peppers in a tortilla with soy chile sauce—are so full of rich flavor and so beautifully presented that the absence of meat isn't noticed. Ditto for entrees such as seitan piccata, made with panko-crusted seitan cutlets in a lemon white wine caper sauce and served with quinoa. Sunday brunch at Luna 61 is a real treat, featuring the imaginative use of eggs in dishes such as McLunatic, the restaurant's delicious version of eggs Benedict. The desserts are all baked in-house without white flour or white sugar. By all means try the banana cream pie. Luna 61 has an enjoyable terrace for outdoor dining in the warmer weather. Inside, the decor is on the funky side; the upper dining room is reached by a spiral staircase. Open for dinner every night except Wed; brunch on Sun from 10 a.m. to 4 p.m.

Murray's, 76 Broadway, Tivoli, NY 12583; (845) 757-6003; murraystivoli.com; Vegetarian; $. Murray's is a favorite spot for breakfast and lunch in Tivoli. The mostly vegetarian menu features breakfast dishes and lunch sandwiches made with fresh local produce. Sandwiches such as the celeriac Reuben, made with roasted celery root, swiss cheese, sauerkraut, and home-made Russian dressing, are interestingly different. Murray's offer a short wine list and a good selection of craft beers. The restaurant is open daily from 8 a.m. to 5 p.m.

Osaka, 74 Broadway, Tivoli, NY 12583; (845) 757-5055; osaka sushi.net; Japanese; $$$. This Japanese restaurant is the sister restaurant to the one in Rhinebeck—see listing description on p. 118. It's a bit more spacious, with some booth seating, but it's still quite small. Expect a wait during busy times.

Panzúr Restaurant and Wine Bar, 69 Broadway, Tivoli, NY 12583; (845) 757-1071; panzur.com; Spanish; $$$. The cuisine at Panzúr is remarkable—sophisticated, inventive, delicious, and served by a very capable staff. The dishes are primarily tapas-style small plates, with emphasis on homemade charcuterie, aged hams, and artisanal cheeses, both local and imported. Dishes rarely if ever seen on other menus, such as black fried squid with black aioli, scallion, garlic, chile, and *pimentón,* make Panzúr an adventure in eating. The *cocas,* a type of Spanish pizza on flatbread, change daily—they're all excellent. The interesting empanadas (rabbit confit, for example) change daily as well. The burgers here are outstanding: half a pound of local Hudson Valley beef served on a house-made brioche bun with special sauce, served with *patatas fritas.* Additional toppings, such as bacon jam or seared *foie gras,* give the burger even more flavor. The large whiteboard at the back of the elegantly rustic dining room lists the specials for the evening, which might include unusual items such as duck pastrami or apple bread pudding with maple bacon ice cream. The beer list, drawn from local craft breweries, is short (six brews on tap) but focused. The wine list is much more extensive, with over a hundred choices, drawn mostly from regional Spanish vintages. The cocktails from the bar match the menu for imagination. They're unusual to the point of being off-putting to some, but they're all worth trying. The dinner menu at Panzúr is served from 5:30 p.m. to 9 p.m. Tues through Thurs and from 5:30 p.m. to 10 p.m. on Fri and Sat. The late-night menu takes over from the dinner menu and is served until 10 p.m. on Tues through Thurs and until 11 p.m. on Fri and Sat. Panzúr is open for dinner only; closed Sun and Mon. Reservations suggested.

Santa Fe, 52 Broadway, Tivoli, NY 12583; (845) 757-4100; santafe tivoli.com; Mexican; $$. This lively restaurant is a local favorite for outstanding Tex-Mex cuisine. The menu is extensive and crisply covers all the usual bases. The grilled tacos here are a good choice. They have just the right crispiness—the grilled Oaxacan tacos, made with grilled chicken and served with homemade *mole poblano,* caramelized onions, and white cheddar cheese, are particularly good. Santa Fe offers a good range of fish and vegetarian dinner dishes, such as grilled fish tacos and *enchiladas de San Miguel,* made with blue corn and mushrooms, spinach, fresh tomatoes, *queso fresco,* white cheddar cheese, and salsa verde. Many dishes at Santa Fe can be made gluten-free—ask your server. The frozen strawberry margaritas at Santa Fe are legendary. The extensive tequila list contains a number of rare and interesting choices. Open for dinner only; closed Mon.

Specialty Stores & Producers

Tivoli Bread and Baking, 75 Broadway, Tivoli, NY 12583; (845) 757-2253; facebook.com/tivolibreadandbaking. Tivoli Bread and Baking offers a great range of excellent baked goods, including scones both sweet and savory, baguettes, loaf breads of all sorts, bialys, blueberry muffins, lemon squares, sticky buns, brownies, and even pretzels. They're open from 6:30 a.m. to noon Wed through Fri and from 6:30 a.m. to 3 p.m. on the weekends. On Sat and Sun, you can also order a sandwich on a baguette. Closed Mon and Tues.

Farm Bounty

Mead Orchards, 15 Scism Rd., Tivoli, NY 12583; (845) 756-5641; meadorchards.com. A beautiful 185-acre farm, Mead Orchards has many acres of fruit trees and berries and also grows vegetables. The farm has been in the Mead family since 1916. In 2001, development rights to the farm were sold so that land will remain forever open—no housing subdivisions ever! Today the farm operates a large u-pick operation, sells its produce at local markets, and has a farm stand on the property that's open weekends only from mid-July to the end of the season in Oct. Call ahead to find out what's ripe and ready to pick.

Northwind Farms, 185 E. Kerley Corners Rd., Tivoli, NY 12583; (845) 757-5591; northwindfarmsallnatural.com. Pasture-raised, all-natural eggs, poultry, rabbit, goat, pork, and beef. Northwind Farms eggs and meat are sold at the Red Hook farmers' market and at the farm. Not all meats and cuts are always available, so call ahead to order. Pork is available at the farm by the whole or half pig; beef is available in whole, half, or quarter sections.

Wappingers Falls

Aroma Osteria, 114 Old Post Rd., Wappingers Falls, NY 12590; (845) 298-6790; aromaosteriarestaurant.com; Italian, $$$. A consistent award winner, Aroma Osteria is one of the best Italian restaurants in the region. The restaurant is lovely, with four elegantly furnished dining rooms. The large outdoor terrace is lined on one side with the restaurant's own herb and vegetable garden and a pergola for grapevines; fruit trees dot with landscaping. Fresh ingredients are taken very seriously at Aroma Osteria; what isn't grown here is purchased from local farmers whenever possible. The food here is classic country Italian, the sort of food Italians in Italy cook for themselves. All the dishes on the broad menu are prepared with care and imagination—the chicken *nostrano,* for instance, made with breast of free-range chicken, wild mushrooms, pearl onions, and peas, is a blend of flavors that could make you completely reevaluate your thinking about peas. You also can't go wrong with any of the pastas, but it's the daily specials that keep customers coming back. Based on what's fresh at the market that day, these dishes, such as pork osso buco, braised rabbit or quail, or zucchini blossoms, are always interesting and well crafted. Leave room for a piece of the outstanding tiramisu for dessert. The wine cellar at Aroma Osteria contains more than 20,000 bottles, so there's always a bottle to pair perfectly with your meal. Aroma Osteria is a popular place for celebratory meals; the dining rooms are well-suited for larger groups and the expert staff knows how to handle them. Open for lunch and dinner every day but Mon; reservations recommended.

Cafe Maya, 2776 W. Main St., Wappingers Falls, NY 12590; (845) 632-3444; mayacafecantina.com; Mexican; $$. See listing description on p. 46 for Maya Cafe in Fishkill.

Le Express Bistro and Bar, 1820 New Hackensack Rd., Wappingers Falls, NY 12590; (845) 849-3565; leexpressrestaurant.com; French; $$$. Upscale French cuisine in a strip mall may seem like a contradiction in terms, but Le Express Bistro and Bar simply proves that hungry foodies should never judge by outward appearances. Inside, Le Express has an open, airy feel. The friendly bar has a comfortable seating area, while the simply decorated, spacious dining area never feels crowded. The food here is well-executed, traditional French bistro fare; the chef uses local ingredients wherever possible. This shows in appetizers such as the excellent charcuterie plate, made with local cheese and local cured meats, and in side dishes made with fresh local vegetables. Classic bistro dishes, such as short rib beef bourguignon, duck confit, *croque monsieur,* and grilled hanger steak, are the mainstays of the menu. The chef also prepares at least four different appetizer and entree specials each evening; the well-trained and friendly servers are always happy to explain them. Desserts here are excellent. The chocolate lava cake is prepared exactly right and served promptly, while it's still molten in the center. Le Express also offers an amazingly good version of the humble bread pudding. The excellent wine list means that there is always a good pairing for the table and always something new to try. Open for lunch and dinner every weekday; open for dinner only Sat; brunch and dinner on Sun. Reservations suggested.

Palace Dumpling, 1671 Rte. 9 (Lafayette Plaza), Wappingers Falls, NY 12590; (845) 298-8886; palacedumplings.com; Chinese; $. The emphasis at Palace Dumpling is on very good, very authentic noodles and dumplings, Chinese style. The excellent soups and salads make good starters, but don't order more than one, because the dumpling and noodle portions are substantial. The dumplings here are handmade in the northern Chinese style, meaning they have thin, delicate wrappers and interesting, well-spiced fillings. Choose from more than 25 varieties, including some good vegetarian choices. An order contains 12 dumplings, steamed or panfried. The noodle menu is much shorter but equally authentic. The noodles are handmade and carefully prepared—the lo mein, for example, is quickly stir-fried with a minimum of oil, leaving the flavors clear and fresh.

Cafes & Quick Bites

The Ground Hog, 2703 W. Main St., Wappingers Falls, NY 12590; (845) 298-9333; groundhogcoffee.com; Coffeehouse; $. Some coffeehouses have books; others have folk singers. The Ground Hog has motorcycle parts and gear, along with really good coffee, a wide selection of teas, and great food. The breakfast omelets, pancakes, and other choices are always very well prepared; at lunch, the freshly made sandwiches and paninis, salads, and soups are impressive. At all times, The Ground Hog has a great selection of baked goods from local suppliers. The very welcoming atmosphere, comfortable seating, and free Wi-Fi make this spot in the center of the village a local favorite. Open Mon through Sat, 7:30 a.m. to 3 p.m.; Sun 8 a.m. to 1 p.m. Cash only.

Specialty Stores & Producers

Adams Fairacre Farms, 160 Old Post Rd., Wappingers Falls, NY 12590; (845) 632-9955; adamsfarm.com. See listing description on p. 95.

Corsino Cakes, 653 E. Main St., Wappingers Falls, NY 12590; (845) 632-6300; corsinocakes.com. The specialty here is specialties— artistically designed cakes for special occasions. Wedding cakes are a big part of the business, but pastry chef Derek Corsino will design and make one-of-a-kind hand-crafted special cakes for any event, including birthdays, anniversaries, graduations, corporate occasions, or anything else. Cakes need to be special-ordered in advance, but cookies, cupcakes, brownies, and assorted other goodies are available daily at the store from noon to 4 p.m. Wed is cookie day.

Los Hornitos Bakery, 1582 Rte. 9 (Dutchess Plaza), Wappingers Falls, NY 12590; (845) 298-8683; loshornitosbakery.com. A tiny bakery/cafe with a South American accent, Los Hornitos uses a brick oven to bake its wonderful breads, cakes, cookies, and pastries. They're all for sale at the bakery at very reasonable prices. The cafe is a popular breakfast and lunch spot, both to stay and to go. At breakfast, try any of the several variants on the basic egg sandwich. At lunch, all the sandwiches are great, but the truly outstanding offering is the *churrasco,* or steak sandwich, made with avocado, tomato, cheese, and mayo. Have it on Chilean country bread. For dessert, try a Chilean pastry, such as an *alfajor,* a sandwich cookie with *dulce de leche* in the middle. Open Mon through Sat, 7 a.m. to 7:30 p.m.; Sun from 8 a.m. to 6 p.m.

Viscount Wines and Liquor, 1173 Rte. 9, Wappingers Falls, NY 12590; (845) 298-0555; viscountwines.com. A large, well-stocked, friendly store with a great selection of New York State wines. The store offers wine tastings almost every weekend. Viscount is a major sponsor and organizer of one of the region's premier foodie events, **The Taste of Hudson Valley Bounty** (see p. 305).

Meadowbrook Farm, 29 Old Myers Corners Rd., Wappingers Falls, NY 12590; (845) 297-3002; meadowbrookfarmmarket.com. Home-grown fresh fruits and vegetables in season, along with locally grown produce. Also for sale are Meadowbrook's own salsa, local honey, McCutcheon jams, jellies, and preserves, freshly pressed sweet cider, fresh baked goods, and apple cider doughnuts. Visit with the goats and chickens while you decide what to buy.

Secor Strawberries, 63 Robinson Ln., Wappingers Falls, NY 12590; (845) 452-688; www.facebook.com/secorfarm. U-pick some of the best strawberries, blueberries, and other berries in the region. Call ahead for picking conditions and availability.

Wappingers Falls Farmers' Market, Mesier Park, Wappingers Falls, NY 12590; (845) 529-7283. The market is set up in lovely Mesier Park, in the center of the village, every Fri from 4 p.m. to 7 p.m. from June through Oct.

Wingdale

Big W's Roadside BBQ, 1475 Rte. 22, Wingdale, NY 12594; (845) 632-6200; bigwsbbq.com; Barbecue; $$. Wingdale is a bit outside the scope of this book, but because hungry barbecue lovers make pilgrimages to Big W's from all over the region, the point needs to be stretched a bit. The meats here are prepared with a dry rub of spices and brown sugar and prepared out back in a vast tank smoker that weighs well over a ton. They're slow-smoked over a wood fire for up to 20 hours. Diners here have the option of ordering their barbecue by the pound or choosing among the spareribs, chicken, smoky hot wings, sandwiches, or massive combination platters. Even the one-person combination is enough for two hungry people: a quarter rack, quarter chicken, quarter pound of any meat, plus two sides. The sides are the usual barbecue joint choices, including excellent mac and cheese, hush puppies, coleslaw, beans, and dirty rice. Open from noon to whenever they run out food, usually around 8 p.m. (they close at 7 p.m. on Sun). Closed Mon and Tues.

Cousin's Pizza, **1815 Rte. 22 (at Route 55), Wingdale, NY 12594; (845) 832-6510; cousinspizzawingdale.com; Italian/Pizza; $$.** Cousin's Pizza offers a full menu of standard Italian dishes, but the reason to go here is for the pizza made in a wood-fired oven. The pizzas range in size from 20 inches down to a personal pizza that's just 10 inches across. All the usual variations on the theme of pizza toppings are available, and they're all carefully prepared, use fresh ingredients, and taste great. What makes Cousin's Pizza stand out, however, is their special pizza of the month. The flavor combinations, such as bacon and clam or grilled chicken, roasted peppers, red onions, fresh mozzarella, and fresh basil are refreshingly different and very flavorful.

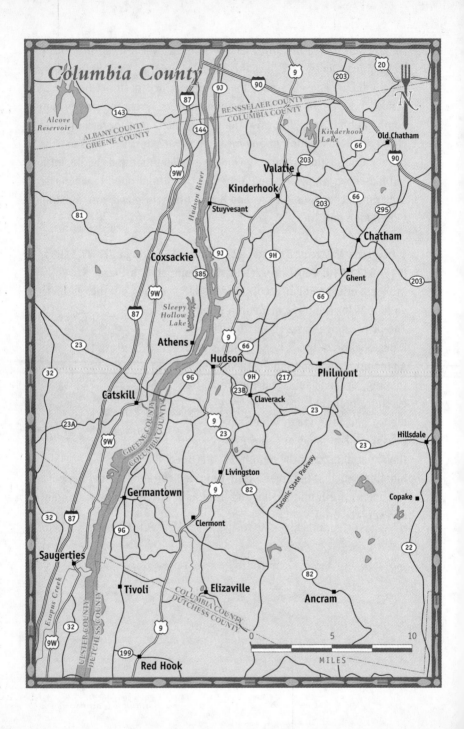

Columbia County

Columbia County is the most rural of all the areas covered in this book. Some 850 working farms covering well over 100,000 acres make up most of the land here. The little city of Hudson, directly on the river, is the only real urban area, followed by the town of Chatham. The rest of the county is dotted with small towns scattered among orchards, farms, and pastures.

In the first half of the 1800s, the historic river city of Hudson was, surprisingly, home to a fleet of whaling ships. The fleet turned Hudson into a prosperous port city with a number of elegant homes and commercial buildings. As whaling declined, other industries such as textiles took over, and more elegant new homes and buildings went up. But by the early 1900s, economic changes and the loss of river traffic meant Hudson slowly faded, becoming best known for its tawdry red light district (shut down in the 1950s). In the 1980s, Hudson's distinctive architecture and low prices began to attract artists, weekenders, and antiques dealers. The city began a remarkable transformation into a lively arts locale and an antiques-hunter's destination. What happens when a charming small city surrounded by wonderful farms experiences a revival? Restaurants—and lots of them—spring up. The food scene in Hudson today is innovative, interesting, and changing all the time.

A surprising number of outstanding restaurants, farm markets, and food shops are found scattered throughout Columbia County. Some are in the town of Chatham and the surrounding area; others are spread across the region, in faded rural towns and off winding country roads.

They're all worth visiting, whether for a great meal or an enjoyable afternoon of apple picking. Columbia County is also the home of Hawthorne Valley Farm, a large biodynamic farm and dairy in rural Ghent. Over the past several decades, Hawthorne Valley has provided much of the inspiration and training that has led to the resurgence of organic farming in the Hudson Valley and beyond.

Ancram

Foodie Faves

Miller's Tavern, 920 Rte. 82, Ancram, NY 12502; (518) 851-7230; millerstavernny.com; Traditional American; $$. Located in a historic building that was a tavern dating back to before 1770—and with the plaque from New York State to prove it—Miller's Tavern continues to serve good food and drink. It's a local favorite for eating and socializing. The menu offers a solid selection of standards. Soups, salads, pasta, burgers, sandwiches, and a handful of good entrees are all available for lunch and dinner. There's also a full bar with a good selection of bottled beers. Open for lunch and dinner Thurs through Sat.

Cafes & Quick Bites

The Farmer's Wife, 3 County Rte. 88, Ancramdale, NY 12503; (518) 329-5431; thefarmerswife.biz; Traditional American/Sandwich Shop; $. This little take-out shop and cafe with very good food is extremely popular locally. The ingredients are all sourced locally as much as possible and freshly prepared with skill and imagination. For breakfast, most choose the fresh coffee and something from the baked goods selection. At lunch, sophisticated sandwiches such as grilled **Herondale** sausage (see p. 146) with sautéed broccoli rabe and melted provolone on a roll keep everyone coming back. A blackboard lists the day's selection of entrees; if buttermilk fried chicken is available that day, order it. The shop has only a handful of tables and it can get crowded here at lunch. Open 7 a.m. to 4 p.m. (5 p.m. on Sat); closed Tues.

Specialty Stores & Producers

Hillrock Estate Distillery, 408 Pooles Hill Rd., Ancram, NY 12502; (518) 329-1023; hillrockdistillery.com. The ingredients that go into Hillrock Estate whiskies are all grown on the property, an estate dating back to 1806, when it was the home of a prosperous grain merchant. The original house, beautifully restored, is still on the grounds. The lovely fields around it are sustainably managed to grow the heirloom grain varieties used to make the whiskies. The artisan spirits are produced at a complex of buildings containing the malt house, granary, distillery, and barrel house. The malt house was the first to be built in New York State since Prohibition. Hillrock Estate is one of the very few field-to-glass whiskey producers in the world. The current products at Hillrock include the world's first solera-aged bourbon (the bourbon is aged in a stack of old sherry casks), along with estate single-malt whiskey and estate rye whiskey. Hillrock has a very nice visitors' center with a tasting room and bar; tours of the distillery are by appointment only. Bottles can be purchased at the visitors' center. The bottles are also sold in many spirits shops in the area and also in shops in Albany, Westchester County, and Manhattan.

Fox Hill Farm, 887 E. Ancram Rd., Ancramdale, NY 12503; (518) 329-2405; foxhillfarmgrassfedbeef.com. Grass-fed British White, Murray Grey, Red Devon, and cattle crosses are raised on the 315 rolling acres of this farm. Halves, quarters, and cuts are available, along with all-beef, additive-free hot dogs. Orders can be picked up at the farm (visitors welcome, but call ahead) or shipped UPS.

Herondale Farm, 90 Wiltsie Bridge Rd., Ancramdale, NY 12503; (518) 329-3769; herondalefarm.com. At beautiful Herondale Farm, the British White and Murray Grey cattle thrive in the grassy pastures. So do the sheep, pigs, and chicken. All are raised sustainably, free to roam and without any antibiotics or hormones. Meat from Herondale can be purchased at the farm store or online; shipping is by UPS. The farm store also sells fresh produce and flowers from nearby **Sol Flower Farm** (see p. 69). In season, the farm store is open Thurs through Sun, 10 a.m. to 5 p.m. Call ahead to check on hours. Not all meat cuts are always available. Call ahead to check or to place a special order.

Ronnybrook Dairy, 310 Prospect Hill Rd., Ancramdale, NY 12503; (518) 398-MILK (6455); ronnybrookfarm.com. The Osofsky family at Ronnybrook Dairy have been milking prize-winning Holsteins for more than 70 years. The milk comes from happy, pastured cows raised using organic methods. The milk at Ronnybrook isn't homogenized, which makes it creamier, and it's sold in reusable, recyclable glass bottles. The dairy also offers yogurt, ice cream, butter, and spreads. Tradition counts, but the farm also uses a solar thermal system to produce the hot water needed for bottling. Ronnybrook products can

The Hudson-Berkshire
Beverage Trail

The Hudson-Berkshire Beverage Trail (hudsonberkshire experience.com) is a trade organization that promotes wineries, breweries, and distilleries in Columbia County, the Capital District (Albany region), and the Berkshires region in western Massachusetts. Technically speaking, only Columbia County is within the geographic region covered by this book, but the line is somewhat artificial. If you'd like to follow the trail, especially during one of the many events sponsored by Hudson-Berkshire Experience, here's the full list of participants:

Brookview Station Winery, 1297 Brookview Station Rd., Castleton, NY 12033; (518) 732-7317; brookviewstationwinery.com. Brookview Station Winery uses fruit from Goold Orchards to make award-winning wines from apples, pears, strawberries, cherries, and other fruits, as well as traditional grape wine.

Furnace Brook Winery at Hilltop Orchards, 508 Canaan Rd. (Route 295), Richmond, MA 01254; (413) 698-3301; furnace brookwinery.com. Wine from grapes and from their own apples, grown at Hilltop Orchards, a century-old farm set on 200 acres in the Berkshires.

Harvest Spirits Farm Distillery, 3074 Rte. 9, Valatie, NY 12184; (518) 253-5917; harvestspirits.com; see listing description on p. 192.

Hudson–Chatham Winery, 1900 Rte. 66, Ghent, NY 12075; (518) 392-WINE (9463); hudson-chathamwinery.com; see listing description on p. 161.

Tousey Winery, 1774 Rte. 9, Germantown, NY, 12526; (518) 567-5462; touseywinery.com; see listing description on p. 158.

be purchased at the farm, at many regional retail stores, and at many farmers' markets in the region and in Manhattan.

Thompson-Finch Farm, 750 Wiltsie Bridge Rd., Ancram, NY 12502; (518) 329-7578; thompsonfinch.com. A family-run fruit farm, Thompson-Finch has been growing certified organic strawberries, raspberries, blueberries, and apples since 1988. You can pick your own strawberries here every day from the second week of June to the second week of July. (If you visit, please leave the dog at home.) The farm stand sells their own vegetables and strawberries and meat, cheese, and eggs from nearby farms. The farmers at Thompson-Finch are very aware of their carbon footprint. Among other conservation approaches, the farm runs mostly on biodiesel fuel and solar electric. They offer a discount to visitors who carpool or arrive by foot or bike.

Chatham

Foodie Faves

Blue Plate Restaurant, 1 Kinderhook St., Chatham, NY 12037; (518) 392-7711; chathamblueplate.net; Traditional American; $$. If ever a restaurant had a signature dish, it's the legendary Blue Plate meat loaf, topped with bacon and served with mashed potatoes and gravy. This alone makes a trip to this comfortable restaurant worthwhile, but the other items on the short menu here are equally good, including meatless dishes such as the black bean veggie burger and the stuffed eggplant. The fresh vegetables that accompany the dishes are always beautifully prepared. The nightly specials make up for the short standard menu—there are always several and they are always interesting, seasonal, and made with local products whenever possible. To find out what's on for that evening, call after 5:30 p.m. Live music in the bar on Wednesday evening. The restrooms and bar are downstairs at the Blue Plate, which could be a problem for people with limited mobility.

Destino Cucina Mexicana and Margarita Bar, 1 Church St., Chatham, NY 12037; (518) 392-6663; facebook.com/destino restaurant; Mexican; $$$. Is finding an upscale Mexican restaurant in a little town in rural Columbia County a bit of a surprise? Not really. In the Hudson Valley, small and rural doesn't mean unsophisticated. The food at Destino Cucina is definitely at a high level. Dishes such as *chile en nogada,* featuring a pan-seared poblano pepper stuffed with chicken, apples, peaches, raisins, tomato, onion, garlic, and plantains, and served with a walnut and goat cheese cream sauce, aren't found in most Mexican restaurants in the region. Even the more standard offerings, such as lobster tacos and *tacos de puebla,* are similarly different—elegantly plated and delicious. Desserts here are unusually good, especially the tres leches cake. The bar makes excellent margaritas and also offers some interesting Mexican-style cocktails, such as the Paloma, made with tequila, lime juice, and grapefruit Jarritos (a traditional Mexican soda pop brand).

Peint O Gwrw, 37 Main St., Chatham, NY 12037; (518) 392-2337; facebook.com/FriendsofPeintOGwrwWelshPub; Pub Grub; $$. In Welsh, *peint o gwrw* (pronounced PINT oh ger-ROO), means a pint of good ale The excellent selection of brews at this friendly, comfortable pub includes the full line of products from **Chatham Brewing** just down the street (see p. 150). The food here is quite good and varied for pub grub. Burgers, fish-and-chips, wings, and Irish bangers and mash are the expected menu items. More unusually, the pub offers choices such as wild boar ribs, fresh lobster rolls, and a kimchi burger. Game nights and other fun stuff on weeknights; live music on the weekends.

Yianni's Restaurant, 29 Hudson Ave. (Route 66), Chatham, NY 12037; (518) 392-7700; facebook.com/yiannischathamhouse; New American; $$$. Years ago, the Chatham House was a dilapidated railroad hotel with a somewhat dubious reputation. Today, the beautifully restored building with a soaring central dining area contains Yianni's Restaurant (this restaurant replaces the old Lippera's). The menu here is fairly standard American bistro, but with the addition of a raw bar and a large selection of sushi dishes. The cooking at Yianni's is reliably good, with flashes of excellence in the seafood dishes. Many ingredients are sourced locally, including from Yianni's own family farm.

Specialty Stores & Producers

Chatham Brewing, 59 Main St., Chatham, NY 12037; (518) 697-0202; chathambrewing.com. Chatham Brewing has been making small batches of beer and ale since 1997. The only brewery in Columbia County, Chatham Brewing is also one of the best in New York State. In 2012, the brewery won the coveted Matthew Vassar Brewers' Cup for Best Craft Beer Brewery in the Hudson Valley. The brewmasters think their excellent beer has something to do with using nothing but hops, barley, malt, yeast, and Chatham water. The current brews include Amber Ale, 8 Barrel Ale, Golden, IPA, Scotch Ale, OC Blonde Ale, Porter, and Maple Amber. They brew the beers every week and sell them at the brewery on Saturday from 11 a.m. to 5 p.m. They're available in growlers (bring your own if you wish) and kegs ranging from pony to corny to bubba. Some beers are also available in bottles. The brews are also on tap at many regional restaurants and are sold at many local farmers' markets.

The Gluten-Free Bakery & Our Daily Bread Cafe, 54 Main St., Chatham, NY 12037; (518) 392-9852; theglutenfreebakery

chatham.com. Our Daily Bread bakery and cafe was long the home of a traditional bakery that sold most of its products to the restaurant and retail market. The lucky residents of Chatham got to buy the excellent breads and pastries at the shop and also enjoy a vegetarian lunch menu in the cafe. When the bakery moved to larger quarters at 116 Hudson Street, the old oven at 54 Main Street was put to a new use: making wonderfully normal-tasting gluten-free breads and pastries. The gluten-free products also mostly go to restaurants and retailers, and they're sold at the shop, along with the regular baked goods (kept carefully apart from the gluten-free products). The cafe menu is now a bit different. Breakfast and lunch are still served. The menu 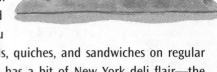 offers homemade soups, salads, quiches, and sandwiches on regular or gluten-free bread. The cafe has a bit of New York deli flair—the pastrami on rye sandwich here is very authentic. Both regular and gluten-free products from Our Daily Bread are sold at many local farmers' markets. Special gluten-free treats such as the flourless chocolate cake and fresh fruit tarts are sold only at the cafe.

Farm Bounty

The Berry Farm, 2309 State Rte. 203, Chatham, NY 12037; (518) 392-4609; thechathamberryfarm.com. Family-owned and -operated, The Berry Farm is a farm stand selling natural, organic, and local produce and products from more than a hundred local vendors. This is a great spot for finding fresh fruits and veggies in season, along with ethnic foods, gluten-free and dairy-free products, and local eggs and dairy products. The stand also carries free-range, antibiotic- and hormone-free meats and poultry (fresh, frozen, and smoked) from a number of local growers. All year round, The Berry Farm sells no-spray, pesticide-free greens and vegetables from their own greenhouses. The Berry Farm has more than 15 acres of berries in production. In season, this is a very popular u-pick destination, because the strawberries, blueberries, blackberries, and raspberries are never sprayed and no pesticides are used. The stand is open daily from 8 a.m. to 6 p.m.; until 7 p.m. on Thurs and Fri. Call ahead for u-pick information on what's ripe and how the weather is.

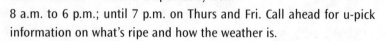

Chatham Farmers' Market, 15 Church St. (Route 203), Chatham, NY 12037; (518) 392-3353; chathamrealfoodcoop.net. Early June through mid-Oct, Fri, 4 p.m. to 7 p.m.

Chatham Real Food Market, 15 Church St. Chatham, NY 12037; (518) 392-3353; chathamrealfoodcoop.net. A community-owned food cooperative, the Chatham Real Food Market brings together the products of more than 50 local farms and kitchens in one retail outlet, open every day year-round. The market is a wonderful community program for educating the public about agriculture in Columbia County and promoting a sustainable local food system. Anyone can shop here, but co-op members get rebates based on their purchases. Closed Mon.

Claverack

Foodie Faves

Coyote Flaco, 6032 Rte. 9H, Claverack, NY 12613; (518) 851-7430; mycoyoteflaco.com; Mexican; $$. A good Mexican restaurant, the sort of place where local Mexican families go to eat, is an unexpected find in rural Claverack. Coyote Flaco isn't much to look at from the outside—or from the inside, for that matter—but the food here is authentic and prepared for people who know what real Mexican food should be. Popular selections here are the chile rellenos, the fajitas, the *pollo Oaxaqueno* (grilled chicken cutlet with mole sauce) and the combo plates. The bar has a good selection of tequilas and makes a great margarita. The service here is courteous and efficient and the prices are very reasonable.

Farm Bounty

Common Hands Farm, Route 23B and Webb Road, Claverack, NY 12513; (518) 929-7544; commonhandscsa.com. Primarily a CSA with over 150 members locally and in New York City, Common Hands Farm uses biodynamic methods to grow over a hundred varieties of fruits, vegetables, herbs, and flowers. The farm sells the surplus at local farmers' markets and at a farm stand on 370 Rte. 23B. The stand is open in season Thurs and Fri from 4 p.m. to 7 p.m. and on Sat from 10 a.m. to 3 p.m.

Philip Orchards, 270 Rte. 9H, Claverack, NY 12613; (518) 851-6351; philiporchards.com. Fifteen apple varieties and five pear varieties are grown here on the historic Talavera estate (the 1807 Greek revival mansion isn't open to the public). The u-pick season begins in early September and usually goes into early November or until the first frost. Picking is available every day, 8 a.m. to 6 p.m. Call ahead to check on the weather, what's ripe, and picking hours.

COLUMBIA COUNTY DINERS

Martindale Chief Diner, 1000 Rte. 23, Craryville, NY 12521; (518) 851-2525; Diner; $. A 1958 Silk City model with a sign featuring a Native American, the Martindale Chief diner is just off the Taconic Parkway at the exit for Route 23—almost but not quite roadside. In case there's any doubt, the word diner is spelled out in huge letters on the roof. Good standard diner food, efficient service. Open 7 days a week starting at 6:30 a.m.; closing time is 8:30 p.m. on weeknights and 9 p.m. on weekends.

O's Eatery, 309 Rigor Hill Rd., Chatham, NY 12037; (518) 392-1001; oseatery.com; Diner; $. In the entire length of the Taconic Parkway, only one diner is directly visible and accessible from the road: O's Eatery. It's a classic 1952 Colonial-style Fodero design. The menu here isn't as extensive as in many diners, but the food is very good, with some good daily specials. Open every day from 7 a.m. to 9 p.m.; until 11 p.m. on Fri and 10 p.m. on Sun.

Plaza Diner, 300 Fairview Ave. (Route 9), Hudson, NY 12534; (518) 822-0356; Diner; $. The only non-chain place to eat on this long stretch of Route 9. Standard diner food, fast service. Open daily, 7 a.m. to 11 p.m.

West Taghkanic Diner, 1016 Rte. 82, Ancram, NY 12502; (518) 851-7117; taghkanicdiner.com; Diner; $. The classic Art Deco design and neon Indian chief sign at West Taghkanic Diner have been gracing the roadside of this rural area since 1953. The interior design is still the same, right down to the stools at the counter. The diner is popular with locals and with drivers on the nearby Taconic Parkway looking for a good, quick meal. The food is standard well-prepared diner fare. Breakfast and dinner served all day. Open 7 a.m. to 9 p.m. on weeknights; until 11 p.m. on Fri and until 10 p.m. on Sat and Sun.

Clermont

Farm Bounty

Clermont Farmers' Market, 1820 Rte. 9, Clermont, NY 12526; (845) 464-3598; clermontny.org. This market is located where the old Hettling's Farm stand used to be. It's open Fri, 3:30 p.m. to 7:30 p.m., from Memorial Day to the end of Oct.

Copake

Foodie Faves

The Greens at Copake Country Club, 44 Golf Course Rd., Copake Lake, NY 12521; (518) 325-0019; copakecountryclub.com; New American; $$$. Restaurants at country clubs tend to be on the boring side, but not this one. The Greens is an excellent restaurant tucked away in one of the most rural parts of Dutchess County. The food here is well-executed contemporary American, using ingredients drawn extensively from local producers. The main dinner menu offers serious entrees such as a grilled thick-cut pork chop with sweet potato and onion gratin, swiss chard, and apple-cranberry chutney. Alternatively, guests can order from the club menu, which offers choices such as grilled flat-bread pizzas, excellent sandwiches, and burgers. The carefully chosen wine list assures a good pairing with whatever is ordered. The dining area here is lovely. The deck overlooking the golf course is great for outdoor eating in the warmer weather. When it's cold out, the comfortable indoor dining room has a great circular fireplace in the middle. The service here is excellent. Reservations suggested.

Farm Bounty

Copake Farmers' Market, Church St. (next to First Niagara Bank), Copake, NY 12516; (518) 329-0384; facebook.com/copake farmersmarket. Every Sat, June to Oct, from 9 a.m. to 1 p.m.

Hill-Over Farm, 7441 Rte. 22, Copake, NY 12516; (518) 329-MILK (6455); hilloverhealthyandfresh.com. One of the very few independent dairy farms left in the region, Hill-Over Farm sells hormone-free milk from pastured cows. The Barringer family has been farming in the area for nine generations, dating back to when Johannes Barringer left Germany and settled in Rhinebeck in 1710. The farm store sells fresh, creamy milk, yogurt, ice cream, and cheese from **Amazing Real Live Food Co.** (see p. 74). Also sold at the  store are other farm products, including maple syrup, honey, and free-range eggs. The self-serve store is open in the winter from 7 a.m. to 6 p.m.; in summer, the hours are 5 a.m. to 8 p.m. Ice cream and milk shakes are available in summer from noon to 8 p.m.

Pigasso Farms, 500 Farm Rd. (at Route 22), Copake, NY 12516; (518) 929-3252; pigassofarms.com. Cattle, sheeps, pigs, and poultry are all found on the pastures at Pigasso Farms. This farm uses only sustainable methods; the animals roam free and are never given hormones or antibiotics. Pigasso Farms meat is available at the Hudson Farmers' Market and at the farm store, open Fri, Sat, and Sun from 10:30 a.m. to 5 p.m. Call ahead for to check on availability and special orders.

Sir William Farm Stand, 4160 County Rte. 7, Craryville, NY 12521; (518) 325-3105. Free-range, grass-fed Black Angus beef and Berkshire hogs are raised at Rasweiller Farm on Sir William Road—hence the name of the farm stand here. In addition to fresh and frozen meat, the stand offers excellent homemade sausage, fresh fruit and vegetables in season, eggs, cheese, and toothsome homemade pies. The stand operates on the honor system. Put your money in the can or swipe your credit card. Open every day from 8 a.m. to 6 p.m. Call ahead for special orders.

Germantown

Specialty Stores & Producers

Block Factory Tamales, 15 Block Factory Rd., Germantown, NY 12526; (518) 537-3398; facebook.com/blockfactorytamales. Block Factory makes gourmet tamales using only the finest ingredients sourced from local farms. The succulent fillings go way beyond the traditional to include tomatillo chicken, peanut chipotle beef, vegetarian black bean chili, grilled veggies with goat cheese, and even turkey with cranberry chipotle salsa. Look for the fresh and frozen versions at many local retailers, farmers' markets, and outdoor events. Frozen tamales can also be ordered directly and shipped.

Otto's Market, 215 Main St., Germantown, NY 12526; (518) 537-7200; ottosmarket.com. Germantown is a small place, so it's no surprise that practically everyone in town passes through Otto's Market. A breakfast, they come to enjoy the bagels, store-baked pastries, and breakfast burritos. At lunch, they come to enjoy the great sandwiches, salads, pastas, and daily hot specials. Otto's works hard to be a local products emporium, so at all times, people stop by to get fresh local produce and locally made specialties (including Jane's ice cream—see p. 245). The store also carries high-quality groceries and a good selection of gourmet items. The seating area is small here and it can get busy at lunch time. Open Mon through Sat, 7 a.m. to 7 p.m.; Sun 7 a.m. to 3 p.m.

Tousey Winery, 1774 Rte. 9, Germantown, NY, 12526; (518) 567-5462; touseywinery.com. Tousey Winery began as a small experiment in turning black currants into wine. That worked out well—today Tousey's crème de cassis, blending four varieties of black currants and sweetened with honey from the winery's own bees, is a very popular dessert. The next step was to try wine from grapes, an experiment that started working out well in 2006. Today Tousey has 16 acres of grapes and fruit under cultivation and produces about 1,600 cases of wine each year. The winery produces blends such as the Queen of Clermont white and The Riot red. Varietals, including Riesling, Chardonnay, and Cabernet Franc, are also produced. The tasting room at Tousey is open Fri from noon to 7 p.m., Sat and Sun from noon to 5 p.m. The wines can be purchased at the winery or online; the winery will ship anywhere in the US.

Field Apothecary and Herb Farm, 245 Main St., German-town, NY 12526; (917) 202-3443; fieldapothecary.com. The 3 acres of Field Apothecary and Herb Farm are dedicated to growing organic healing and medicinal herbs and other plants. Most are made into healing products, such as tinctures, extracts, tonics, infused oils and salves, and teas. The farm sells fresh medicinal herbs at local farmers' markets and has a CSA. Workshops and classes on herbal medicine and techniques are also offered. See Field Apothecary and Herb Farm's recipe for **Fire Cider Margarita** on p. 320.

Hearty Roots Community Farm, 1830 Rte. 9, Germantown, NY 12526; (845) 943-8699; heartyroots.com. One of the largest and oldest community-supported agriculture (CSA) farms in the region, Hearty Roots uses sustainable practices to grow 25 acres of vegetables for its members. The CSA has pickups at the farm in Clermont and in Red Hook, Kingston, and Beacon. In New York City, pickups are at three locations in Brooklyn and one in Riverdale.

Highland Farm, 283 County Rte. 6, Germantown, NY 12526; (518) 537-6397; eat-better-meat.com. Highland Farm produces grass-fed, farm-raised venison and mouflon sheep. The meat is sold as prime cuts, such as steaks and loins; the rest is made into jerky and sausages of various types at the **SmokeHouse of the Catskills** in Saugerties (see p. 279) and at Mountain Products in LaGrangeville. All the products, along with buffalo, elk, ostrich, and some other meats, are available at the farm or online. The availability of meats and cuts varies from week to week; call ahead to check or place an order.

Klein's Kill Fruit Farm, 469 Rte. 10, Germantown, NY 12526; (518) 828-6116; kleinskillfruit.com. The u-pick operation at Klein's

Kill Fruit Farm gets under way around the third week of July, when the peaches, plums, and nectarines start coming in. After that come the pears and 20 kinds of apples, with picking that goes into October. This 600-acre farm has been in family operation since 1921. The orchards are open for picking in season every day from 8 a.m. to 6 p.m. Call ahead for hours, weather conditions, and what's ripe.

Ghent

 **Specialty Stores & Producers**

The Creamery at Twin Maple Farm, 416 Schnackenberg Rd., Ghent, NY 12075; (201) 370-2301; twinmaplefarm.com. Dairy cows have been grazing the pastures at Twin Maple Farm since 1801. In 2009, The Creamery at Twin Maple Farm began, with the conversion of the old milk house in the Twin Maple Farm dairy barn into an artisan cheese production facility and aging cave. The Creamery quickly began producing award-winning cheese using raw milk sourced from grass-fed Jersey cows at local, family-owned dairy farms. Preserving these farms by buying their milk is a central part of The Creamery's mission. Hudson Red is a washed-rind, raw cheese with a dusky red rind; aged 60 to 90 days, it resembles a pungent Taleggio in flavor. Hudson Gold is a cheddar-like cheese aged for at least 60 days and sold as nuggets. Hudson Truffle includes a thin layer of Italian truffles in the wheel. The Creamery cheeses are sold at the farm at the self-serve cheese shop— call ahead for hours. They're also sold at **Hawthorne Valley Farm** (see opposite page), at local farmers' markets, and at cheese shops in 26 states. The farm holds an annual open house in May; tours of the cheesemaking operation can be arranged by appointment.

Hawthorne Valley Farm, 327 County Rte. 21C, Ghent, NY 12075; (518) 672-7500; hawthornevalleyfarm.org. A national leader in organic, biodynamic farming since 1972, Hawthorne Valley Farm raises dairy cows, chickens, pigs, and sheep and grows vegetables on 400 acres in the heart of Columbia County. The store sells products from the farm, including vegetables, baked goods from the organic bakery, yogurt, cheese, and other dairy products from the creamery, and Hawthorne Valley's famous sauerkraut. In addition, the store carries locally grown or produced fruits, vegetables, grocery products, and household items. The organic deli offers hot food, cold sandwiches, soups, and salads. The store is open Mon through Sat from 7:30 a.m. to 7 p.m. From Memorial Day to Labor Day, the store is also open on Sun from 7:30 a.m. to 7 p.m. Hawthorne Valley Farm has been a vendor at the Union Square Greenmarket in New York City since 1980. Farm products are also sold at other greenmarkets in New York and at some local farmers' markets. Hawthorne Valley Farm welcomes visitors to tour the property and participate in the many enjoyable educational events for kids, adults, and families. Check the website for details. See the recipe for **Hawthorne Valley Farm Rye Strudel** on p. 322.

Hudson-Chatham Winery, 1900 Rte. 66, Ghent, NY 12075; (518) 392-WINE (9463); hudson-chathamwinery.com. The small-batch wines from Hudson-Chatham Winery are consistent award-winners at the regional and national level. The wines are mostly made with red and white grapes sourced from New York State growers, with some grapes from the winery's own vineyard. One of their signature wines is Baco Noir, made from a grape variety that was used to replace Pinot Noir vines during the phylloxera epidemic in the 1880s. Other wines from Hudson-Chatham include Seyval Blanc, Riesling, and several excellent white and red blends. Visitors are welcome to tour the winery and the vineyard and enjoy the wines, cheeses, and desserts at the tasting room. The wines are also sold at a number of regional farmers' markets and wine shops and are served at a number of local restaurants, including the prestigious **St. Andrew's Cafe** at the Culinary Institute of America in Hyde Park (see p. 55). In the summer, the winery is open on Friday, noon to 7 p.m., Sat, 11 a.m. to 6 p.m., Sun, noon to 5 p.m., and whenever the OPEN flag is flying. Call ahead for hours the rest of the year.

Farm Bounty

Cedar Ridge Farm, 72 George Rd., Ghent, NY 12075; facebook .com/cedarridgefarm. A small, family-owned farm, Cedar Ridge Farm grows vegetables using sustainable methods and sells them at local farmers' markets.

Cool Whisper Farm, 1011 Rte. 21, Ghent, NY 12075; (518) 672-6939; facebook.com/coolwhisper farm. Pastured beef, pork, chicken, and eggs are the main products here, along with flavorful homemade bacon, Canadian bacon, kielbasa, sausages, and ham steaks. Products are sold at the farm and at local farmers' markets. Call ahead to set up a farm visit.

Grazin Angus Acres, Bartel Road, Ghent, NY 12075; (518) 392-3620; grazinangusancres.com. The cattle, pigs, and poultry at Grazin Angus Farm are all pastured; the meat is certified 100 percent organic. The eggs, milk, and dairy products also all come from pastured animals. All Grazin Angus products are certified Animal Welfare Approved, meaning the animals are raised humanely on pasture and allowed to exhibit natural behavior with minimal environmental impact. In keeping with this philosophy, Grazin Angus products are sold only at two farmers' markets in New York City, some local retail markets, and at the farm. They're also served at the farm's sister operation, **Grazin** diner in Hudson (see p. 171), and at **Local 111** in Philmont (see p. 189). To avoid creating a larger carbon footprint, the farm does not ship its products. Sales at the farm are by appointment—call ahead.

Kinderhook Farm, 1958 County Rd. 21, Ghent, NY 12075; (518) 929-3076; kinderhookfarm.com. With over a thousand rolling acres of pasture, Kinderhook Farm is one of the largest producers of grass-fed beef and lamb in the Hudson Valley. The farm also raises chickens and heritage pigs. Family-owned Kinderhook Farm has been awarded the Animal Welfare Approved certificate, meaning the animals are raised on pasture with the highest animal welfare standards. Kinderhook Farm products are available every day at the farm store year-round, from 7 a.m. to 7 p.m. For special orders or to find out what cuts are available, call ahead. The farm is open for tours every Saturday and Sunday at 1 p.m. Guests can also arrange a farm stay at the child-friendly restored barn on the property. The barn is much like renting a vacation home, including a fully equipped kitchen. Guests can participate as much or as little as they wish in the daily activities of the farm. Farm stays are available from May to Oct.

Loveapple Farm, 1421 Rte. 9H, Ghent, NY 12075; (518) 828-5048; loveapplefarmcom. At Loveapple Farm, the u-pick season for strawberries, raspberries, apricots, apples, cherries, nectarines, plums, peaches, and pears starts in mid-June and runs to the end of Oct. The farm is open for picking every day in season from 8 a.m. to 6 p.m. While you're there, have some of the great tamales and other Mexican food they make at the cafe. You can buy fruit, local vegetables, and home-made pie at the farm stand. Call ahead for weather conditions, hours, and what's ripe.

Hillsdale

CrossRoads Food Shop, 2642 Rte. 23, Hillsdale, NY 12529; (518) 325-1461; crossroadsfoodshop.com; New American; $$$. CrossRoads Food Shop sounds like it's a deli or maybe a farm stand, but it's actually a farm-to-table restaurant operating on locavore principles. The food is fresh, local, seasonal, and simply prepared to bring out its full flavor. The chef has a wonderful way with eggs and the coffee here is truly excellent, making this a popular breakfast and lunch spot. At dinner, the menu offers a short but select list of interesting and beautifully prepared dishes, such as pork chop with rhubarb gastrique, farro, kale, and pancetta. The day's menu always includes seafood and vegetarian choices. At breakfast and lunch, order at the counter, get your own utensils and so forth, and take a seat. The staff will bring your food. Dinner offers standard waiter service. Open for breakfast and lunch Wed through Sun, 8:30 a.m. to 2:30 p.m.; dinner Thurs through Sun starting at 5:30 p.m.

Swiss Hütte Inn and Restaurant, Route 23, Hillsdale, NY 12529; (518) 325-3333; swisshutte.com; Continental; $$$. Set against the background of the distant Berkshires, Swiss Hütte's chalet architecture doesn't seem out of place among the rolling hills of Columbia County. This combination inn and restaurant serves impeccably prepared Continental cuisine. Traditional dishes such as wiener schnitzel, medallions of beef with béarnaise sauce, and veal in white wine and cream sauce with morels (Zurich-style *geschnetzeltes Kalbfleisch*) are prepared with care and the finest ingredients and served by a friendly, professional staff. All the baking is done on the premises.

The desserts are also made in-house—this is the rare restaurant that serves dessert soufflés.

Cafes & Quick Bites

Village Scoop, 2640 Rte. 23, Hillsdale, NY 12529; (518) 325-6455; villagescoop.com; **Ice Cream; $.** Jane's ice cream (see p. 245) is featured at this fun little shop. Have your favorite flavor in a cone or in a milkshake, sundae, banana split, or for a really special treat, in a root beer float made with Virgil's root beer. The shop also offers fresh fruit smoothies, good, freshly brewed coffee and tea, and great baked goods from Sweet Sam's Baking Company in the Bronx. In the winter, Village Scoop adds a rotating selection of wonderful homemade soups. Open daily in the warm weather; call to check the hours in the winter.

Farm Bounty

Hawk Dance Farm, 362 Rodman Rd., Hillsdale, NY 12529; (518) 325-1430; facebook.com/hawkdancefarm. A small farm—only 3 acres—Hawk Dance grows organic vegetables for sale at the farm stand and at local farmers' markets. The farm also operates a small CSA.

Hillsdale Farmers' Market, Roe Jan Park, 9140 Rte. 22, Hillsdale, NY 12529; (518) 325-4165; facebook.com/hillsdalefarmers market. Sat from 9 a.m. to 1 p.m., beginning of June to mid-Oct.

Markristo Farm, 2891 Rte. 23, Hillsdale, NY 12529; (518) 325-4261; markristofarm.com. A family farm growing organic vegetables, herbs, and a great array of cut flowers, Markristo Farm sells primarily to local restaurants and wholesalers. Locally, the farm products are sold at the **Copake** (see p. 295) and **Hillsdale** (see p. 295) farmers' markets.

Mountain Brook Farm, Route 22, Hillsdale, NY 12529; (914) 874-4459; mountainbrookfarmny.com. This 330-acre farm mostly raises pastured Angus beef cattle, heritage-breed laying hens, turkeys, and organic fruits, vegetables, mushrooms, and honey. The farm products are sold at local farmers' markets and are delivered to regular clients. On-farm pickups of meat, eggs, and other products can easily be arranged—just call.

White Oak Farm, 65 Whippoorwill Rd., Hillsdale, NY 12529; (518) 325-3384; whiteoakfarmny.com. Specializing in blueberries, raspberries, and fresh corn, White Oak Farm also produces preserves and barbecue sauce. These products and other fresh vegetables and fruit are sold at the farm stand and at the **Hillsdale Farmers' Market** (see p. 295). You can also pick your own blueberries—call ahead for ripeness, hours, and weather conditions. In addition to the plant products, White Oak Farm is also a fish hatchery offering a variety of fish for stocking ponds.

Hudson

Foodie Faves

American Glory BBQ, 342 Warren St., Hudson, NY 12534; (518) 822-1234; americanglory.com; Barbecue; $$. Maple-smoked barbecue is a central part of the menu at American Glory, but this fun restaurant with a lively bar is really more about American comfort food. The menu offers the usual barbecue choices, including ribs, brisket, chicken, and pulled pork, along with the traditional barbecue sides of collards, mac and cheese, and slaw. The non-barbecue choices on the menu are actually more interesting. They include a good selection of po' boy sandwiches, nicely done flame-grilled burgers, sliders, and enjoyable entrees such as pecan-crusted tilapia, meat loaf, and stuffed cabbage. The bar at American Glory is 30 feet long and serves a good selection of icy-cold draft beers, including some local brews. Live music and other performances happen at American Glory every night. The performances are downstairs in this restored old firehouse and can get noisy. If you prefer conversation with your fellow diners, ask to be seated in the spacious upstairs dining room.

Ca' Mea Ristorante, 333 Warren St., Hudson, NY 12534; (518) 822-0005; camearestaurant.com; Italian; $$$. Consistent excellence is the mark of a fine restaurant, and Ca' Mea hits it every time. This restaurant specializes in a fairly traditional menu of expertly prepared northern Italian dishes. The pasta and ravioli are homemade here and very good, especially in dishes such as pappardelle with shiitake and porcini mushroom sauce and the spinach and ricotta ravioli. There's also always a pasta special, such as lobster and shrimp ravioli in a mushroom and saffron broth with leeks, fresh tomato, and pan-seared scallops. The entrees include flavorful dishes such as grilled beef medallions in a brandy reduction and a lovely pan-seared chicken breast with prosciutto, grilled red onion, and smoked mozzarella in a Marsala sauce. The fish specials each evening, such as pan-seared halibut with an asparagus emulsion, are very worthwhile. For dessert, try the outstanding tiramisu or the day's variation on cheesecake. The lunch menu offers really good panini, a large selection of pasta dishes, and the always-intriguing omelet of the day special. The wine list at Ca' Mea focuses, not surprisingly, on Italian bottles. The very professional and accommodating staff will happily help you choose a good pairing. Ca' Mea has two cozy dining rooms and a lovely back patio for outdoor dining in the nicer weather. The restaurant has an attached elegant nine-room inn for those staying in Hudson. Closed Mon. Reservations strongly suggested.

The Crimson Sparrow, 746 Warren St., Hudson, NY 12534; (518) 671-6565; thecrimsonsparrow.com; New American; $$$. The Crimson Sparrow is one of the newest additions to the bustling Hudson restaurant scene. The restaurant is physically impressive. It's in the beautifully restored 1850s Keystone building, which has been an elegant residence, a bakery, and shops before becoming The Crimson Sparrow. The old carriage house in the back has been converted into the kitchen, which has a glass wall looking out onto a beautifully rebuilt enclosed flagstone courtyard (big enough to seat nearly 100). A dining counter looks into the kitchen; nearby tables offer a look into the kitchen as well. Inside, the stainless-steel bar is backed by salvaged ironwork. Past the bar is the dining room, with the original tin ceiling, exposed brick walls, and simple but elegant furnishings. A private dining is in the rear. The food at The Crimson Sparrow is a foodie's delight: sophisticated and often surprising. The traditional menu categories of starters, entrees, side dishes and so on have been dispensed with here and are replaced simply by large and small dishes. Every dish innovatively combines flavors, textures, and presentation in ways that challenge the taste buds—and are delicious. A daring dish such as octopus with cauliflower, pine nuts, *arancini,* and white chocolate combines disparate ingredients, yet every element of the dish comes together beautifully. Other dishes, such as pork belly with *yuzu,* pistachio, and grape, are equally innovative, and probably equally different from anything the diner has ever eaten before. The Crimson Sparrow serves a prix-fixe brunch on Sunday that offers familiar dishes with interesting twists, such as fried green tomatoes with spicy sambal aioli and breakfast sausage with zaatar. The restaurant also offers a multicourse prix-fixe Sunday Supper that has become very popular. The Crimson Sparrow tops off the foodie experience with an excellent bar, good wine list, and attentive, professional staff. Closed Mon and Tues. Reservations strongly recommended.

DABA, **225 Warren St., Hudson, NY 12534; (518) 249-4631; facebook.com/dabahudson; Scandinavian; $$$.** The Scandinavian-influences on the extraordinary cuisine at DABA make this restaurant one of the more exciting dining experiences in the region. The entire approach to a meal is a little different here. The usual menu categories are replaced by libations, essentials, roughage, sustenance, staples (the food kind), and afters. The house cocktails on the libation list are extremely good. On the food front, only at DABA could an essential appetizer be pickled herring with mustard, dill, and espresso. Skagen, another Scandinavian house specialty, is sometimes on offer. Made with shrimp, red onions, cream, lots of dill, and golden whitefish roe, it's a rare and delicious treat. The sustenance section lists one fabulous dish after another, such as grilled filet mignon with blueberry vodka sauce, potato puree, fava beans, asparagus, and pepper foam. The awe-inspiring Swedish meatballs are also in this section. The daily specials, however, are where the real surprises come. Dishes such as seared filet mignon with langoustine summer rolls, pickled carrots, and spinach, served with lemongrass emulsion and sesame soy, or seared fluke with salsify, chestnuts, spinach, and nectarines, are perfectly cooked and beautifully presented. The chef at DABA has a real Scandinavian feel for fish—the seafood dishes here are consistently excellent and original. The staples part of the DABA menu is simpler and offers an excellent burger. Vegans can try the tempeh sandwich or the hummus plate. The afters menu is just as interesting as the rest of the menu, with desserts such as whipped brie with blueberry ginger marmalade. DABA has a Scandinavian spareness and calm to it—it's a good restaurant for conversation over dinner. Open for dinner only; reservations suggested.

Fish & Game, 13 S. 3rd St., Hudson, NY 12534; (518) 822-1500; fishandgamehudson.com; New American; $$$$. Famed chef Zak Pellacio's Hudson restaurant, eagerly anticipated by seemingly every foodie on the East Coast, opened in June 2013. A carefully restored 19th-century blacksmith shop, the handsome brick building is largely unaltered on the outside; the only addition is a front patio for outdoor dining. Inside, the building was gutted to the walls. The decor is now a mix of exposed brick and stone, with wooden floors and rustic yet sophisticated furnishings designed just for the restaurant. The cozy bar features comfy leather sofas, a working fireplace, and a good view into the kitchen. The comfortable dining room, also with a working fireplace, is also cozy, seating only 36. (A private dining room is upstairs.) Most importantly, the renovation put a wood-burning oven in the kitchen, a tool that is used here with consummate skill. The operating concept of Fish & Game is to use local ingredients as much as possible, and to use as much as possible of the local ingredients. Farm-to-table, nose-to-tail, and seasonal ingredients come together here with finesse. The many different house-made condiments, pickles, preserves, and sauces are used to added zings of extra flavor. The dining room menu

is a prix-fixe tasting menu that includes six or seven courses and comes in vegetarian and meat versions. For an additional cost, the menu offers excellent wine pairings from the eclectic wine list. To dine a la carte here, eat at the bar—and sample one of the perfectly mixed house cocktails. The menu at Fish & Game changes every single day, depending on what's available from the restaurant's own garden and from the many farms and producers who supply it. The one constant is creativity. Open for dinner Wed through Sun. Reservations strongly recommended for the tasting menu.

Grazin, 717 Warren St., Hudson, NY 12534; (518) 822-9323; grazindiner.com; Traditional American; $$. The Grazin building is an old diner that dates back to 1946, when it arrived in halves by barge up the Hudson River. Today, Grazin is still a diner, sort of. The decor is still diner-style, the jukeboxes are still there and still work, and the old-fashioned soda fountain is still in operation. Otherwise, however, Grazin has a very up-to-date focus on farm-to-table dining. The main menu items at lunch and dinner are wonderfully flavorful burgers made with grass-fed Angus beef from the diner's sister operation, **Grazin Angus Acres** in nearby Ghent (see p. 162). In addition to the basic burger, toppings drawn from local producers, such as cheese from **Hawthorne Valley Farm** (see p. 161) can be added. Also on the menu are farm-fresh, free-range eggs, and great sandwiches that use locally made products and locally baked bread, and really good hand-cut french fries. Dinner specials at Grazin vary with the season and what's available from local producers. Brunch at Grazin is on weekends only. The menu then offers eggs, pancakes, french toast, and, naturally, a terrific breakfast burger topped with cheddar cheese, country ham, and a fried egg. Closed Tues and Wed.

Helsinki Hudson, 405 Columbia St., Hudson, New York 12534; (518) 828-4800; helsinkihudson.com; New American; $$$. Helsinki Hudson is primarily a very popular music and performance venue that happens to have a very good restaurant in it. Helsinki is in an old industrial building that has been carefully restored to have two performance spaces, the restaurant, a nice gallery space, an outdoor dining patio, and even a recording studio. The restaurant is very warm and inviting, with lots of wood and a nice bar. The food here is carefully prepared New American with a Southern accent. The appetizers, for instance, include both fried okra and gravlax. Likewise, the entrees range from Low Country shrimp and grits to lemonade-poached halibut over chilled fava bean puree with Jonah crab meat and Canadian lobster. Whenever possible, the ingredients are sourced from local providers. The service at Helsinki is friendly and professional, even when the restaurant is very busy. Open for dinner only. Reservations suggested.

Hudson Food Studio, 610 Warren St., Hudson, NY 12534; (518) 828-3459; facebook.com/hudsonfoodstudio; Asian; $$. The richly varied cuisine of southeast Asia is the inspiration at Hudson Food Studio. Appetizers such as green papaya salad, steamed buns with pork belly, and summer rolls are made with the freshest possible ingredients, locally grown whenever possible. The same is true for entrees such as caramel chicken, made with lemongrass, greens, jasmine rice, and coriander, and *bun cha,* spicy pork meatballs over noodles. The flavors are exotic but never overwhelming—this is food that lets the ingredients speak for themselves. Hudson Food Studio is small, with only about 20 seats; if it's too crowded, get your order to go. Open for dinner only; closed Tues.

Mexican Radio Hudson, 537 Warren St., Hudson, NY, 12534; (518) 828-7770; mexrad.com; Mexican; $$. A family-friendly, fun place to eat, Mexican Radio offers a broad menu of well-prepared, imaginative Mexican dishes. The usual range of good tortillas, tacos, enchiladas, quesadillas, and burritos are complemented by the more unusual *platos gigantes* entrees, which include dishes such as carne asada fries, carnitas, and stuffed plantains. Under the house favorites heading, Mexican Radio offers a great seafood chimichanga, triple enchiladas mole, and *flautas con crema.* The weekly specials add seasonally based dishes such as cucumber mango soup. Try the creamy flan for dessert. The restaurant is very accommodating for vegetarians, vegans, and the gluten-free. The colorful bar makes knockout margaritas and has a very broad selection of tequilas. Mexican Radio has a lot of fun events and live music; check the website to see what's coming up. Open for lunch and dinner every day; brunch on Sun. Dinner reservations suggested.

(p.m.) Wine Bar, 119 Warren St., Hudson, NY 12534; (518) 301-4398; pmwinebar.com; Tapas; $$. The foods and wines of the Iberian peninsula are featured at this relaxed wine bar. (p.m.) offers a well-chosen selection of Iberian wines, many of them by the glass. By the glass or by the three-wine tasting flight, (p.m.) offers wine lovers a good way to learn more about these relatively unfamiliar wines. There's also a fully stocked bar. The dishes on the tapas menu at (p.m.) are offered in small and large plates. The dishes are authentically Spanish. For example, *bocadillos* (a sort of Spanish panini) made with serrano ham and Manchego cheese with butter and quince marmalade spread or with goat cheese and sun-dried tomato, are enjoyable for being both well prepared and a bit different. Other plates include good selections of Iberian cheese and hot dishes such as *albondigas al ajillo* (meatballs in garlic sauce) and *carne guisada* (traditional Catalonian beef stew). A large communal table in the back room is great for groups or just for getting to know new people. Closed Mon and Tues.

Red Dot Restaurant and Bar, 321 Warren St., Hudson, NY 12534; (518) 828-3657; reddotrestaurant.com; New American; $$. When Red Dot opened on Warren Street in 1999, the area was very different from how it is today—back then, the street was blighted by crack and empty storefronts. Red Dot and the Carrie Haddad Gallery down the street at 622 Warren Street are widely credited with starting the rebirth that has made Hudson into a destination for foodies and art lovers. Red Dot moved down the street a bit to the current space in 2002.

Today, it is the oldest dining establishment in Hudson. The restaurant has a dance floor, a screening room, and a lovely garden dining area. Leaving aside the lively bar scene here, Red Dot is a fun place to eat. The consistently good food is sort of international, with a lot of American classics in the mix. On the dinner menu, the entree of Thai curried vegetables is followed by chicken potpie—and Meatloaf Monday is very popular. For dessert, try the homemade chocolate pudding. At lunch, Red Dot offers mostly sandwiches and burgers. The brunch menu is limited, with good eggs Benedict and omelets; the potato latkes are a fun choice. Red Dot is closed on Tues. Brunch is on weekends only.

Swoon Kitchenbar, 340 Warren St., Hudson, NY 12534; (518) 822-8938; swoonkitchenbar.com; New American; $$$. The chefs at Swoon Kitchenbar are true believers in the imaginative but straight-forward preparation of local and sustainably sourced products. They like to let the ingredients speak for themselves in dishes such as pork chop brined in brown sugar and served with white beans, roasted tomato, and radish greens or pea and ramp risotto with lemon and parsley. The menu here changes daily, depending on what's fresh from the farm and the fishing boats—Swoon does a great job with fish and seafood. The dessert menu offers some intriguing choices, such as the warm red apricot crostata with extra-virgin olive oil ice cream and black currant sauce. The menu also has a really good list of after-dinner drinks. Swoon offers two very popular prix-fixe special nights: Meatless Monday and Burger Thursday. Meatless Monday features a flavorful four-course vegetarian meal with soup, salad, entree, and choice of dessert. Burger Thursday features half-pound burgers made using beef from **Kinderhook Farm** (see p. 163) and served on a toasted brioche with homemade tater tots. At lunch, the menu is mostly the same excellent appetizers selection as at dinner, but with omelets and paninis as the main attractions. Open for lunch Fri through Sun; dinner Thurs through Mon; closed Tues and Wed. Reservations suggested.

Vico Restaurant and Bar, 136 Warren St., Hudson, NY 12534; (518) 828-6529; vicorestaurant.com; Italian; $$$. Vico serves classic northern Italian cuisine in this romantically cozy storefront restaurant, adorned inside with the works of local artists. In the winter, stay warm by the fireplace in the dining room; in the summer, enjoy eating outdoors in the secluded back garden. The menu at Vico is mostly well-prepared standards, including very good homemade pasta dishes. The daily specials menu is where the kitchen gets to stretch a bit, with appetizers such as lobster ravioli in a Marsala-tomato cream sauce and entrees such as *anatra al bergamotto* (grilled boneless breast of duck in a bergamot-scented orange sauce, served with a warm farro cranberry salad). In the winter, wild boar lasagna is often one of the specials. Vico offers a three-course prix-fixe dinner every evening that's a very good value—salad, choice of entrees, and dessert. Dinner Thurs through Mon; lunch on weekends only. Closed Tues and Wed.

Cafes & Quick Bites

Baba Louie's Pizza, 517 Warren St., Hudson, NY 12534; (518) 751-2155; babalouiespizza.com; Pizza; $$. One of the very best pizza places in the Hudson Valley, Baba Louie's is a family-friendly, fun place to eat. Even vegans and the gluten-free can enjoy really good pizza here, plus the soup of the day is always vegan. The wood-fired pizzas come in 10- and 14-inch sizes and are constructed on a sourdough crust; spelt and gluten-free crusts are also available. The pizzas come in a number of wonderfully imaginative topping combinations—the Dolce Vita, made with tomato sauce, spinach, mozzarella, figs, Gorgonzola, prosciutto, and Parmesan, topped with infused rosemary oil, is a good example. The barbecue chicken pizza, made with red onions, mozzarella, smoked Gouda, oregano, and Parmesan is outstanding. If the pizzas on the menu aren't interesting enough—or if they're too interesting—guests can build their own pizzas from the long list of individual toppings. The excellent salads at Baba Louie's are huge—plan on sharing with at least one other person. At dinner, the menu expands to include a special pasta dish created for that day from whatever local ingredients are fresh. The portions are very generous. At lunch, Baba Louie's adds a good selection of paninis and sandwiches to the salads and pizzas. The restaurant is very popular and doesn't take reservations. On a weekend evening, be prepared for a wait. Free Wi-Fi. Closed Wed.

Bonfiglio & Bread, 748 Warren St., Hudson, NY 12534; (518) 822-0277; facebook.com/bonfigliobread; Bakery Cafe; $. After outgrowing several spaces in Hudson, Bonfiglio & Bread seems to have settled down at this cheery storefront location. The bakery part of the operation produces a wonderful range of breads and rolls, including baguettes, challah, brioche, ciabattas, and bialys. The pastries include wonderful cinnamon buns, pies, cupcakes, éclairs, feuilletés and other classic pastries (the choices vary daily). At breakfast, Bonfiglio offers breads, sweets, and amazing breakfast sandwiches, along with very good coffee. At lunchtime, Bonfiglio has freshly baked pizza and strombolis and probably the best, most creative sandwiches on all of Warren Street. The selection changes daily and includes choices such as torta with beef and chorizo, farmer cheese, cabbage slaw, cilantro, and mayo or roast pork with spicy broccoli rabe on focaccia. The shop has counter seating and can get crowded—most people get their sandwiches to go. Open Tues through Sun, 7 a.m. to 6 p.m.

Cafe Le Perche, 230 Warren St., Hudson, NY 12534; (518) 822-1850; cafeleperche.com; Bakery Cafe; $$. Inspired by the Le Perche region of northern France, the owners of this shop imported a 17-ton wood-fired oven from France and opened their own bakery, cafe, and bar in a restored 1830 building. The shop has a baked goods market featuring its own breads, muffins, pastries, pies, tarts, and cakes. The bistro offers dishes built on the artisanal breads, including great sandwiches at lunch and dinner. At dinner, the menu also offers updated bistro classics, such as *steak frites* and coq au vin. A traditional zinc bar and an outdoor terrace make Cafe Le Perche an enjoyable place any time of day, whether it's morning coffee and a *pain au chocolat* or a more substantial lunch, dinner, or just a glass of wine.

The Cascades, 407 Warren St., Hudson, NY 12534; (518) 822-9146; thecascadeshudson.com; Sandwich Shop; $. When it's time to fuel up while antiquing Hudson, the great soups, sandwiches, salads, and **J.B. Peel** coffee (see p. 106) at The Cascades is the place for quick stop. At breakfast, the good range of breakfast sandwiches are augmented by gourmet waffles. At lunch, the well-crafted signature sandwiches will get you ready for another round in the shops—the list includes the Mount McKinley (turkey breast, bacon, Monterey jack cheese, tomato, sprouts, and mayo on mixed grain bread) and the Olympic, made with venison salami from **Highland Farm** (see p. 159) with swiss cheese and spicy mustard, served warm on rye bread. Open Mon through Sat, 8 a.m. to 4 p.m.

The Chai Shop, 444 Warren St. (inside Lillie K Traders), Hudson, NY 12534; (518) 822-0200; hudsonchaishop.com; Indian; $. The Chai Shop serves a limited menu of traditional Indian cuisine and Indian street food in a lovely setting that's more like a living room than a restaurant. The food here is made using organic local ingredients whenever possible. The menu includes dishes that aren't found at standard Indian restaurants, including the Goa sandwich, made with pork vindaloo on Tuscan bread and the vegetarian *kathi* roll, a street food dish from Calcutta made with vegetables in a *paratha,* with or without an egg. The shop is open for lunch only on Fri, Sat, and Sun from 11 a.m. to 4 p.m.

Lick, 253 Warren St., Hudson, NY 12534; (518) 828-7254; lickhudson.com; Ice Cream; $. Jane's ice cream (see p. 245) in all its many flavors is the featured attraction at this tiny shop (only 10 feet wide). The shop is open seasonally from Memorial Day to Columbus Day. Summer hours are daily from 1 p.m. to 10 p.m.; fall hours are daily from 2 p.m. to 9 p.m.

Nolita Bakery and Cafe, 454 Warren St., Hudson, NY 12534; (518) 828-4905; Bakery Cafe; $. This welcoming little shop is a local favorite for breakfast and lunch. The excellent coffee is fair trade and organic; it's brewed fresh all day long. The breads and pastries are baked on the premises and are very popular with the morning crowd; so are the breakfast wraps. At lunchtime, the excellent sandwiches and wraps are made to order with high-quality ingredients. The shop is small and can get crowded at busy times. Open from 8 a.m. to 4 p.m.; closed Wed.

Park Falafel and Pizza, 11 N. 7th St., Hudson, NY 12534; (518) 828-5500; parkfalafel.com; Middle Eastern/Pizza; $. Park Falafel is the first kosher food shop in Hudson in over 70 years and is the only kosher restaurant in town; the food is prepared under rabbinical supervision. In addition, the food here is halal, meaning it's prepared to the Muslim dietary code. The vegetarian and mostly vegan menu is limited, but what's there is outstanding. The generous falafel sandwich, for instance, is on homemade pita bread and contains six perfectly spiced and cooked falafel balls, hummus, cucumber salad, and tahini. In addition to the fresh sandwiches, Park Falafel also offers platters, very good pizza, calzones, and salads. Open Sun through Thurs from 11 a.m. to 9 p.m. On Fri and Sat, Park Falafel is open until 11 p.m., making this one of the very few places in Hudson to get something good to eat late in the evening.

Spotty Dog Books and Ale, 440 Warren St., Hudson, NY 12534; (518) 671-6006; thespottydog.com; $. Books and beer in the same shop—brilliant! Spotty Dog is in the beautifully restored C.H. Evans Fire Company firehouse, which served the community from 1889 to 2002. The bookstore part of Spotty Dog carries over 10,000 new titles in all categories, including a good section featuring local authors. The ale part of the store is the bay area that once held the fire trucks; the original tin ceiling and many other architectural details are still in place. The lounge offers a rotating selection of very good and mostly local beers and ales. The list includes beers made at The Pump Station in Albany, a restaurant and craft brewery operated by a direct descendant of Cornelius H. Evans, who himself was a prominent brewer in Hudson for decades until his death in 1902. A limited selection of pub grub snacks, including knishes and cheese plates, is available. Spotty Dog has an active schedule of music performances and other events; check the website for details. Free Wi-Fi; dogs welcome.

Tanzy's, 223 Warren St., Hudson, NY 12534; (518) 828-5165; tanzyshudson.com; Breakfast/Brunch; $. Tanzy's is one of the most popular spots in Hudson for breakfast—the blueberry pancakes are legendary. It can get crowded (packed, actually) on weekends. The lunch menu offers good hot and cold sandwiches, soups, salads, and homemade desserts. Two or three daily specials made with local products are usually on the lunch menu as well. Tanzy's also offers afternoon teas that are a really enjoyable alternative to a coffee break. High tea is a full meal, with a cup of soup, a delicious scone with cream and jam, and assorted finger sandwiches, tea breads, and sweets. The simpler afternoon tea, lady's tea, and cream tea all feature the shop's scones. The staff at Tanzy's are uniformly friendly and attentive. The gift room sells a good selection of tea-related items. Hours are 8 a.m. to 3 p.m. Mon, Tues, and Thurs through Sat; 8 a.m. to noon on Sun; closed on Wed.

Tortillaville, 347 Warren St., Hudson, NY 12534; (518) 291-6048; tortillaville.com; Taco Stand; $. Tortillaville is a taco stand with an address: it's located in a spruced-up vacant lot with some picnic tables for outdoor eating. The simple menu here is mostly tacos, burritos, and quesadillas in a variety of options, including vegetarian, vegan, and gluten-free. Thursday is shrimp day—get there early. Tortillaville is open seasonally, from mid-May to late Oct. In season, the hours are 11 a.m. to 7 p.m., Thurs through Sun. The stand is usually open rain or shine, but sometimes has to close due to severe weather.

Specialty Stores & Producers

Christopher Norman Chocolates, 73 N. 2nd St., Hudson, NY 12534; (518) 822-0300; christophernormanchocolates.com. Christopher Norman Chocolates offers innovative, beautiful, and delicious handmade chocolates. The boxed collections, crunches, hand-painted truffles and chocolate hearts, extraordinary chocolate bars, and more can all be purchased at the showroom.

Hudson Chocolate Bar, 135 Warren St., Hudson, NY 12534; (518) 828-3139; hudsonchocolatebar.com. Sharing premises with **Verdigris Tea** (see p. 182), Hudson Chocolate Bar offers an extensive collection of chocolates, ranging from local to international manufacturers. The cafe area has wonderful hot and cold chocolate drinks and a good selection of chocolaty baked goods. Hudson Chocolate Bar is open Sun through Wed from 11 a.m. to 6 p.m.; Thurs through Sat from 11 a.m. to 8 p.m. Closed Tues.

Hudson Wine Merchants, 3411/2 Warren St., Hudson, NY 12534; (518) 828-6411; hudsonwinemerchants.com. A well-stocked wine store with a strong selection of wine from international boutique winemakers, Hudson Wine Merchants offers frequent tastings and excellent advice from the knowledgeable staff. The store carries many products from local wineries and distilleries, including **Hillrock Estate Distillery** (see p. 145).

Olde Hudson Specialty Food, 421 Warren St., Hudson, NY 12534; (518) 828-6923; oldehudson.com. A town full of visiting foodies needs a store like Olde Hudson Specialty Food. The store has a good selection of artisanal cheese, *salumi,* and charcuterie, and locally grown meat and poultry. A wide array of epicurean pantry items is offered, including rare olive oils and vinegars. The store also offers personalized gourmet gift baskets.

Vasilow's Confectionery, 741 Columbia St., Hudson NY 12534; (518) 828-2717; vasilows.com. Back in 1923, brothers Louie and Jim Vasilow opened their store in Hudson and began producing chocolates and candy, using their own secret recipes. In 1969, the brothers finally retired, to the dismay of their Hudson neighbors. In 2002, Louie's grandson decided to revive the family business. Vasilow's reopened, using the old recipes to make classically

excellent chocolates and confections, while adding new ideas to the mix. The shop today sells its own handmade products, including boxed samplers, truffles, barks, peanut brittle, marzipan, fruit slices, peppermint patties, and the store's famed cinnamon squares.

Verdigris Tea, 135 Warren St., Hudson, NY 12534; (518) 828-3139; verdigristea.com. This delightfully aromatic shop carries over 120 teas, including an extensive library of loose teas. The shop also carries a wide range of teapots, tea accessories, preserves, and spices. The shop offers a good selection of international chocolates as well. Tea lovers can stop in at the cafe area for freshly brewed tea and tea drinks, accompanied by chocolates, scones, or pastries. The shop is shared with **Hudson Chocolate Bar** (see p. 180), where chocolate drinks and treats rule. Verdigris is open Sun through Wed from 11 a.m. to 6 p.m.; Thurs through Sat from 11 a.m. to 8 p.m. Closed Tues.

Farm Bounty

The Barn, 2510 Rte. 27, Hudson, NY 12534; (518) 851-7346. Pick-your-own apples in season here or buy some from the roadside stand. Call ahead for hours, weather conditions, and what's ripe.

Eger Brothers, Rte. 9 at Route 23, Hudson, NY 12534; (518) 828-3510. The Eger Brothers' well-known farm stand on wheels sells fresh fruit and vegetables from their own orchards and farm. The stand opens with spinach in the early spring and stays open until the apples are all in, usually around the end of October. Open every day from 9 a.m. to 6 p.m. in season, but call ahead in bad weather

Fix Brothers Fruit Farm, 215 White Birch Rd., Hudson, NY 12534; (518) 828-7560; fixbrosfruitfarm.com. The Fix Brothers farm dates back to 1899. Today, the fourth generation of the Fix family grows cherries, peaches, pears, and apples. The pick-your-own operation starts with cherries in mid-June, moves on peaches in early August, and ends with apples and pears from September into October. In season, the orchards are open for picking every day from 8 a.m. to 5 p.m. Call ahead to find out what's ready to be picked and how the weather is.

Holmquest Farms, 516 Spook Rock Rd., Hudson, NY 12534; (518) 851-9629; holmquestfarms.com. Holmquest has been a family farm since 1943; before that, it was a dairy farm. Today, the Holmes family grows a broad selection of fruits and vegetables on 500 acres of fields and greenhouses. The market is open from June through Oct, from 8 a.m. to 5:30 p.m. Mon through Sat and from 8 a.m. to 5 p.m. on Sun.

Hudson Farmers' Market, 6th and Columbia Streets, Hudson, NY 12534; hudsonfarmersmarketny.com. Open from the beginning of May to Thanksgiving, Sat from 9 a.m. to 1 p.m.

Shortcake Farm, Route 23B, Hudson NY, 12534; (518) 851-7676. Pick your own strawberries here in June. There's also a farm stand with seasonal fresh fruits and vegetables and fresh-pressed apple cider. Open every day from June through Oct, 9 a.m. to 6 p.m. Call ahead to check on the strawberries and the weather.

Smith Farms, 200 White Birch Rd., Hudson, NY 12534; (518) 828-1228; smithfarmshudson.com. The small, friendly operation has a big range of pick-your-own fruit, including cherries, raspberries, and blackberries, six varieties of peaches, nectarines, and seven varieties of apples. Picking begins in early July when the cherries come in and continues into October. The fields are open for picking every day from 9 a.m. to 5 p.m. Check the website or call ahead for weather conditions and what's ripe.

Sparrowbush Farm, 2409 Rte. 9, Hudson, NY 12534; (518) 537-4401; facebook.com/sparrowbushfarm. Agriculture has been happening at Sparrowbush Farm ever since 1853. After many years primarily as fruit orchards, Sparrowbush today grows most field crops, with a special emphasis on winter root crops. The farm products are sold at local farmers' markets. The farm also has a popular winter CSA that provides its members with fresh winter greens, root vegetables, eggs, milk, bread, and meat.

Taconic Orchards, 591 Rte. 82, Hudson, NY 12534; (518) 851-7477; taconicorchards.com. Pick your own tree-ripened apples (20 different varieties), plums, raspberries, cherries, apricots, nectarines, pears, and peaches at Taconic Orchards. The farm shop sells deli sandwiches, ice cream, apple cider, and homemade baked goods. Open daily in season from 10 a.m. to 5 p.m. Call ahead to check on the weather and what's ripe.

Van Wie Natural Foods, 6798 Rte, 9, Hudson, NY 12534; (518) 828-0533; vanwienaturalmeats.com. Certified by the USDA as producers of natural pork and beef, Van Wie Natural Foods also raises free-range chickens and turkeys. Whole, custom, and individually cut animals are available, along with artisan products such as smoked chicken legs and thighs, smoked turkey breast, smoked beef bacon, and a variety of flavorful sausages. The artisan products are entirely natural; no artificial ingredients, preservatives, nitrates, or nitrites are used. Van Wie products are sold at the farm store Thurs through Sat, from 10 a.m. to 5 p.m. or by appointment. Call ahead before visiting to be sure someone is there to help you.

Kinderhook

Foodie Faves

Carolina House, 59 Broad St., Kinderhook, NY 12106; (518) 758-1669; carolinahouserestaurant.com; New American; $$$. Carolina House serves contemporary American food with a slight Southern accent. The menu of well-prepared standards is livened up by dishes such as the 1,000 Spice Caribbean chicken and creamy Cajun chicken, made with sun-dried tomatoes and asparagus and served over ricotta ravioli. Dirty rice is a popular side dish, and the bread basket contains corn bread and good Southern-style biscuits. The pleasant dining room and good service make eating here very enjoyable.

Farm Bounty

Katchkie Farm, 745 Fischer Rd., Kinderhook New York 12106; (518) 758-2166; katchkiefarm.com. Katchkie Farm is a 60-acre, NOFA-NY–certified organic farm. It's owned by Great Performances, a catering company in New York City. Vegetables and preserves from the farm go primarily to the catering operation and its cafes, with some sales to restaurants, a CSA, and farmers' markets in the city. Locally, Katchkie Farm products aren't really available. The farm also houses The Sylvia Center, an educational nonprofit that introduces children to the pleasures and benefits of healthy, sustainable food through farm visits and cooking workshops.

Kinderhook Farmers' Market, 7 Hudson St. (Village Green at Route 9), Kinderhook, NY 12106; (518) 755-9293; kinderhook farmersmarket.com. Open from early May to mid-Oct, Sat from 8:30 a.m. to 12:30 p.m.

Roxbury Farm, 2501 Rte. 9H, Kinderhook, NY 12106; (518) 758-8558; roxburyfarm.com. Roxbury Farm is one of the largest community-supported agriculture operations in the region. The farm grows vegetables, herbs, and grass-fed meat on 300 historic acres, some of which were originally part of Lindenwald (nps.gov/mava), the estate of Martin Van Buren, the eighth president. Because Roxbury is an organic, biodynamic farm, the farming methods used here are in some ways very similar to those in Van Buren's time. The farm has over a thousand CSA members and feeds over 1,200 families in Columbia County, the Capital Region, Westchester County, and Manhattan. The farmland at Roxbury has been placed in permanent conservation—it can only ever be used for farming, and can never be used for subdivisions and sprawl.

Samascott Orchards, 5 Sunset Ave., Kinderhook, NY 12106; (518) 758-7224; samascott.com. Manhattanites will recognize the Samascott name from their presence at many greenmarkets; they also sell their products in Albany and local Columbia County farmers' markets. The pick-your-own season starts in July at Samascott Orchards with

sugar snap peas and strawberries. It continues on with farm produce and fruit throughout the growing season. Apple picking (more than 50 varieties) begins in September and continues to the end of October. Samascott also has a large farm market selling their produce and nursery plants. The fields and farm market

are open every day from June to Nov from 8 a.m. to 6 p.m. Call ahead or check the website for an update on what's ripe.

Livingston

Foodie Faves

Historic Blue Store Restaurant, 2215 Rte. 9, Livingston, NY 12534; (518) 537-6658; bluestorerestaurant.com; Traditional American; $$. The restaurant isn't really blue, and it wasn't ever a store, and although it's been in operation for years, it's not historic. It is, however, located in Blue Store, a hamlet of the historic town of Livingston, which dates back to an original land grant in 1686. The hamlet gets its name from the blue-painted store that once stood at the intersection of what's now Route 9 and Route 31. The restaurant serves a solid menu of traditional American fare, including good, build-your-own burgers, steaks, pastas, and a light bar menu of sandwiches and pub food such as sliders, onion rings, and loaded french fries. The three attractive dining areas in the restaurant are very pleasant, with brick walls and fireplaces. The bar area has its own two fireplaces. The restaurant offers karaoke nights and live bands on weekends.

Farm Bounty

The Farm at Miller's Crossing, 81 Roxbury Rd., Hudson, NY 12513; (518) 851-2331; farmatmillerscrossing. This 200-acre farm gets its name from the old Albany–Boston Railroad, which used to run through the northwestern end of the property. The farm was owned by the Millers at the time, giving it the name Miller's Crossing. Today the farm grows certified organic vegetables, plants, and flowers and raises a small beef herd on 75 acres of pasture. The farm operates a popular

CSA program. The produce is also sold at local farmers' markets, at some local farm stands, and to nearby restaurants and wholesalers.

Mister Cider, 2279 Rte. 9, Livingston, NY 12541; (518) 537-5788; mistercider.com. As the name says, farm-fresh pasteurized cider is all that's sold at Mister Cider. Each pressing is made from fresh, locally grown apples and flash-pasteurized to preserve the flavor. The cider is sold from the roadside barn stand, in the hamlet of historic Livingston known as Blue Store.

Old Chatham

Cafes & Quick Bites

The Old Chatham Country Store, 639 Albany Turnpike Rd., Old Chatham, NY 12136; (518) 794-6227; oldchathamcountrystore .com; New American/Sandwich Shop; $$. This charming food shop and cafe isn't really a store at all, although it does carry grocery items, local products such as cheese from **Old Chatham Sheepherding Company** (see opposite page), and local and national publications such as the *Wall Street Journal* and the *Chatham Courier*. What brings in most customers is the food, whether it's the breakfast eggs and wonderful home-baked pastries or the lunchtime soup, salad, and sandwich specials. On Fri and Sat, the shop serves dinner as well, featuring local produce. Breakfast every day from 7 a.m. to 11 a.m.; lunch from 11 a.m. to 2:30 p.m.; the store closes at 3 p.m. Dinner Fri and Sat from 5 p.m. to 8:30 p.m. Dinner reservations recommended. The shop also offers Sunday dinner to go—a full meal from that month's special menu, prepared to order and ready to pick up between 3 p.m. and 4 p.m.

Old Chatham Sheepherding Company, 155 Shaker Museum Rd., Old Chatham, NY 12136; (888) 743-3760; blacksheep cheese.com. From its small start in 1993, Old Chatham Sheepherding Company has grown to become the largest sheep dairy farm in the US, a leader in producing domestic sheep's milk cheese and yogurt. Old Chatham Sheepherding is a beautiful farm, located on 600 grassy acres in the rolling hills of eastern Columbia County. Visitors are welcome at the farm any time; the barn complex includes a beautiful restored Shaker barn from the original Shaker community near Albany. (The Shaker Museum just down the road is well worth a visit—shaker museumandlibrary.org.) Cheese can be purchased in the Shaker barn from the 24/7 self-serve store. Old Chatham cheeses are sold at many fine retailers in the region, including **Adams Fairacre** (see pp. 95, 138) and **Hawthorne Valley Farm** (see p. 161). Many stores in New York City, such as Citarella and Fairway, carry the cheese; nationally, it's found in Whole Foods stores.

Philmont

Foodie Faves

Local 111, 111 Main St., Philmont, NY 12565; (518) 672-7801; local111.com; New American; $$$. Local 111 is located in a converted former gas station in the center of Philmont, a mill town that lost its mills many years ago. Philmont is in the geographic heart of Columbia County's rich farm country, and that proximity has helped make Local 111 into an outstanding farm-to-table restaurant. The kitchen takes the plentiful ingredients from the farms and other producers seriously and creates clean, simple dishes that let them shine. Dishes such roasted chicken breast with arugula pesto, fried potato, and seasonal greens are expertly prepared so that every flavor comes through clearly. Dishes here have a definite seasonal slant. In the winter, for example, root vegetables are key ingredients, as in the seared scallops with smoked bacon, sweet potato cream, caramelized onion, and root chips. The dinner menu includes a number of sandwich options, including an excellent burger made with local beef and the very sophisticated chicken confit with Hudson red cheese, oregano aioli, candied onion, bacon, and spinach. Desserts here are all homemade and very good. The thoughtfully chosen wine list includes a good selection of local wines and a number of good choices for wine by the glass. On the weekend, Local 111 serves a really good brunch, with a long menu of egg choices, sandwiches, and salads, along with sweeter choices such as the extravagant waffle topped with white chocolate sauce, house-made granola, blackberry preserves, and whipped cream. The lunchbox special at Local 111, ordered at the counter, is a very good value. The menu gives a choice of soup or salad with a sandwich. That can be a difficult choice when the soup is potato ale soup and the salad is fingerling potato and pear with tarragon and blue cheese. It's available on Fri and Sat from 11 a.m. to 1 p.m. Brunch at Local 111 is offered Sat and Sun from 8:30 a.m. to 2 p.m. Dinner is served Wed through Sun.

Vanderbilt House, 161 Main St., Philmont, NY 12565; (518) 672-9993; vanderbilt-house.com; New American; $$$. Vanderbilt House was built back in 1860 as a hotel and restaurant to serve employees of the Vanderbilt-owned New York and Harlem Railroad. The hotel was sold in 1890 to Leverett Mansfield, whose family operated it until 1937. In 2009, Leverett's great-grandson Bob Mansfield bought the hotel back from the later owners. Today, Vanderbilt House is once again an active hotel and restaurant, with renovated guestrooms and a renovated restaurant area. The old tavern, parlor, and dining room have been lovingly renovated and a two-story deck with fabulous views of Summit Lake has been added. The menu here is New American, with an emphasis on seasonality and local products. It includes tasty burgers (including an excellent salmon burger) and a good choice of well-prepared standards, such as grilled pork loin with Champagne cranberry sauce and mashed sweet potatoes. Beers from nearby **Chatham Brewing** (see p. 150) are on tap. Friday night is prime rib dinner night. Closed Mon and Tues.

Farm Bounty

Philmont Farmers' Market, 93 Main St. (Tripp Center parking lot), Philmont, NY 12565; pbinc.org/revitalization. Open from mid-June to mid-Oct, Sun, 10 a.m. to 1 p.m.

Threshold Farm, 16 Summit St. Philmont NY 12565; (518) 672-5509. Agriculture began on the Threshold Farm property back in the late 1700s. Since then, the land has never been subjected to chemicals or pesticides. Today, Threshold Farm is a community-supported agriculture (CSA) farm that operates on organic, biodynamic principles to raise vegetables and fruit from a 600-tree orchard.

Stuyvesant

Farm Bounty

Red Oak Farm, 1921 Rte. 9, Stuyvesant, NY 12173; (518) 799-2052; redoakfarmny.com. At this NOFA-NY Certified Organic farm,

CSA members get plenty of fresh vegetables and herbs. The surplus is sold at the Hudson farmers' market. Red Oak also specializes in herbal teas that are grown, processed, and blended on the farm. Red Oak also makes seasonal body oils and salves. The products are available at the farmers' market and by special order.

Valatie

Specialty Stores & Producers

Harvest Spirits Farm Distillery, 3074 Rte. 9, Valatie, NY 12184; (518) 253-5917; harvestspirits.com. Using fruit from Golden Harvest Farms, Harvest Spirits makes outstanding vodka, applejack, pear brandy, grappa using grape pressings from nearby **Hudson–Chatham Winery** (see p. 161), and other flavorful distilled fruit spirits. The distillery's flagship product is their award-winning Core vodka. It's distilled from hard cider made from Golden Harvest apples and retains an intriguing apple flavor. The tasting room is open on weekends year-round for tastings, tours of the distillery, and sales. Tasting room hours are noon to 5 p.m. Harvest Spirits products can also be purchased at a number of liquor stores in the region and in New York State—check the website for store locations and links to those who sell online.

Farm Bounty

Golden Harvest Farms, 3074 Rte. 9, Valatie, NY 12184; (518) 758-7683; goldenharvestfarms.com. Pick your own apples at Golden Harvest Farms every weekend in September and October. The retail farm market is open daily year-round from 8 a.m. to 5 p.m. The market sells the farm's own apples, peaches (unusually good even for Hudson Valley fruit), blueberries, cherries, raspberries, and strawberries. Golden Harvest is one of the few places that sell Concord grapes. Local vegetables in season are also available. The farm stand is well known in the area for fruit pies baked daily—order early for the holidays. Call ahead to find out what apple varieties are ripe for picking and how the weather is.

Staron Farm Stand, 162 Merwin Rd., Valatie, NY 12184; (518) 392-2920. This well-stocked stand carries products from the Staron Farm, including vegetables, beef, and pork. Open Mon through Fri from 9 a.m. to 6 p.m.; 9 a.m. to 5 p.m. on weekends.

Yonder Fruit Farms, 37 Maple Ln., Valatie, NY 12184; (518) 573-1654. Tree-ripened apples and pears from Yonder Farm are sold here. The stand is actually on Route 9 just north of Maple Lane. It's open daily from Labor Day through Oct 30, 9 a.m. to 6 p.m.

Orange County

N

Wallkill

87

300

ULSTER COUNTY
ORANGE COUNTY

9W

Wappingers
Falls

9

376

Walden

52

208

32

9D

Fishkill

82

52

84

17K

Gardnertown

17K

Newburgh

Beacon

9

DUTCHESS COUNTY
PUTNAM COUNTY

Montgomery

84

300

32

416

207

New Windsor

207

208

94

Vails Gate

Cornwall-
on-Hudson

218

Garrison

301

Clarence
Fahnestock
Memorial
State Park

208

Cornwall

32

9W

94

208

West Point
Military Academy

West Point

9

6

293

Highland
Falls

Fort
Montgomery

87

0   5   10

Monroe

17M

6

Hudson River

MILES

Orange County

Compared to the other counties in this book, Orange County is densely populated. At the same time, it's second only to Columbia County in the number of working farms—about 800—and agricultural acreage. Most of Orange County is oriented toward the Wallkill Valley, which contains a mixture of working farms and suburban sprawl (the area is within commuting distance of New York City) but is geographically out of the range of this book. This chapter focuses on and around the area along the banks of the Hudson: the interesting city of Newburgh, nearby New Windsor, and the town of Cornwall.

Newburgh, much like its sister city Beacon directly across the Hudson, is a former industrial city, but with a longer history. It was, among other distinctions, the first city in the country to be electrified. The city has a lot of interesting architecture, lovely Downing Park (designed by Frederick Law Olmstead and Calvin Vaux, the creators of Central Park in New York City), and several fascinating Revolutionary War sites. Newburgh experienced a period of steep decline in the 1960s, when misguided urban renewal led to the destruction of much of its waterfront area for development that never happened. In the 1990s, revival finally came to the Newburgh waterfront, which now contains a diverse string of excellent restaurants. The surrounding area is also slowly making a comeback, with new investments such as the Newburgh Brewing Company leading the way. Beyond the waterfront, the Newburgh and New Windsor area has many great places to eat, ranging from hot dog stands to some of the best Italian restaurants in the region.

Cornwall

Foodie Faves

Avocado, 2576 Rte. 9W, Cornwall NY 12518; (845) 534-3350; avocadorestaurant.com; Mexican; $$. This Mexican restaurant with a very pleasant, high-ceilinged dining room has an unusually extensive menu. Even less adventurous eaters will find something good here, and so will vegetarians and vegans. In addition to well-prepared standards, Avocado has a number of interesting—even surprising—items on the menu. As might be expected, the guacamole here, made tableside, is excellent. More unusual is the intriguing avocado fries appetizer—slices of avocado breaded, fried, and served with a honey chipotle dipping sauce. Those who love avocado will love this. Similarly, the sophisticated *flautas de pato* appetizer, made of flour tortillas filled with roasted duck, deep-fried, and topped with cilantro, onions, cabbage, hoisin sauce, and sour cream, is not something seen on most Mexican menus. It's delicious. Among the entrees, *crepas de langosta* (crepes filled with lobster and topped with corn cream sauce, melted cheese, fresh cilantro, and roasted poblano strips) is a standout, as is the *lomo de puerco cacahuates* (pork loin braised in peanut and Guajillo sauce). At the colorful bar, the Mexican-style sangria and margaritas are very good. The lunch menu at Avocado is only a little shorter than for dinner and includes good combination plates.

Canterbury Brook Inn, 331 Main St., Cornwall, NY 12518; (845) 534-9658; thecanterburybrookinn.com; Continental; $$$. Continental dining Swiss-style is enhanced here by the romantic setting and attentive service—guests can enjoy two lovely candlelit dining rooms, each with a fireplace, the rustic Pub Room, and a terrace overlooking Canterbury Brook in the warmer weather. The food here is expertly prepared, with a number of traditional Swiss dishes, such as homemade spaetzle, classic Wiener schnitzel, pan-seared pork tenderloin Zürichoise (pork tenderloin in a brown mushroom sauce), and in the colder weather, a genuine Swiss cheese fondue for two. The complete dinner specials on Tues, Wed, and Thurs are an excellent value. Reservations suggested. Closed Sun and Mon.

Painter's, 266 Hudson St., Cornwall-on-Hudson, NY 12520; (845) 534-2109; facebook.com/theriverbankny; International/Fusion; $$. The menu at Painter's is international, perhaps the better to match the international beer list—the restaurant offers over a hundred choices—and solid international wine list. The excellent selection of brews and bottles means Painter's has a lively bar. The all-day menu and brunch menu here are best described as eclectic. The featured cuisines range from Mexican to Italian (a good choice of pastas and focaccia) to Asian and to the American heartland (very good sandwich selection). Despite the lack of specialization (less kindly, the lack of focus), the food here is overall quite good.

The River Bank, 3 River Ave., Cornwall-on-Hudson, NY 12520; (845) 214-4929; New American; $$. The River Bank was in fact once a bank. The Cornwall Bank opened in 1897 and closed abruptly 6 years later when the bank manager ran off with all the money. The building went on to other incarnations, including being the village hall, before it was transformed into a restaurant in 2006. Despite the years and the changes, most of the dark wood, architectural details, and decorative elements remain, including the bank vault (now a wine cellar). The green walls and copper-topped bar evoke the money that was once here. Today The River Bank is a small, cozy restaurant with a well-prepared menu of standards, such as strip steak with peppercorn sauce, and excellent thin-crust pizzas. In the back, the restaurant has a very pleasant outdoor patio with a fountain, a great spot for outdoor dining in the warmer weather. Open for lunch and dinner, The River Bank is a popular local spot for family celebrations. Closed Tues.

Cafes & Quick Bites

Fiddlestix Cafe, 319 Main St., Cornwall, NY 12558; (845) 534-3866; fiddlestixcafe.com; Cafe; $. This small breakfast and lunch spot is so popular that there's often a line at breakfast. Get there early so you can get your eggs, omelets, waffles, pancakes, and french toast without waiting. At lunch, the menu expands to include a creative range of sandwiches, paninis, and wraps. The portions here are very generous, but be warned: Service can be slow. Open 7 a.m. to 3 p.m. Mon through Fri; 8 a.m. to 3 p.m. Sat and Sun.

Hudson Street Cafe, 237 Hudson St., Cornwall-on-Hudson, NY 12520; (845) 534-2450; hudsonstreetcafe.com; Cafe; $$. The breakfast, lunch, and brunch menus at the Hudson Street Cafe feature ingredients that are local, organic, and made in-house whenever possible. The food here is very good; the standard breakfast and lunch offerings include pancakes made with the restaurant's own mix (available for sale), waffles, a very good buttermilk fried chicken sandwich, and organic hamburgers served on brioche buns. The menus are complemented by seasonal specials, such as fried green tomatoes. Many dishes are vegetarian or vegan. On the second Saturday of many (though not all) months, Hudson Street Cafe opens for dinner and works with local farmers to serve a farm-to-table meal. Reservations are needed for the dinners, so call ahead for details. Hudson Street Cafe is very dog friendly—canine companions can join their families on the patio. The staff will even bring a bowl of water. Open Mon through Fri 6 a.m. to 3 p.m.; Sat 7 a.m. to 3 p.m.; Sun 7 a.m. to 2 p.m.

Cornwall Farmers' Market, 183 Main St. (Town Hall lawn), Cornwall, NY 12558; (845) 527-1084; cornwallcoop.com. Memorial Day through the end of Oct, Wed, 9 a.m. to 1 p.m.; Sat, 10 a.m. to 2 p.m.

Cornwall Winter Farmers' Market, 66 Clinton St. (St. John's Episcopal Church), Cornwall, NY 12558; (845) 527-1084; corn wallcoop.com. Nov through Apr, first and third Sat, 11 a.m. to 3 p.m.

Edgwick Farm, 348 Angola Rd., Cornwall, NY 12558; (845) 401-2301; facebook.com/edgwickfarm. The happy pastured Alpine and Nubian goats at Edgwick Farm provide the milk for the artisan goat cheese produced here. The farm makes several goat cheeses in different styles, including fresh ricotta, Canterbury marinated chèvre, Firthcliffe (cheese with a coating of vegetable ash), Sackett Ridge cheddar, Trestle (dill, rosemary, black pepper), and Moodna feta. The farm is also licensed to sell raw goat's milk. Edgwick Farm cheeses are sold at a number of regional farmers' markets and at the farm. To buy goat's milk or cheese at the farm, call ahead for hours and availability.

The Shops at Jones Farm, 190 Angola Rd., Cornwall, NY 12558; (845) 534-4445; www.jonesfarminc.com. The Shops at Jones Farm is a complex of a country store, gift shop, art gallery, and bakery. The Jones family farm has been in continuous operation since 1914. The country store sells a wide range of fresh produce from the farm. Also on hand are gourmet products from local and regional producers. Fresh baked goodies, including very good carrot cake, are sold at Grandma Phoebe's Bakery. The Shops are fun to visit—chickens roam, ducklings swim, ponies and pigs can be petted, hayrides are offered in the fall, the demonstration beehive is fascinating, and the gallery has lots of beautiful art.

New Windsor

Foodie Faves

Citrus, 1004 Rte. 94, New Windsor, NY 12553; (845) 787-4947; citrusny.com; Indian/Thai; $$. Citrus is two very good restaurants in one: This attractive space serves both Indian and Thai cuisine from separate menus. Citrus takes both seriously, so there's no fusion cuisine here, although dishes from both menus can be ordered at the same meal. The food is very well-prepared and perfectly spiced, making this restaurant one of the very few in the area where both authentic Indian and Thai cuisine can be found. Both menus include an unusually large number of vegetarian choices. On the Indian side, the tandoori dishes are particularly good; on the Thai side, try the curries. The lunch buffet is an excellent value. Don't be put off by the undistinguished strip-mall exterior—the restaurant is much nicer on the inside.

Schlesinger's Steakhouse, 475 Temple Hill Rd., New Windsor, NY 12553; (845) 561-1762; schlesingerssteakhouse.com; Steak House; $$$. The historic Brewster House, built in 1762, today forms part of Schlesinger's Steakhouse—the fieldstone walls and original fireplace are now visible in the main dining room. Schlesinger's is a serious steak house with a solid menu of high-quality steaks, seafood, pasta, and well-prepared salads and side dishes, plus their famous raisin bread and homemade pickles. The dining room is quietly elegant, with attentive service. After dinner, those who wish can smoke a cigar in the cigar bar; those who prefer a smoke-free environment can enjoy a drink and live entertainment in the Elephant Bar. In the warmer weather, Schlesinger's sets up an outdoors bar called The Beach. Open every day for dinner only. Reservations suggested.

Specialty Stores & Producers

Mama Theresa's Italian Deli, 357 Old Forge Hill Rd. (New Windsor Mall), New Windsor, NY 12553; (845) 568-3375; mama theresas.com. This family-owned deli offers a full range of Italian specialties, including meats, cheeses, *salumi,* baked goods, and imported gourmet items. The mozzarella, sausages, and soups are made fresh every day. The extensive take-out menu offers Mama Theresa's famous overstuffed sandwiches, Italian-style heros, paninis, and hot entrees, including house specialty pasta dishes.

Farm Bounty

Continental Organics, 320 Mt. Airy Rd., New Windsor, NY 12553; (845) 567-0385; conorgnx.com. In many ways, Continental Organics is the future of agriculture. This company is an official service-disabled veteran-owned small business committed to producing fresh, locally grown food using aquaponic, hydroponic, and conventional organic field farming. The farm combines high-tech, closed-loop aquaponics with traditional organic farming to produce healthy, sustainable food year-round. Fish are a part of the closed-loop aquaponics system. The system reuses almost all its water and produces very high yields per acre, with no effluent discharges and very little greenhouse gas emission. The produce and fish from this amazing new player in the local food chain go to a number of local restaurants; it's also available at **Adams Fairacre Farms** locations (see pp. 95, 138) and at a number of regional farmers' markets.

Newburgh

Foodie Faves

Billy Joe's Ribworks, 26 Front St., Newburgh, NY 12550; (845) 565-1560; riboworks.com; Barbecue; $$. This lively restaurant on the Newburgh waterfront has a good barbecue menu featuring ribs prepared with Billy Joe's secret spice blend. The rest of the barbecue items are the usual standards, all well prepared, as are the sides and appetizers. The Carolina fries appetizer, for instance, is topped with pulled pork, onions, baked beans, cheddar, and scallions. The portion is very generous, making this addictive appetizer almost a meal in itself. Those who don't like smoke have a good range of options, including very

ORANGE COUNTY DINERS

Alexis Diner, 5023 Rte. 9W, Newburgh, NY 12550; (845) 565-1400; thealexisdiner.com; Diner; $. The food at this very clean 24-hour diner is reliably good; the service is friendly and efficient. In addition to the usual towering baked-on-the-premises desserts, the display case offers good chocolate candy specialties. The Egypt Room is available for large groups.

New Windsor Coach Diner, 351 Windsor Hwy., New Windsor, NY 12553; (845) 562-9050; Diner; $. Family-operated; the look is preserved-in-amber 1970s; good food. Open 6 a.m. to 11 p.m. Mon through Thurs, 24 hours on weekends.

good burgers and sandwiches. Billy Joe's is as much bar as restaurant. The inside bar features five 55-inch TVs. The outside terrace bar, open in the warmer weather, offers live music and dancing on weekends and some weeknight evenings. When the bar is open late, order from the late-night menu. Billy Joe's doesn't take reservations, so there may be a wait on Fri and Sat nights. Open for lunch and dinner every day.

Cafe Pitti, 40 Front St., Newburgh, NY 12550; (845) 565-1444; cafepitti.com; Italian; $$. Sandwiches Italian style (paninis and focaccia) and gourmet individual thin-crust pizzas baked in a wood-burning brick oven are the  chief menu items at this casual waterfront restaurant. The antipasti selections here include some excellent specialty meat and cheese items. The paninis are more interesting than most, with combinations such as the Amarcord, made with *bresaola,* goat cheese, lemon, and peppers. Enjoy the food indoors in the pleasant dining room or on the terrace overlooking the Hudson. Open every day for lunch and dinner.

Captain Jake's Riverhouse, 40 Front St., Newburgh, NY 12550; (845) 565-3939; facebook.com/captainjakes; Seafood; $$$. At Captain Jake's Riverhouse, the decor is nautical and the food is seafood. The solid menu has a good choice of raw seafood and shellfish, pastas, and classic seafood entrees, such as sole française and shrimp scampi. The excellent lobster roll is a popular favorite—so is the lobster fettuccine. Those who don't want seafood can choose from a number of other menu items, including good steaks. If the weather is good, eat on the outside terrace and enjoy the lovely views over the Hudson. The good food, lively bar, and live music on some evenings mean that Captain Jake's can sometimes get crowded and noisy. Open for lunch and dinner every day.

Cena 2000 Ristorante and Bar, 50 Front St., Newburgh, NY 12550; (845) 561-7676; cena2000.com; Italian; $$$. Elegant Italian cuisine and waterfront dining make Cena 2000 a favorite destination for a special meal among the Front Street restaurants. The terrace overlooking the Hudson is open in the warmer weather and glassed in when it's cold, giving diners spectacular views year-round. The menu here presents one well-prepared classic dish after another.

The antipasti go beyond the usual, with choices such as grilled polenta topped with Gorgonzola and hot and sweet sausage. The homemade pasta dishes here are particularly interesting and delicious as shown by the black tagliatelle tossed with mushrooms, lobster, and tomato and by the garganelli with wild boar *ragú*. Entrees include northern Italian specialties, such as grilled veal scaloppine with sautéed spinach. Open for lunch and dinner every day; reservations suggested.

El Solar Cafe, 346 Broadway, Newburgh, NY 12550; (845) 561-3498; facebook.com/elsolarcafe; South American; $$. The cuisine at this cozy storefront restaurant is a bit hard to describe. It's mostly South American, but the menu also has Spanish and Italian dishes. No matter—narrow categories shouldn't be applied to dishes such as *avocado y relleno* (avocado stuffed with shrimp, diced tomatoes, red onions, and scallions in lemon, mayo, and yogurt sauce) or *pernil* (roasted pork) sandwiches. El Solar is that rare place where the osso buco and the homemade ravioli are as good as the *patacones y camarones* (fried plantains with shrimp). El Solar isn't just about interesting food, friendly service, and reasonable prices, however. The restaurant also regularly hosts flamenco performances by Sol Koeraue, Latin dancers from the Newburgh-based Dojo Dance Company, and other Latino dance and jazz performers. On special-event nights, the restaurant offers special menus to complement the performances. The restaurant is open from 11 a.m. to 10 p.m. every day; the kitchen stays open late.

Havana 59, 50 Front St., Newburgh, NY 12550; (845) 562-7767; havana59newburgh.com; Cuban; $$$. Cuban-American fusion cuisine is on the menu at Havana 59. The mix leads to intriguing combinations such as the house specialty, the Havana Platter—homemade roast pork, Jamaican jerk chicken, and citrus-chipotle flank steak served with Spanish rice, black beans, pineapple-mango salsa, *salsa roja,* and tortillas. Other dishes worth trying include shrimp and scallop tequila scampi, quesadilla rolls, and of course, the Cuban sandwiches. Havana 59 hosts karaoke night on Wednesdays and a lively Baggo (horseshoes played with beanbags, sorta) scene on Thursday. The restaurant has a very nice outdoor terrace and bar overlooking the river. During the season, Havana 59 is closed on Mon and Tues. In winter, it's closed end of Dec to middle of Mar.

Il Cenácolo, 228 S. Plank Rd., Newburgh, NY 12550; (845) 564-4494; ilcenacolorestaurant.com; Italian; $$$. Il Cenácolo isn't much to look at from the outside, but on the inside, this is an elegant restaurant with some of the best Italian food in the region. The antipasto and dessert displays near the entrance give a clue as to what awaits. The food is classic Tuscan cuisine, masterfully prepared and served with panache by well-trained waiters. The straightforward menu here lists only a handful of classics for each course; the waiters recite, without missing a single detail, easily a dozen specials for the day, many seasonally based. There's no such thing as a dish that's less than really good at Il Cenácolo, but some dishes stand out for being rarities as well. Among them are *risotto alla pirata,* made with spicy seafood. Properly prepared risottos are hard to find in the region, and this one is particularly interesting. Also outstanding are the roasted veal shoulder and the *filetto al pepe nero,* filet mignon in a sauce of black peppercorns, brandy, and cream. The fish of day, served *arrosto,* is another rarity:

fish roasted to simple perfection with fresh rosemary. Open for lunch and dinner every day but Tues. Il Cenácolo is very popular in the area; reservations are strongly suggested.

Lakeview House, 343 Lakeside R., Newburgh, NY 12550; (845) 566-7100; thelakeviewhouse.com; Traditional American; $$$. Lots of great restaurants in the region have great waterfront views of the Hudson River. Lakeview House has great waterfront views as well, but of Orange Lake, a lovely spot just to the west of Newburgh. A century ago, Orange Lake was a resort destination and Lakeview House was known as O'Malley's. Local lore says the restaurants was a speakeasy during Prohibition. Today, Lakeview House preserves a turn-of-the-20th-century resort feel, with wraparound porches and the original carved wood bar. The original liquor license from 1899—the first ever issued in Orange County—is framed on the wall. The attractive dining room has floor-to-ceiling windows looking out over the lake. The menu at Lakeview House has few surprises. It's mostly well-executed favorites, such as steaks and seafood, with good pasta dishes and a daily veal special. Lakeview House is one of the few remaining restaurants to seriously offer oysters Rockefeller as an appetizer. Lunch is served here on weekdays only. The menu includes good sandwiches and burgers and a good choice of entrees, including the quesadilla du jour. Lakeview House is locally quite popular; dinner reservations are suggested. Closed Tues.

Machu Picchu Peruvian Restaurant, 301 Broadway, Newburgh, NY 12550; (845) 562-6478; machupicchurest.com; Peruvian; $$. Peru has a lengthy Pacific coastline and a surprisingly large population of people of Chinese descent. That explains a lot about the interesting and delicious menu at Machu Picchu, perhaps the only Peruvian restaurant in the region—this is the original fusion cuisine.

This is a great restaurant for adventurous eaters. The restaurant serves many intriguing fish dishes, such as *jalea mixta* (lightly breaded and fried calamari, shrimp, and fish pieces served atop crispy fried yucca) and *arroz chaufe de marisco* (Peruvian-style stir-fried rice with calamari, shrimp, and fish). The restaurant also serves dishes such as *carapulcra*, an Incan stew made with chicken, dried Andean potatoes, and onion in a smoky *aji panca* sauce (red chile pepper paste, a staple of Peruvian cuisine). On the less exotic side, the rotisserie chicken here is outstanding. Machu Picchu is decorated with Peruvian art and has a full bar serving excellent pisco sour cocktails. Closed Tues.

North Plank Road Tavern, 30 Plank Rd. (Route 53), Newburgh, NY 12550; (845) 562-5031; northplankroadtavern.com; New American; $$$. The roots of this historic restaurant go back to 1801, when the site was a tavern at a stagecoach stop. Food and drink have been served here ever since. In the early 1900s, the building was Mrs. Sauer's boardinghouse, serving vacationers back when Newburgh was a resort area. Later, the building became a tavern again. During Prohibition, the owner had his own still on the third floor, where he produced "Gordons' Gin." The counterfeit labels he used now decorate the bar area. Trapdoors for hiding bottles are still in place in the mahogany bar, which was salvaged from the United States Hotel, an old resort hotel on the waterfront. Today, North Plank Road Tavern is far from its speakeasy days. The beautiful building has been carefully restored to its turn-of-the-20th-century appearance. It's also far from its boardinghouse days. The contemporary American menu uses lots of local and seasonal ingredients. It encompasses skillfully executed dishes such as cockles steamed in Captain Lawrence ale with chile pepper and hominy, Hudson Valley duck confit salad with charred grapefruit, spiced walnuts, and shaved Great Hill blue cheese, and crisped citrus Wellington Farm chicken with mixed grain sauté and fennel pollen. With three cozy dining rooms, a

Shawangunk Hudson Valley Wine Trail

The Shawangunk Hudson Valley Wine Trail (shawangunkwinetrail
.com) includes 14 wineries in Orange and Ulster counties, almost
all in the lush Wallkill River valley between the Shawangunk ridge
and the Hudson. This is the oldest wine region in the country, established more than 300 years ago when French Huguenot settlers
brought their winemaking skills to the New World. Wineries on the
trail include Benmarl, the oldest vineyard in America, Brotherhood
Winery, the oldest winery in America, and Robibero Winery, one of
the newest wineries in the region. Although every winery is different,
they all offer beautiful scenery and interesting, often historic, architecture. All welcome visitors to their tasting rooms.

The Shawangunk Hudson Valley Wine Trail organizers
put together a series of events each year that promote the wineries through tasting tours, festivals, performances, prizes, and the
annual Bounty of the Hudson wine and food festival in July. The
trail is 80 miles long and winds through some of the most beautiful
scenery in the state; the route is marked with a distinctive grape
cluster sign. Many of the restaurants discussed in the Ulster County
and Orange County sections of this book are easily reached from
the trail route.

Some of the wineries on the Shawangunk Hudson Valley Wine
Trail are discussed in this book, but most are outside the geographic
region. Because touring the wineries is such a popular and enjoyable
activity, all of them are listed below.

Adair Vineyards, 52 Allhusen Rd., New Paltz, NY 12561; (845) 255-
1377; adairwine.com. See listing description on p. 260.

Applewood Winery, 82 Four Corners Rd., Warwick, NY 10990;
(845) 988-9292; applewoodwinery.com.

Baldwin Vineyards, 176 Hardenburgh Rd., Pine Bush, NY 12566; (845) 236-4265; baldwinvineyards.com.

Benmarl Winery, 156 Highland Ave., Marlboro, NY 12542; (845) 236-4265; benmarl.com. See listing description on p. 248.

Brimstone Hill Winery, 61 Brimstone Hill Rd., Pine Bush, NY 12566; (845) 744-2231; brimstonehillwinery.com.

Brotherhood Winery, 100 Brotherhood Plaza Dr., Washingtonville, NY 10992; (845) 496-3661; brotherhood-winery.com.

Clearview Vineyard, 35 Clearview Ln.,Warwick, NY 10990; (845) 651-2838; clearviewvineyard.com.

Demarest Hill Winery, 81 Pine Island Tpke., Warwick, NY 10990; (845) 986-4723; demaresthillwinery.com.

Glorie Farm Winery, 40 Mountain Rd., Marlboro, NY 12542; (845) 236-3265; gloriewine.com. See listing description on p. 249.

Palaia Vineyards, 10 Sweet Clover Rd., Highland Mills, NY 10930; (845) 928-5384; palaiavineyards.com.

Robibero Winery, 714 Albany Post Rd. New Paltz, NY 12561; (845) 255-9463; rnewyorkwine.com. See listing description on p. 262.

Stoutridge Vineyard, 10 Ann Kaley Ln., Marlboro, NY 12542; (845) 236-7620; stoutridge.com. See listing description on p. 249.

Warwick Valley Winery, 114 Little York Rd., Warwick, NY 10990; (845) 258-4858; wvwinery.com.

Whitecliff Vineyard, 331 McKinstry Rd., Gardiner, NY 12525; (845) 255-4613; whitecliffwine.com.

kitchen that turns out reliably excellent food, and a high level of professional service, this restaurant is a very good choice for a special meal. Dinner reservations recommended. Closed Sun.

Cafes & Quick Bites

Caffe Macchiato, 99 Liberty St., Newburgh, NY 12550; (845) 565-4616; caffemacchiatonewburgh.com; Coffeehouse; $. Newburgh is a historic city, even by the demanding standards of the Hudson Valley. Caffe Macchiato is located right across the street from Washington's Headquarters State Historic Site (nysparks.com/historic-sites). Hasbrouck House, a small fieldstone structure, was the longest-serving headquarters of George Washington during the Revolutionary War. It's also the oldest house in Newburgh, dating back to at least 1750, and it was the first property ever acquired and preserved by a state for historic reasons. The site is well worth a visit. Afterward, rest up and recharge with coffee and a snack or lunch at Caffe Macchiato. The simple menu here offers really good freshly baked pastries (with many Italian specialties), breakfast egg dishes, lunchtime paninis, daily lunch specials, and a good range of coffee drinks. The brunch menu on weekends is more extensive—try the coconut waffles. Open Tues through Fri, 10 a.m. to 4 p.m.; Sat and Sun from 9 a.m. to 4 p.m.

Cherry Top Dairy Bar, 949 Rte. 32, Newburgh, NY 12550; (845) 564-6340; facebook.com/cherrytopdairybar; Ice Cream; $. A longtime family favorite, Cherry Top Dairy Bar carries 25 varieties of Hershey's hard ice cream and an ever-changing array of homemade soft-serve flavors (the orange creamsicle is wonderful). Sundaes, milk shakes, ice cream sodas, floats, and egg creams are also available. For those who insist ice cream is only for dessert, the shop also sells hot dogs, chili, and a few other non–ice cream foods. Open seasonally, from mid-March to the end of Oct, Sun through Thurs, noon to 10 p.m.; Fri and Sat, noon to 11 p.m.

Ixtapa Taco Truck, 423 Broadway, Newburgh, NY 12550; Food Truck; $. Quick, friendly service, very reasonable prices, and great Mexican food make this taco truck a popular lunchtime stop. Don't be put off by the line—it moves fast. The truck offers excellent tacos, very generous burritos with a choice of chicken or beef, quesadillas, and *tortas* (Mexican sandwiches).

Pete's Hot Dogs, 293 S. William St., Newburgh, NY 12550; (845) 561-0211; Hot Dogs; $. Pete's Hot Dogs has been in the same corner shop since 1932, when Newburgh was a major manufacturing city. The city has changed a lot since then, but at Pete's it's still pretty much 1932. At this Newburgh institution, Boar's Head hot dogs with various toppings, including a Texas-style chili sauce, are the only items on the menu. With only a few tables in a cramped space and a line out the door at lunchtime, Pete's isn't a place for leisurely dining. Get your dogs to go. Open 8 a.m. to 5 p.m. every day except Sun. Cash only.

Specialty Stores & Producers

Adams Fairacre Farms, 1240 Rte. 300, Newburgh, NY 12550; (845) 569-0303; adamsfarm.com. See listing description on pp. 95, 138.

Commodore Chocolatier, 482 Broadway, Newburgh, NY 12550; (845) 561-3960. Commodore Chocolatier offers handmade specialty chocolates from a long-standing (since the early 1900s) family-owned shop. The solid chocolates are especially good, but Commodore also makes excellent small-batch filled chocolates, truffles, and all the other standards. The very friendly staff loves to help customers make up custom boxes. Commodore sponsors an annual make-your-own-candy-cane event every year that is a must-go for local families.

Newburgh Brewing Company, 88 S. Colden St., Newburgh, NY 12550; (845) 569-BEER (2337); newburghbrewing.com. Located in a historic old factory building near the waterfront, Newburgh Brewing Company is both a commercial brewery and a very enjoyable taproom. The brewing operation is on the lower floors. The company brews more than twenty different beers in a variety of styles, including its signature cream ale. Newburgh Brewing products are carried by more than 200 restaurants in the region and in New York City. At the brewery, the high-ceilinged tap room on the fourth floor is set up like a Bavarian beer hall, with long tables and benches. The atmosphere here is relaxed and even family-friendly. On the weekends, the taproom rocks to live music of all sorts; Wednesday is trivia night. The short menu is well-crafted pub grub, made with local ingredients whenever possible. For special events, the taproom brings in local food truck artisans, such as **Kosiner Brothers** organic hot dogs (see p. 258). Closed Mon and Tues.

Farm Bounty

Lawrence Farms Orchards, 39 Colandrea Rd., Newburgh, NY 12550; (845) 562-4268; lawrencefarmsorchards.com. Three generations of Lawrences run this pick-your-own farm. The season here starts with strawberries, peas, and greens in mid-June, moves on to cherries, apricots, peaches, and vegetables, and ends up with apples and pumpkins in the fall, plus Christmas trees in December. To add to the family fun, the farm offers a hay-bale maze, horse-drawn carriage rides, and other activities. The farm stand sells refreshments, including local ice cream, and fresh fruits and vegetables. Open every day in season from 9 a.m. to 4 p.m. Call ahead or check the website to find out what's ready to be picked, what the weather is doing, and what the hours are.

Newburgh Farmers' Market, Downing Park, Rte. 9W and South St., Newburgh, NY 12550; (845) 565-5559. Fri, 10 a.m. to 4 p.m., July through the end of Oct.

Newburgh Farmers' Market, 131 Broadway, Newburgh, NY 12550. Tues, 10 a.m. to 4 p.m., July through the end of Oct.

Newburgh–Healthy Orange Farmers' Market, Broadway between Johnston Street and Lander St., Newburgh, NY 12550; (845) 568-5247. Tues, 10 a.m. to 3 p.m., July through the end of Oct.

Newburgh–Newburgh Mall Farmers' Market, Route 300 at Route 84, Newburgh, NY 12550; (845) 564-1400. Sat, 10 a.m. to 2 p.m., July through the end of Sept.

Overlook Farm Market and Country Store, 5417 Rte. 9W (at Route 84), Newburgh, NY 12550; (845) 562-5780; overlookfarm market.com. Overlook Farm is a fourth-generation family farm growing fruits, vegetables, berries, and garden plants. The farm market carries farm-fresh produce in season, including a lot of apple varieties. Also sold here are very good homemade baked goods and pastries, fresh eggs, milk, cider, honey, maple syrup, preserves, and other farm products, plus freshly made, very good sandwiches. Visitors are welcome to buy something at the stand or bring their own picnic and enjoy it on the picnic tables by Blossom Pond. Kids love the petting zoo here. Open year-round 8 a.m. to 6 p.m.; closed Tues.

West Point/Highlands

Foodie Faves

The Thayer Hotel at West Point, 674 Thayer Rd., West Point, NY 10996; (845) 446-4731; thethayerhotel.com; **Traditional American; $$$.** The imposing Thayer Hotel offers commanding views of the United States Military Academy and the Hudson River; it's actually on the grounds of the academy. It dates back to 1926 and is listed on the National Registry of Historic Places. The hotel has several dining venues, but the real reason for eating here is to dine in MacArthur's Restaurant. The dining room here has a sense of grandeur, with massive pillars, gold leaf decoration, and chandeliers; in season, the outdoor terrace has spectacular views over the river. Dining here is dining with history—presidents, heads of state, generals, and many celebrities have all been guests. The food is well-prepared traditional American. As might be expected, there are no surprises on the menu. The restaurant is best known for its popular Sunday Champagne brunch, featuring carving stations, waffle stations, a wide range of other hot and cold buffet options, and huge dessert tables. Brunch on Sunday is from 10:30 a.m. to 2:30 p.m. The restaurant is open for breakfast, lunch, and dinner every day. Breakfast and lunch are prix-fixe; dinner is a la carte. Reservations recommended for dinner and Sunday brunch. *Note:* Because the Thayer Hotel is on the grounds of the USMA, guests must pass through two security check-points. Allow extra time.

Farm Bounty

West Point–Town of Highlands Farmers' Market, parking lot across from West Point Visitors Center (45 Main St.), Highland Falls, NY 10928; (917) 509-1200; facebook.com/Westpointtownof highlandsfarmersmarket. Sun, 9 a.m. to 2 p.m., mid-June through the end of Oct.

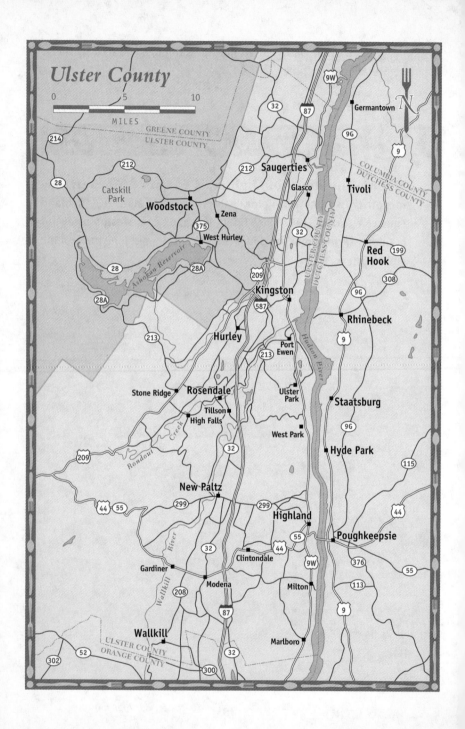

Ulster County

0   5   10
MILES

GREENE COUNTY
ULSTER COUNTY

214

212

28

Catskill
Park

212   Saugerties

Woodstock   Zena

375

West Hurley

28A

Ashokan Reservoir

28A

213

Hurley

Glasco

Tivoli

COLUMBIA COUNTY
DUTCHESS COUNTY

32

87

9W

Germantown

9G

9

Red
Hook   199

308

9G

Rhinebeck

9

209

Kingston

587

Port
Ewen

213

Ulster
Park

Stone Ridge   Rosendale

Tillson

High Falls

32

West Park

Staatsburg

9G

Hyde Park

115

209

Rondout   Creek

New Paltz

44   55

299

299

Highland

Poughkeepsie

44

32

Clintondale

44

55

376

55

Wallkill   River

Gardiner

208

Modena

9W

Milton

113

9

87

Wallkill

ULSTER COUNTY
ORANGE COUNTY

302   52

32

300

Marlboro

Hudson River

ULSTER COUNTY

DUTCHESS COUNTY

N

Ulster County

Ulster County contains some of the most historic farmland in America, including the oldest vineyard in the country and many century farms: farmsteads and orchards that have been in the same family for over a hundred years. The county also contains the historic city of Kingston, the first capital of New York State, the lively and also historic university town of New Paltz, and the very cool small town of Saugerties. (Woodstock, another lively town, is geographically part of the Catskills region and can't be included in this book.) Most importantly, however, Ulster County is also home to the DePuy Canal House restaurant in scenic Highland Falls. That's where Chef John Novi, universally acknowledged as the father of New American cuisine, changed contemporary cooking forever back in the 1970s. Chef Novi still cooks imaginative, delicious food for his guests, making this beautiful part of Ulster County the epicenter of some of the best cooking in America.

There's plenty of good cooking elsewhere as well. Kingston is home to some truly outstanding restaurants, such as Le Canard Enchaîné, and probably offers a wider range of food from a wider range of origins than anyplace else in the region. In Kingston you can choose from many different cuisines and eat well at every level, from white tablecloth restaurants to takeout noodle shops. To a lesser extent, and only because they're smaller, the same is true of New Paltz, Saugerties, and the surprising number of small towns with great restaurants, such as tiny Milton, the home of the famed Ship Lantern Inn.

The lush farmland of the Walkill Valley that runs into Ulster County around New Paltz is included in this book. The region includes over 400 working farms, apple orchards, and some outstanding vineyards and wineries. Many restaurants in the area pride themselves on sourcing ingredients from local growers. All that farm bounty is also available to individuals at the many farm stands and u-pick orchards in the area.

Clintondale

Foodie Faves

Gunk Haus Restaurant and Biergarten, 387 South St., Clintondale, NY 12528; (845) 883-0866; gunkhaus.com; German; $$. The Gunk in Gunk Haus is short for the Shawangunk Ridge, a ridge of bedrock that rises abruptly in the western part of Ulster County. The Gunks are ruggedly beautiful and are a major draw for rock climbers and hikers. The deck of Gunk Haus offers spectacular views of the ridge. In season, the chance to sit here and admire the view while enjoying a cold beer is reason enough to visit this restaurant. The food, however, is what brings guests here even in the middle of the cold, gray Hudson Valley winters. Gunk Haus serves authentic, well-prepared German food, starting with the very popular pretzel and *obatzda* (Bavarian cheese spread) appetizer. The wurst entrees are excellent; the options include currywurst, bratwurst, and chicken sausage. The currywurst and the great burgers are served on the amazing pretzel rolls that are the specialty here. The jaeger schnitzel (breaded sautéed boneless pork loin with a wild mushroom ragout over spaetzle) is outstanding. The meats and perfectly spiced sausages at Gunk Haus are prepared for the restaurant at nearby **Elia's** meat market (see p. 227). Other ingredients are sourced locally whenever possible. As befits a German restaurant,

Gunk Haus has a very good beer selection, including a number of local brews, and rotates them regularly. The service here is notably friendly. Open for lunch and dinner every day but Tues.

Farm Bounty

Minard Farms, 250 Hurds Rd., Clintondale, NY 12515; (866) 632-7753; minardfarms.com. This pick-your-own operation offers apples and pumpkins, along with a good farm store selling homemade cider, cider doughnuts, baked goods, and lots of jams, jellies, local cheeses, and other good stuff. The farm has great views of the Shawangunk Ridge and the Catskills. Bring a picnic lunch or get something from the snack bar and enjoy the view while you eat. Open weekends from the end of Aug to the end of Oct. Call ahead for weather conditions, hours, and to learn which apple varieties are ripe.

High Falls

Foodie Faves

DePuy Canal House, 1315 Main St., High Falls, NY 12440; (845) 687-7700; facebook.com/DepuyCanalHouse; New American; $$$. The beautifully restored stone building that houses DePuy Canal House dates back to 1797, when it was a tavern. When the Delaware and Hudson Canal was built right by it in the 1820s, the tavern prospered; when the abandoned canal was finally closed in 1899, the building became derelict. Chef John Novi bought it in 1964. By 1970, the DePuy Canal House restaurant was pioneering New American cuisine and Chef Novi was famous. Today, he's a living legend who still cooks up eclectic, delicious food, but now only on weekends. The menu at DePuy Canal House is remarkable. Only Chef Novi has the imagination to come up with dishes such as cold watermelon consommé with a gruyère cheese marshmallow or beef tenderloin on a Liège waffle, served with ratatouille and fresh farm vegetables with maitake mushroom sauce. To experience the full range of Chef Novi's talent, try the five-course prix-fixe dinner. Cooking classes at DePuy Canal House are taught by the master himself. Classes begin at 11 a.m. with brunch, followed by menu orientation and preparation, and end with a sit-down dinner with Chef Novi in the kitchen. Open for brunch and dinner weekends only; reservations suggested. Cash preferred.

The Egg's Nest Saloon, 300 Rte. 213, High Falls, NY 12440; (845) 687-7255; theeggsnest.com; International/Fusion; $$. The colorful decor at the Egg's Nest is often described as eclectic. It is, maybe to an extreme, but don't let the funky appearance put you off. The food here is eclectic as well. There's a sort of Southwestern fusion orientation and a strong selection of vegetarian choices. The casual menu sticks mostly to quesadillas, burgers, and overstuffed sandwiches, but also has a lot of interesting choices that are well worth trying. The most unusual offering is *praeseux* (pronounced pray-sue), a sort of thin-crust pizza on a crispy tortilla base, with a choice of Mexican, Greek, or vegetarian toppings. Perhaps the most popular offering at The Egg's Nest is the justly famous Thanksgiving sandwich. It's made with turkey breast, apple walnut stuffing, and provolone on whole wheat bread; the sandwich is dipped in egg batter and grilled. It's served with salad, honey mustard gravy, and cranberry sauce. Other good choices here include the spicy chicken Arizona and the vegetable stir-fry wrap. Open every day for lunch and dinner. Cash only.

High Falls Cafe, 12 Stone Dock Rd., High Falls, NY 12440; (845) 687-2699; highfallscafe.com; Traditional American; $$. The High Falls Cafe is primarily a music venue—there are live performances most nights—that also happens to have good food. The menu is straightforward American, with excellent burgers and sandwiches. The flatbread pizzas made with pita bread are a refreshing change from the usual pizza. The house specialties include homemade meat loaf and country-fried steak, something of a rarity in the region. High Falls Cafe serves an unusually broad breakfast on weekend mornings, including wraps and eggs Benedict in a lot of different ways. Relaxed, friendly service and a good bar make this a good choice for a casual meal or dinner before the music starts. Open for lunch and dinner every day but Mon; breakfast on weekends only.

Hopped Up Cafe, 2303 Lucas Tpke., High Falls, NY 12440; (845) 687-4750; hoppedupcafe.com; New American; $$. Farm to table also means brewery to table at the Hopped Up Cafe. Serving a menu of comfort foods drawn from local farms and producers, this friendly, rustic restaurant also has six rotating taps featuring New York State craft brews; growler fills are available. The beer menu also has a good selection of bottles and cans, mostly of beers that are hard to find in the average store. The food here is mostly salads and sandwiches made using local products, including good cheeses and charcuterie. To sample them, try the ploughman's lunch, which offers an assortment of local cheese, smoked meats, pickled vegetables, and an egg, along with home-baked warm bread. An espresso bar, fresh fruit juices, homemade desserts, and free Wi-Fi make this a good spot for an afternoon coffee break. The Hopped Up Cafe strongly supports local artists: the walls are lined with rotating exhibits of artwork and there's live music most weekends. Open noon to midnight; closed Tues and Wed.

Historic Restaurants

In 1609, Henry Hudson in the *Half Moon* explored the river that came to bear his name. By 1620, Manhattan had Dutch settlements and the first Europeans were moving into the Hudson Valley. Today, the long history of the region is surprisingly well preserved; the region is dotted with many historic sites and restored mansions. The entire region was designated as the Hudson River Valley National Heritage Area by Congress in 1996 (hudsonrivervalley.com).

Because the Hudson River was a major water highway from New York City to Albany and points beyond, and because major roads such as the Albany Post Road ran along the shores, today the region has a number of restaurants with deep historic roots serving travelers. Good food aside, eating in these beautifully restored, antique-filled establishments is interesting. It's possible to imagine yourself, just for a moment, back in time.

Many restaurants in the region are in well-preserved older buildings with interesting architecture. A handful of restaurants are in buildings that have some serious history. The Beekman Arms in Rhinebeck, for example, is the oldest inn in America. Below is a list of the most historic of the historic—see their full listing descriptions for the details.

Northern Spy Cafe, Route 213 and Old Route 213; High Falls, NY 12440; (845) 687-7298; northernspycafe.com; New American; $$$. Tucked away among the apple orchards of High Falls, Northern Spy Cafe is a casually elegant restaurant with well-crafted food and an outstanding wine list. The historic building has a charming dining room with a fireplace, a separate bar area with seating, and a very enjoyable screened patio for outdoor dining in season. The menu here focuses on updated American favorites, including a number of well-prepared

Dutchess County
Beekman Arms and Delamater Inn, 6387 Mill St., Rhinebeck, NY 12572; see p. 111.

Stissing House, 7801 S. Main St. (Route 199 and Route 82), Pine Plains, NY 12567; see p. 73.

Orange County
The Thayer Hotel at West Point, 674 Thayer Rd., West Point, NY 10996; see p. 214.

Putnam County
The Bird & Bottle Inn, 1123 Old Albany Post Rd. (Route 9), Garrison, NY 10524; see p. 20.

Hudson House River Inn, 2 Main St., Cold Spring, NY 10516; see p. 12.

Ulster County
Hoffman House, 94 N. Front St., Kingston, NY 12401; see p. 233.

Mohonk Mountain House, 1000 Mountain Rest Rd., New Paltz, NY 12561; see p. 255.

Ship Lantern Inn, 1725 Rte. 9W, Milton, NY 12547; see p. 250.

vegetarian and vegan versions. Three different kinds of tofu wings, for example, are available as appetizers—and real chicken wings are nowhere on the menu. Diners have the option of a vegetarian meatless loaf, made with lentils, mushrooms, rice, and onions in a tomato mushroom gravy, or Marco's Mama's meat loaf, made with ground beef, pork, and andouille sausage. (Marco Ochoca is the executive chef.) While the menu includes a succulent pan-roasted duck breast with port glaze, it also includes pizza, burgers, and very good sandwiches. Quality food and attentive, friendly service aside, a primary reason for visiting Northern Spy Cafe is to appreciate the award-winning wine selection. Over 150 bottles are available, including 12 wines by the glass every night—an excellent value. Open for dinner only every day but Mon. Reservations suggested.

Cafes & Quick Bites

The Last Bite, 103 Main St., High Falls, NY 12440; (845) 687-7779; thelastbite.com; Sandwich Shop; $. The Last Bite is a great place to refuel while enjoying a day exploring the charming High Falls area (hiking, biking, swimming, antiquing, farmers' markets, apple picking). The cafe serves a simple breakfast (variations on bagels and rolls) all day. Starting at lunch, fresh salads, sandwiches, and paninis are the specialties. If you can't find a sandwich you like on the menu, build your own from the broad selection of deli counter ingredients. If you prefer vegetarian versions, the staff will happily oblige. The coffee here is excellent; so are the fresh juices and smoothies. Open every day until 6 p.m.

Farm Bounty

Clove Valley CSA at Outback Farm, 81 Clove Valley Rd., High Falls, NY 12440; (845) 687-0535; clovevalleycsa.org. This small-scale CSA operates on sustainable principles, including no-till agriculture and permaculture. The farm is also a cut-flower and herb operation, a learning center with an extensive program for interns and students on living with a small footprint, and home to Wild Earth (wildearth.org), a local nature-awareness school.

Highland

Mariner's on the Hudson, 46 River Rd., Highland NY 12528; (845) 691-4711; marinersonhudson.com; Seafood; $$$. Located directly on the west bank of the Hudson between the Mid-Hudson Bridge and the Walkway Over the Hudson (walkway.org), Mariner's offers spectacular river views. (The restaurant is only minutes away from the entrance to the Walkway.) This is the only waterfront restaurant in the region that is truly on the waterfront—there's a large patio that actually extends into the river. The menu here focuses mostly on seafood, with enough steaks, burgers, and pasta dishes so that even seafood haters can enjoy a good meal. The house-made lobster ravioli, bathed in a brandy tomato cream sauce, is worth trying. Other good seafood choices here include the citrus haddock and the fish-and-chips. Mariner's on the Hudson has a busy schedule of live music, barbecues, special events, and trivia night every Thursday—check the website to see what's happening.

The Would, 120 North Rd., Highland, NY 12528; (845) 691-9883; thewould.com; New American; $$–$$$. Flavorful, innovative combinations of fresh, local ingredients are the basis of New American cooking—as The Would exemplifies. The menu here is full of interesting dishes, such as the appetizer of ravioli filled with wild mushrooms and fontina in a sauce of roasted tomatoes, jalapeños, and sour cream. The food at The Would is good every night of the week, but weeknights here are special. Thursday is pasta night, with a prix-fixe menu that includes homemade bread, salad, and a choice of pastas dishes such as fettuccine Alfredo, linguine with white clam sauce, and penne arabiatta, all very fairly priced. The three-course prix-fixe menu, offered on Tuesday, Wednesday, and Thursday, offers entrees such as sautéed chicken medallions with wild mushrooms in a mustard cream sauce, again at a very fair price. The lighter bistro menu offers excellent hot sandwiches. Open for dinner only; closed Sun and Mon.

Cafes & Quick Bites

Frozen Caboose, 6 Haviland Rd., Highland, NY 12528; (845) 234-0138; facebook.com/frozencaboose; Ice Cream; $. Conveniently located at the Highland entrance to the Walkway Over the Hudson (walkway.org) and the Hudson Valley Rail Trail (hudsonvalleyrailtrail .net), the Frozen Caboose serves up treats of all kinds: soft serve and hard ice cream, sorbet, gelati, milk shakes, and fresh fruit smoothies. The shop carries **Jane's** ice cream (see p. 245). Hot dogs and hamburgers are also on the menu.

Specialty Stores & Producers

Bad Seed Cider Company, 341 Pancake Hollow Rd., Highland, NY 12528; (845) 691-2339; facebook.com/badseedcider. An offshoot of the famed **Wilklow Orchards** (see p. 228), Bad Seed Cider Company uses apples from the family orchards to make hard cider. The products include India Pale Cider (made with hops and beer yeast) and Bourbon Barrel Reserve, cider aged in used bourbon barrels. The ciders are all naturally fermented and tend to be on the dry side. They're sold at some local farmers' markets, at the Brooklyn Greenmarkets, and in selected liquor stores and wine shops in the region.

Elia's Catering Company & House of Sausage, 85 Vineyard Ave., Highland, NY 12528; (845) 691-9312; eliasmeatmarket .com. The homemade sausages at Elia's are favorites with both customers and restaurateurs in the area. Elia's offers a full range of authentic German sausages, including *weisswurst,* three kinds of kielbasa, knockwurst, bratwurst, and German hot dogs. Elia's also makes a range of American-style sausages, including maple breakfast sausage, turkey sausage, a terrific tomato, basil, garlic, and mozzarella sausage, and even broccoli rabe sausage. Chef Mark Elia also offers hands-on classes in the art of sausage-making. If you can't stop by, the online store offers the full range of Elia's products.

Farm Bounty

Dubois Farms, 209 Perkinsville Rd., Highland, NY 12528; (845) 795-4037; duboisfarms.com. Dubois Farms isn't quite as historic as some other farms in the area, but the picking here is just as good. The farm lets visitors pick apples, nectarines, plums, pears, peaches, grapes, tomatoes, eggplant, peppers, and pumpkins from mid-August to early November. Kids can enjoy the many family activities at Dubois Farms, including the 2-acre corn maze, visiting with the farm animals, and having a pony ride. There's also a farm stand if you don't want to pick your own and a nice cafe that offers homemade baked goods, including cider doughnuts, fresh cider, and a wide array of local honey, preserves, pickles, and relishes, along with condiments such as salsas, barbecue sauces, hot sauces, and specialty ketchups. Call ahead to check on weather conditions, what's ready to pick, and what family activities are on the schedule.

Highland Farmers Market, Route 9W and Haviland Rd., **Highland, NY 12528; (845) 691-2144.** Wed from 3 p.m. to 7 p.m., mid-June through mid-Oct.

Liberty View Farm, 340 Crescent Ave., Highland, NY 12528; (845) 399-9545; libertyviewfarm.biz. Liberty View Farm offers pick-your-own apples with a bit of a twist: you can lease your very own apple tree and harvest all the apples from it. This approach isn't for everyone, because it yields a lot of apples—around 100 pounds or even more. Those who want a more manageable amount are welcome to pick their own from the other trees on the farm or buy some at the farm stand. Also at the stand are homemade baked goods, preserves, and vegetables and eggs from the farm. The owners of Liberty View Farm are leaders in the organic growing movement in the area. Open weekends in Sept and Oct—call ahead for hours, weather conditions, and to find out which varieties are ripe.

Wilklow Orchards, 341 Pancake Hollow Rd., Highland, NY 12528; (845) 691-2339; wilkloworchards.com. The Wilklow family has been growing apples in Highland since 1855. They've been a fixture at the Brooklyn Greenmarkets since 1984 and also sell their fruit at local farmers' markets. Visitors are welcome to pick their own apples and pumpkins at the farm starting Labor Day weekend and running through October 31. During the picking season, Wilklow is open 9 a.m. to 5 p.m. every day. In addition to picking apple varieties such as Macintosh, Gala, Cortland, Jonamac, Empire, Jonagold, Mutsu, Red Delicious, Golden Delicious, Winesap, Rome, and Northern Spy, visitors can go on hayrides and visit the petting zoo, the children's fun house, the hay jump, and spooky tunnels. The farm stand sells apples, apple cider, apple cider doughnuts, caramel apples, a good assortment of baked goods and preserves, and vegetables from the farm. Call ahead to check on the weather, what's ripe, and what family activities are planned.

Kingston

Foodie Faves

Armadillo Bar and Grill, 97 Abeel St., Kingston, NY 12401; (845) 339-1550; armadillos.net; Mexican; $$. Armadillo Bar and Grill opened in the historic Rondout district when the area was still an undeveloped, sort of scary swath of old industrial buildings. Armadillo is often credited with starting the revival that has made the Rondout home to a lively array of great restaurants, art galleries, and shops. Tex-Mex is the specialty here, all made from scratch with the finest local ingredients. The margaritas are legendary and the fajitas are outstanding. The rest of the menu offers a good range of well-prepared standard choices—tostadas, burritos, tacos, chimichangas, enchiladas—with many good vegetarian options. Armadillo is a fun place to eat. The walls are adorned with colorful beaded lizards and kokopelli figures, and every hand-painted tabletop is different; also, the diners are unusually friendly. Armadillo has a large outdoor patio and garden for dining. In the nicer weather, there's also an outdoor space where dogs can play while their owners eat. Open for dinner only Tues through Sun; open for brunch, lunch, and dinner Sat and Sun.

Boitson's, 47 N. Front St., Kingston, NY 12401; (845) 339-2333; boitsons.com; Traditional American; $$$. The decor at Boitson's has a 1940s nautical feel, with navy blue walls and remarkable murals in the bathrooms, inspired by World War II sailors' tattoos. The name of the restaurant commemorates the owner's late benefactor, a sailor from that era. The food at Boitson's is straightforward contemporary American, done very well. The menu entrees stick to basics such as fried chicken and a very good burger. The specials vary weekly and maintain the same well-prepared approach, with dishes such as Creole shrimp and grits. Boitson's offers some excellent values on weeknights. On Monday, check out the Blue Plate Special. Wednesday night is prime rib dinner night; Thursday night is fried chicken night. At the sleek bar, choose one of the outstanding house cocktails from the rotating seasonal menu; the Kingston, made with local honey vodka, mint simple syrup, and lemon juice, is a popular spring choice. A good selection of local craft beers is available. Open for dinner every night but Tues; Sun brunch from noon to 4 p.m. Reservations suggested.

Le Canard Enchaîné, 276 Fair St., Kingston, NY 12401; (845) 339-2003; le-canard.net; French; $$$. Le Canard Enchaîné is considered one of the best French restaurants north of Manhattan. It's certainly one of the best restaurants of any sort in the region. The classic French bistro cuisine here is overseen by Chef Jean-Jacques Carquillat, formerly of La Reserve and Le Bernardin in New York City. His skills mean perfectly prepared bistro dishes, such as braised lamb shanks in port wine and raisin sauce, *steak frites,* and calf's liver Lyonnaise. The daily specials, based on what's fresh and local at the market, are always worthwhile alternatives to the menu. If you can, save room for dessert, bearing in mind that Chef Jean-Jacques trained as a pastry chef. The lunch menu at Le Canard is simpler, sticking mostly to sandwiches French-style (smoked turkey sandwich with apricot mayonnaise, for example) and a couple of always interesting and delicious two-course prix-fixe offerings. The cozy atmosphere, skilled service, and extensive wine list make eating here a real pleasure—it's serious French food without any pretentiousness, enjoyed in a pleasant, relaxed setting that could be somewhere in Paris instead of the Hudson Valley. Open every day for lunch and dinner. Dinner reservations recommended.

Casa Villa, 395 Albany Ave., Kingston, NY 12401; (845) 331-7646; casavilla845.com; Mexican; $$. This family-friendly, laid-back Mexican restaurant is a stalwart supporter of Kingston's very enjoyable annual Cinco de Mayo celebration. It's a good place for high-quality, authentically prepared Mexican food. The house specialties are worth trying—the *paella de la casa* and the *tamales de puebla* are richly flavorful. The combination dinners offer generous portions of traditional choices such as tacos and enchiladas, with the addition of flautas, corn tortillas stuffed with chicken or beef and deep-fried. This dish, also known as *taquitos*, is inexplicably rare on Mexican menus—Casa Villa is almost the only one in the area to offer it. For those who want tamer food, the menu offers a broad selection of steaks and, a bit surprisingly, Italian specialties (they're very good).

Duo Bistro, 50 John St., Kingston, NY 12401; (845) 383-1198; facebook.com/DuoBistroBar; New American; $$. Located in the uptown Stockade area of Kingston, Duo Bistro is a popular breakfast and lunch spot with locals; in the evening, dinner at Duo draws customers from all over the area. The food is extremely good, from the breakfast egg scrambles and brioche French toast with lemon curd and berries to the dinnertime rib eye steak served with mashed potatoes, poached eggs, asparagus, shrimp, and gravy. The lobster mac and cheese at brunch is wonderful. Portions here are generous and reasonably priced; the presentations are always beautiful; the service is friendly and efficient. Duo Bistro has a monthly prix-fixe event called the Groaning Table, usually the last Monday of the month. Guests dine family-style on a themed meal, such as a seafood boil or Moroccan cuisine. Check the website or call for updates on dates and themes; reservations are a must for the Groaning Table events.

Ecce Terra, 288 Fair St., Kingston, NY 12401; (845) 338-8734; ecce-terra.com; Mediterranean; $$. Ecce Terra fits in nicely in the historic Stockade district of uptown Kingston. This small, charming restaurant is nicely serene, even romantic. The cuisine is Mediterranean, with an emphasis on seafood. The appetizers showcase the Mediterranean offerings, with excellent grilled octopus, *tirokafteri* (feta with kalamata and green olives and Florina red peppers), and *gigandes* (butter beans roasted in olive oil and tomatoes with feta and dill). The grilled haloumi cheese is an unusual offering—cheese from Cyprus doesn't find its way to the Hudson Valley very often. The entrees at Ecce Terra are more European than Mediterranean, with well-prepared dishes such as veal scaloppine and flounder à la Française. The specials, based on what's fresh and interesting at the market that day, are always good. Open for dinner only every night but Sun. Reservations suggested.

Elephant Wine Bar, 310 Wall St., Kingston, NY 12401; (845) 339-9310; elephantwinebar.com; Tapas; $$$. The menu at Elephant Wine Bar is tapas and more tapas, served in a funky, narrow storefront (only 30 seats). The tapas here are authentically Spanish. They're simple—most use no more than a handful of simply prepared ingredients—and boldly flavorful. The 30 or so regular selections on the menu, which includes charcuterie classics such as Spanish *jamón serrano* and the house specialty, chorizo and chocolate, are supplemented by an array of daily specials. The wine list at Elephant is chosen to complement the tapas. It's short (some might even say spare) and focuses mostly, but not exclusively, on wines from Spain and Portugal. The ambience here is very friendly. Evenings only; closed Sun and Mon.

Hickory BBQ and Smokehouse, 743 Rte. 28, Kingston NY 12401; (845) 338-2424; hickoryrestaurant.com; Barbecue; $$$. Hickory BBQ and Smokehouse is on the road from Kingston to Woodstock. This is Texas-style barbecue, slow-smoked and served plain—diners add their own sauces from the flavorful selection of homemade options on the table. (With the exception of Heinz ketchup and Frank's Red Hot sauce, all sauces, condiments, dressings, and pickles are made fresh in-house.) The barbecue offerings here are extensive, including appetizers such as rib tips and wings (there's also award-winning chili, but it's not barbecued). The main courses include all the usual barbecue offerings, such as pulled pork, ribs, brisket, and chicken. Turkey thighs are an unusual offering (why other barbecue places ignore them is a mystery). The truly hungry can order the Kingston Trio platter: turkey thigh, beef brisket, and pulled pork. The sides are all the usual barbecue place choices as well; try Ma Hickory's (yes, there is such a person) slaw. Astonishingly, some people don't like barbecue. The menu here accommodates them gracefully with a good selection of comfort foods, such as homemade meat loaf and shrimp in a basket. Hickory BBQ has an excellent beer selection, including some local brews. Open for lunch and dinner every day.

Hoffman House, 94 N. Front St., Kingston, NY 12401; (845) 338-2626; hoffmanhousetavern.com; Continental; $$$. Eating at Hoffman House is like taking a step three centuries into the past. The stone building, located in the historic Stockade district, is a National Historic Landmark dating back to 1679; the first Hoffman bought the property in 1707. It's a beautifully restored example of early American Dutch architecture, with random-width plank floors, a fireplace in each of the main rooms, and many small multilevel rooms. At one time, the house was a fortification and lookout against Indian attacks. Since 1977, however, it has been an elegant, impeccably restored, peaceable place to enjoy well-prepared traditional Continental cuisine. In addition to the main dinner menu, the tavern menu offers an excellent burger, along with nachos, wings, grilled sandwiches, and daily specials. In the warmer weather, dine on the lovely outdoor patio. *Note:* Because of the uneven floors and multiple levels here, people with mobility handicaps will have difficulty accessing this restaurant.

Mint, 1 W. Strand St., Kingston, NY 12401; (845) 338-2006; mint loungeandtapas.com; Italian; $$. The cuisine of northern Italy is featured at this casual waterfront restaurant. The homemade pastas and gnocchi are excellent—try the *malfatti di spinaci* in a Gorgonzola cream sauce or the wild goose *ragú* over pappardelle. The perfectly prepared made-to-order risottos are even better for their rarity on menus in the region. The grilled thin-crust pizzas, served in personal sizes, come in a good range of options. The limited list of Italian standard entrees at Mint are all well prepared and worth sampling. The bar offers a short but select list of wines and beer and some interesting house cocktails. Open for dinner only, Wed through Sun. Reservations suggested.

Santa Fe Uptown, 11 Main St., Kingston, NY 12401; (845) 339-7777; santafekingston.com; Mexican; $$. The Kingston outpost of Santa Fe in Tivoli (see p. 134), Santa Fe Uptown has the same good Mexican menu. The large, U-shaped bar here is very lively, perhaps because it has a very large and broad collection of tequilas. Dinner every night; open for lunch on Fri.

Savona's Trattoria, 11 Broadway, Kingston, NY 12401; (845) 339-6800; savonas.com; Italian; $$–$$$. Savona's offers Italian food in a stylishly casual setting on Kingston's historic waterfront. The lunch and dinner menus stick mostly to well-prepared classics served in very generous portions. Some dishes really stand out, such as the salmon limoncello, a salmon filet with panko and finished in a limoncello cream sauce and served with spinach risotto. The specials menu is where things get interesting, with dishes such as veal and ricotta meatballs with a fresh tomato basil sauce, served over bucatini. At lunchtime, Savona's offers a popular three-course prix-fixe pasta menu along with the regular entrees. In the warmer weather, enjoy your meal on the patio. Open for lunch and dinner every day.

Ship to Shore, 15 W. Strand St., Kingston, NY, 12401; (845) 334-8887; shiptoshorehudsonvalley.com; New American; $$$. Ship to Shore calls itself, a bit clumsily, "an American bistro with a taste of old New York steak house." The steak house items on the menu are both the standard grilled chops and steaks, all very nicely prepared, and also more contemporary takes. Steak and Cake, for example, is a pan-seared filet mignon with a crab cake—the restaurant's tribute to surf and turf. Seafood items, including very good fish-and-chips, are the other half of the entree list. The dinner menu and the specials menu at Ship to Shore are full of reliably good appetizers (try the tuna stack), pastas, and entrees, but for great food and great value, try the special nights. Monday is the restaurant's locally famous burger and brew night, Tuesday features tuna au poivre, and Wednesday is wine-lover's night, when bottles of wine are half off with dinner. Thursday is surf and turf night, Friday is bouillabaisse, and Saturday features seafood mac and cheese. Ship to Shore is open for lunch, Sun brunch, and dinner every day from 11 a.m. to 11 p.m., making this one of the rare local restaurants where the kitchen is open late.

Skytop Steakhouse & Brewing Company, 237 Forest Hill Dr., Kingston, NY 12401; (845) 340-4277; skytop.moonfruit.com; Steak House; $$$. The view of the Catskills and the surrounding area from Skytop Steakhouse makes the trip to this slightly out-of-the-way restaurant worthwhile. The restaurant is perched on a hilltop in a chalet-type building with high roof beams, large windows, and a spacious dining room. The reliably good steaks, pastas, and well-prepared seafood and chicken entrees add to the enjoyment of the view. To go with the steaks and the well-stocked antipasto bar (complimentary with an entree), Skytop offers an excellent selection of craft beers, many from local breweries. The taps change weekly, making Skytop a regular stop on the rotation for local beer aficionados. Skytop is also a popular comedy and music venue—there's some sort of entertainment every weekend and some weeknights. Brew Ha Ha comedy nights sell out quickly. Check the website to learn what's coming up. Closed Mon.

Yum Yum Noodle Bar, 275 Fair St., Kingston, NY 12401; (845) 338-1400; yumyumnoodlebar.com; Asian; $. For a quick, inexpensive, and really delicious meal, the noodles and other choices at Yum Yum Noodle Bar are perfect. This restaurant, an offshoot of the original restaurant in Woodstock, specializes in big bowls of four kinds of Asian noodles: ramen (Chinese egg noodle), rice (gluten-free), soba (buckwheat), and udon (thick wheat noodles) with your choice of broth and added protein. Every bowl also contains sautéed vegetables, scallions, nori, mushrooms, and an egg. In addition to noodle bowls, Yum Yum offers Vietnamese *banh mi* sandwiches, excellent steamed buns, and a variety of other Asian-style street food, along with bento boxes and daily specials. The Fair Street special is always attractively priced and delicious. There's also a full bar with house special cocktails. Restaurant descriptions don't usually discuss the restrooms, but Yum

Yum is an exception. Check out the LoveLock wall, a section of chain link fencing adorned with old locks of every kind. Feel free to donate one yourself. Yum Yum has a colorful food truck that is often seen at outdoor events in the region. Open Mon through Sat from 11:30 a.m. to 10 p.m.

Cafes & Quick Bites

Boice Brothers Ice Cream, 62 O'Neil St., Kingston, NY 12401; (845) 340-2018; Ice Cream; $. Fabulous ice cream made using hormone-free milk from the family dairy. The stand offers 30 flavors, including luscious chocolate raspberry. The ice cream cakes are probably the best in the region. Open every day, 8 a.m. to 9 p.m.

Cafe East, 243 Fair St., Kingston, NY 12401; (845) 331-2042; facebook.com/eastfoodcart; Asian; $. The east part of Cafe East refers to Asia. This little cafe serves mostly Asian street food cuisine, such as a variety of Vietnamese *banh mi* sandwiches, kimchi omelets, and pad thai with shredded Asian sausage, all made with fresh, authentic ingredients. To balance things out for adventurous eaters, the menu also includes fusion tacos, such as chipotle fish and marinated tofu with pineapple. The coffee and desserts here are excellent. Open 8 a.m. to 3 p.m. Mon through Sat; 11 a.m. to 4 p.m. Sun.

Dallas Hot Wieners, 51 N. Front St., Kingston, NY 12401; (845) 338-6094; dallashotwieners.com; Hot Dogs; $. An uptown Kingston institution since the 1920s, Dallas Hot Wieners is famed for hot dogs topped with mustard, onion, and secret sauce. If for some strange reason you don't like hot dogs, the menu also offers fries, onion rings, burgers of various sorts, some basic sandwiches, and simple breakfast options. The family that runs Dallas Hot Wieners won't reveal what's in the addictive secret sauce, but you can buy it in half-pints and pints to take home. Open Mon through Sat from 9 a.m. to 8 p.m.

Dallas Hot Wieners, 490 Broadway, Kingston, NY 12401; (845) 331-6311; dallashotwieners.com; Hot Dogs; $. See listing description above. The same hot dogs, secret sauce, and basic menu as the Front Street store, with the addition of some sandwich items and salads. Open Mon through Fri from 10 a.m. to 8 p.m. and on Sat from 11 a.m. to 8 p.m.

Dolce, 27 Broadway, Kingston, NY 12401; (845) 339-0921; face book.com/dolce; Sandwich Shop; $. This little storefront cafe near the Kingston waterfront is a wonderful spot for breakfast or lunch. They make great eggs and pancakes (even vegan pancakes) and wonderful breakfast and lunch sandwiches and paninis. Vegans are not second-class citizens here: The grilled tofu sandwich with tomato, raw onion, avocado, and Vegenaise, served on focaccia, is taken as seriously as the sandwich made with Coach Farm goat cheese, salami, and pesto. A bit unusually, Dolce also makes crepes, both savory and sweet. The fillings for the savory crepes, such as home-baked turkey, avocado, and cheddar cheese, are very satisfying. The sweet crepes are a real treat—try the crepe stuffed with Nutella and a sliced banana. Dolce also offers truly excellent coffee and a good selection of teas and herbal teas. The cafe can get crowded at lunchtime; be prepared for a bit of a wait. Open daily 8 a.m. to 3 p.m.; cash only.

Dominick's Cafe, 34 N. Front St., Kingston, NY 12401; (845) 338-4552; dominickscafe.com; Italian; $. A small cafe featuring Italian specialties, Dominick's is in a beautifully restored turn-of-the-century building in the historic Stockade district. The breakfast menu offers really good egg sandwiches along with all the usual items. The lunch menu features the unique Sisters sandwiches, named for the owners' four grandmothers. In addition, the cafe offers salads, soups, paninis, fresh pasta dishes, and traditional Italian choices, such as eggplant parmigiana. The coffee and home-baked desserts here are very good. Open daily 8 a.m. to 5 p.m.; Sun 9 a.m. to 4 p.m.

El Danzante on Wheels, 654 Broadway, Kingston, NY 12401; (845) 430-9086; facebook.com/eldanzantekingstonny; Food Truck/ Tacos; $. Look for this green and white food truck in midtown Kingston on weekdays and in the Stockade district at 323 Wall St. on weekend nights from 10 p.m. to 2 a.m. El Danzante offers authentic Mexican fare to go, including tacos, burritos, *pupusas, tortas,* and fried yucca. The truck is also occasionally seen in Saugerties at the corner of Main and Market Streets at SpeedyMart.

Gabriel's Cafe, 316 Wall St., Kingston, NY 12401; (845) 338-7161; gabriels-cafe.com; South American; $. Small and friendly, Gabriel's Cafe serves an unusually interesting menu of South American dishes. This is a great place for adventurous eaters. Many of the dishes, such as the *acarajé* (Brazilian black-eyed pea fritters served with a passion fruit dipping sauce) and *carne mechada Chilena* (Chilean pot roast served with quinoa and sweet plantains) will be new to diners. Never fear—the food here may be unfamiliar, but it's really good. The specials are always a great way to eat something you've never eaten before. The dishes are all authentically prepared using organic, seasonal ingredients that are sourced locally whenever possible. A number are gluten-free, vegetarian, or vegan. The scones, croissants, and empanadas are baked fresh daily on the premises. Open Mon through Fri from 10 a.m. to 9 p.m.; Sat 9 a.m. to 9 p.m.; closed Sun.

Hudson Coffee Traders, 288 Wall St., Kingston, NY 12401; (845) 338-1300; hudsoncoffeetraders.com; Coffeehouse; $. At

Hudson Coffee Traders, the coffee drinks are always made by skilled baristas using freshly brewed organic beans. Tea drinkers get equal treatment here—the wide assortment of teas comes from **Harney & Sons** (see p. 68). To go along with the caffeine, Hudson Coffee Traders offers egg wraps at breakfast and a good selection of paninis and sandwiches at lunch. Homemade baked goods are always available. Free Wi-Fi and plenty of outlets make this a good spot for a working meal or coffee break. Open Mon through Fri, 7 a.m. to 5:30 p.m.; 8 a.m. to 3 p.m. on Sat; 9 a.m. to 2 p.m. on Sun.

Joe Beez Famous Sandwiches, 456 Broadway, Kingston, NY 12401; (845) 334-9501; joebeez.com; Sandwich Shop; $. The foot-long sandwiches from Joe Beez are indeed famous, at least locally. This shop offers a broad menu of sandwiches and hamburgers, all with distinctive names and all freshly grilled. How exactly sandwiches like the Buster Douglas (grilled roast beef, chicken, provolone, blue cheese, onion, pepper, lettuce, and hot sauce) got their names is never explained, but no matter—the point is that the sandwiches are really good, freshly prepared, and very reasonably priced. The store can get crowded at lunchtime, and there's no seating. Plan to take your sandwich with you. Open from 7 a.m. to 8 p.m. Mon through Fri; 9 a.m. to 8 p.m. on Sat; 10 a.m. to 6 p.m. on Sun.

The Lunch Box, 275 Fair St., Kingston, NY 12401; (845) 616-2417; facebook.com/thelunchboxofkingston; Sandwich Shop; $. Chef Sean Miller turns out amazing sandwiches, soups, and desserts from his tiny kitchen area at this storefront shop. The menu changes daily and includes items such as smoked ham and roasted red pepper wrap, ham and swiss panini, sliced London broil sandwich with mushrooms and onions, and a very good Reuben sandwich. One constant at the Lunch Box is the locally famous pulled pork sandwich. Dessert here is always good—try the homemade banana or coffee ice cream. Open Mon through Fri from 7:30 a.m. to 4 p.m.

Mickey's Igloo, 416 E. Chester Ave., Kingston, NY 12401; (845) 416-3807; mickeysigloo.com; Ice Cream; $. A Kingston favorite for over 60 years, this popular stand serves 18 flavors of hard ice cream and 25 soft-serve flavors. Cones, milk shakes, ice cream sodas, sundaes, banana splits, malts, egg creams, and ice cream cakes are on the menu. The Colossal Sundaes are exactly that: ten variations on the theme of a lot of ice cream with a lot of toppings. Also available are burgers, hot dogs, chicken nuggets, french fries, and onion rings. On a hot summer evening the line is out the door, but it moves quickly. Open daily, 11 a.m. to 10 p.m. **Additional location:** 193 Hurley Ave., Kingston, NY 12401; (845) 416-3807.

Monkey Joe Roasting Company, 478 Broadway, Kingston, NY 12401; (845) 331-4598; monkeyjoe.com; Coffeehouse; $. The giant coffee roaster opposite the espresso bar at Monkey Joe Roasting Company tells you these people take coffee seriously. The single-origin, sustainably grown green coffee beans come from around the world and are then carefully roasted in small batches. This shop is located in the restored Hutton Building, which dates back to 1906; the shop has the original tin ceiling, wainscoting, and fireplace. The coffee menu includes latte, cappuccino, breve, macchiato, and many more variations. There's also an extensive tea list and other beverages, including Italian sodas. A good selection of locally made baked goods rounds out the menu. Open Mon through Fri from 6:30 a.m. to 6 p.m.; 7:30 a.m. to 4 p.m. on Sat.

Ulster County Diners

Broadway Lights Diner, 713 Broadway, Kingston, NY 12401; (845) 338-4280; broadwaylightsdiner.com; Diner; $. A very clean, family-owned, friendly place with unusually good Greek specialties and good homemade desserts. Free Wi-Fi. Open Sun through Thurs 6 a.m. to 11 p.m.; until midnight Fri and Sat.

College Diner, 500 Main St., New Paltz, NY 12561; (845) 255-5040; thecollegediner.com; Diner; $. Located in the heart of New Paltz. One of the very few places in the area that is open 24 hours a day. Popular with hungry SUNY students late at night.

Dietz Stadium Diner, 127 N. Front St., Kingston, NY 12401; (845) 331-5321; Diner, $. A popular spot, especially after high school football games and other events at nearby Dietz Stadium. Good food, generous portions, friendly service. Open 24 hours a day.

Elena's Restaurant and Diner, 51 Schwenk Dr., Kingston, NY 12401; (845) 331-2767; Diner; $. A neighborhood favorite for breakfast and lunch. Homemade soups. Open daily from 6 a.m. to 3 p.m.

Outdated: An Antique Cafe, 314 Wall St., Kingston, NY 12401; (845) 331-0030; www.facebook.com/outdatedcafecafe; $. A cafe in an antiques store, Outdated is a quiet, unhurried spot in the Stockade district for a great home-cooked breakfast or lunch. The shop has good homemade granola, baked goods (including scones, biscuits, cakes, and tarts), and makes great egg dishes, sandwiches, and salads.

Or just order one of the French press coffee drinks and relax among the vintage objects in the cafe area and the downstairs shop. That comfy chair today might be sold tomorrow, though. Free Wi-Fi. Open Mon, Wed through Sat 9 a.m. to 5 p.m.; Sun 9 a.m. to 3 p.m.; closed Tues.

Kings Valley Diner, 617 Ulster Ave., Kingston, NY 12401; (845) 331-3254; kingsvalleydiner.com; Diner; $. The sleek decor sets this large, clean diner a bit apart from others in the area. Good food, friendly and very efficient service, free Wi-Fi. Open Sun through Thurs, 6 a.m. to midnight; Fri and Sat until 2 a.m.

Michael's Diner, 1071 Ulster Ave., Kingston, NY 12401; (845) 336-6514; Diner; $. Good food, good Greek specialties, and good service. Smaller than the average diner, so there may be a wait at lunchtime. The one-way southbound entrance to the parking area is a little confusing, as is the one-way southbound exit—drive carefully. Open 24 hours a day.

Olympic Diner, 620 Washington Ave., Kingston, NY 12401; (845) 331-2280; Diner; $. Fast, friendly service, plus very good specials and desserts at this local favorite. Open daily 6 a.m. to 11 p.m.

Village Diner, 140 Main St., Saugerties, NY 12477; (845) 246-7747; Diner: $. Conveniently located in the heart of the village, this pleasant diner serves good food with ample portions. Open daily, 6 a.m. to 10 p.m.

Sissy's Cafe, 324 Wall St., Kingston, NY 12401; (845) 514-2336; sissycafekingston.com; Sandwich Shop; $. Breakfast and lunch sandwiches are the specialty at Sissy's (owned by two sisters). This is great place to grab a quick meal to go. For something different at breakfast, try the Greek wrap, made with eggs, spinach, olive tapenade, and feta cheese, or the vegetarian Sunshine breakfast wrap, made with fake bacon, avocado, tomato, sprouts, and hummus. At lunch, the Hot Bird sandwich, made with turkey, bacon, avocado, red onion, cheddar, and spicy mayo is a real treat. Sissy's also offers freshly made juices and smoothies—check the board to see what the daily specials are. Open every day, 8 a.m. to 4 p.m. weekdays, 8 a.m. to 3 p.m. on Sat, and 9 a.m. to 2 p.m. on Sun.

Adams Fairacre Farms, 1560 Ulster Ave., Lake Katrine, NY 12449; (845) 336-6300; adamsfarm.com. See listing description on p. 95.

Cake Box Bakery, 8 Fair St., Kingston, NY 12401; (845) 339-4715. An old-fashioned corner bakery with friendly service and excellent cakes, pastries, cookies, bread, rolls, and bagels. A small cafe area is a good spot for lunch or a coffee break—the menu is mostly soups and sandwiches. Have a cup of their excellent coffee and an almond horn for dessert. The Cake Box building was once a Gulf gas station. Many of the vintage Art Deco details remain, and photos of the station in its heyday are in the cafe area. Closed Mon.

Cheese Louise, 940 Rte. 28, Kingston, NY 12401; (845) 853-8207; cheeselouise-ny.com. Cheese Louise is a gourmet shop with an excellent selection of local and imported cheese, smoked fish, charcuterie, chocolate, and other goodies. Good cheese shops are rare in this area, making Cheese Louise a local foodie destination. The store also offers a daily menu of excellent gourmet takeout. There's a small area for eating in. Open daily from 11:30 a.m. to 7 p.m.

Deising's Bakery, 111 N. Front St., Kingston, NY 12401; (845) 338-7505; deisings.com. An award-winning bakery with deep roots in Kingston, Deising's offers over 400 varieties of freshly baked bread, rolls, cakes, pies, pastries, cookies, and desserts. The bakery is notable for its breads and rolls, including an authentic German rye and a really good cracked wheat loaf. The retail bakery on N. Front Street has an attached restaurant serving breakfast and lunch. A second retail location at 584 Broadway has a smaller restaurant serving only breakfast until 1 p.m.

Fleisher's Meats, 307 Wall St., Kingston, NY 12401; (845) 338-6666; fleishers.com. Josh Applestone of Fleisher's grass-fed and organic meats is nationally known as a master butcher. He's also a driving force behind the growing movement for locally pastured, humanely produced meat, poultry, and eggs. Despite his national fame, the store in uptown Kingston has an intimate, neighborhood feel. All the meat sold here comes from local farmers committed to sustainable practices. Because of this, not all cuts are available all the time—if you want a specific cut of beef, pork, lamb, or poultry, call ahead. The store also offers more than 20 different homemade sausages. Serious home cooks can take Fleisher's Butcher 101 3-day course. This intensive program teaches knife skills, safety techniques, basic anatomy, and sausage making. It includes hands-on carving workshops. The retail store is open Thurs and Fri from 11 a.m. to 7 p.m. and on Sat from 10 a.m. to 6 p.m.

Jane's Ice Cream, 307 Wall St., Kingston, NY 12401; (845) 338-1801; janesicecream.com. Jane's Ice Cream was founded in 1985 in nearby Phoenicia and quickly grew to become a much-loved favorite in the region. This is artisan ice cream, rich and fully flavored, made in small batches using only fresh, local, organic ingredients. New flavors, such as gingersnap molasses, are added regularly. Jane's ice cream has a fanatical local following, but it's actually a bit hard to find. It's sold only at select restaurants and retail outlets in the region—check the website for a list. See Jane's Ice Cream's recipe for **Frozen Raspberry Mojito** on p. 321.

Keegan Ales, 20 Saint James St., Kingston, NY 12401; (845) 331-BREW (2739); keeganales.com. Craft brewing is growing fast in the Hudson Valley, fueled by consumer demand and lots of good restaurants. Keegan Ales joined the movement early on, back in 2003, when

Tommy Keegan took over a defunct brewery in Kingston. He was soon producing three brews, Old Capital (traditional), Hurricane Kitty (India pale ale), and Mother's Milk (dark stout), that quickly became regional and national award-winners. In addition, Keegan Ales produces unusual small-batch seasonal and specialty beers that are sold only at the brewery's lively bar and restaurant. Entertainment and beer are both on tap here every night except Monday. Tours of the brewery are offered once an hour on Fri, Sat, and Sun from 1 p.m. to 6 p.m. Tell the bartender you want to go on the tour.

Kingston Candy Bar, 319 Wall St., Kingston, NY 12401; (845) 901-0341; kingstoncandybar.com. All kinds of candy, including gummi worms in sizes from standard to python. Some 50 varieties of bulk candy by the pound, including lots of fun retro brands. The shop also offers **Jane's Ice Cream** (see p. 245), and home-baked pastries. At the soda fountain, have a milkshake or egg cream or make your own concoction. Open daily, 11 a.m. to 8 p.m.

Kokokobi, 604 Ulster Ave., Kingston, NY 12401; (845) 331-1037; kokokobi.com. The slogan at Kokokobi is "Where Life is Kokolicious and Chocolate is Kokompulsory!" Owner and chocolatier Kobi Pincus takes his chocolates very seriously. He's also pretty serious about his ice cream, his coffee, and his hot chocolate. The wonderfully imaginative chocolates here (many named for movie stars) are matched by the equally wonderful and imaginative ice creams, with flavors such as caramelized banana and sea salt butter pecan. The coffee and hot chocolate are wonderful as well. Take home the chocolates and ice cream or enjoy them in the small, comfortable cafe area. Open Sun through Wed from noon to 8 p.m. and Thurs through Sat from noon to 9 p.m.

La Bella Pasta, 906 Rte. 28W, Kingston, NY 12401; (845) 331-9130; lbpasta.com. With 17 varieties of cheese ravioli alone, La Bella Pasta offers the best and most varied fresh pasta in the region. All are made fresh daily. La Bella Pasta products are used by many restaurants in the region. Retail consumers are welcome at the family-owned shop. It's open Mon through Fri from 10 a.m. to 6 p.m. and on Sat from 11 a.m. to 3 p.m. See the recipe for **Porcini Mushroom Sauce** on p. 325.

Michael's Candy Corner, 773A Broadway, Kingston, NY 12401; (845) 338-6782; candycornerusa.com. This beloved shop is most famous for their handmade Christmas candy canes, produced every year since 1917. In addition, they make excellent chocolates. Many have a holiday theme, such as the very cute chocolate bunnies at Easter time. Others are year-round choices, including truffles and chocolate dinosaurs.

Mother Earth's Storehouse, 300 Kings Mall Court, Kingston NY, 12401; (845) 336-5541; motherearthstorehouse.com Founded in 1978 as a single small store, Mother Earth's Storehouse has grown to three large stores, with a branch in Poughkeepsie (see p. 98) and another in Saugerties (see p. 279). The main Kingston store is the size of a moderate supermarket and about as well stocked, but with only organic products (plus a very large vitamins and supplements section). In all the stores, the selection of fresh organic fruits and vegetables is excellent; most produce comes from local farms. All the stores also have in-house bakeries and delis with many vegan and vegetarian selections. The shelves, dairy cases, and freezers are fully stocked with healthy foods and beverages of all kinds, including bulk foods and a great selection of dried fruit. This is a good place to find unusual foods and spices that can be hard to come by at regular groceries.

Farm Bounty

Kingston Farmers' Market, Midtown Broadway between Henry and Cedar Streets, Kingston, NY 12401; (845) 535-3185; kingstonfarmersmarket.org. Tues from 3 p.m. to 7 p.m., end of May to end Sept.

Kingston Farmers' Market Uptown, Wall Street between Main and John Streets, Kingston, NY 12401; (845) 535-3185; king stonfarmersmarket.org. Sat from 9 a.m. to 2 p.m., May through Nov.

Kingston Winter Market, Bethany Hall at the Old Dutch Church, 272 Wall St., Kingston, NY (845) 535-3185; kingstonfarmers market.org. First and third Sat of the month from Nov to Apr, 10 a.m. to 2 p.m.

Slow Roots Farm, 205 Hidden Valley Rd., Kingston, NY 12401; (845) 339-2731; slowrootsfarm.com. Over 250 varieties of organically grown vegetables. Most produce goes to the CSA members; the surplus is sold at the Rosendale and Saugerties farmers' markets.

Marlboro

Specialty Stores & Producers

Benmarl Winery, 156 Highland Ave., Marlboro, NY 12542; (845) 236-4265; benmarl.com. The oldest vineyard in America, Benmarl holds New York Farm Winery license number 1. Benmarl produces small-batch wines from its own 37-acre estate overlooking the Hudson; some additional grapes are sourced from selected regional vineyards.

The winery turns out red and white varietals, including Cabernet Franc, Chardonnay, and Seyval Blanc, along with proprietary blends. The tasting room is open daily from noon to 6 p.m. from Apr through Dec. In Jan, Feb, and Mar, the tasting room is open Fri through Sun from noon to 5 p.m. The winery is a member of the **Shawangunk Hudson Valley Wine Trail** (see p. 208).

Glorie Farm Winery, 40 Mountain Rd., Marlboro, NY 12542; (845) 236-3265; gloriewine.com. Glorie Farm Winery was established in 2004 as an offshoot of the family fruit farm. The winery remains small, producing only about 850 cases of wine each year. The current wine list has an interesting mix of varietals, blends, and dessert wines. Their 2010 Cabernet Franc was the gold medal winner for best red wine at the 2012 Hudson Valley Wine and Food Festival. The tasting room at Glorie Farm Winery is closed from Jan to Mar, although sales are still available. Tours of the winery and tastings are offered on weekends and Mon holidays from Apr through Dec from 11:30 a.m. to 5:30 p.m. The winery is a member of the **Shawangunk Hudson Valley Wine Trail** (see p. 208).

Stoutridge Vineyard, 10 Ann Kaley Ln., Marlboro, NY 12542; (845) 236-7620; stoutridge.com. Although the vineyard at Stoutridge was originally planted in the late 1700s, the current vineyard dates back to replanting in 2001. The winery was opened in 2006, and the distillery in 2009. Stoutridge today is famed for producing slow wine: wine that is made organically, with minimal processing. The wines produced here include Seyval Blanc, Merlot, and their own excellent varietals and blends. Stoutridge is open for picnics on the grounds, tours of its beautiful building, and tastings on Fri, Sat, and Sun year-round from 11 a.m. to 6 p.m. The vineyard is a member of the **Shawangunk Hudson Valley Wine Trail** (see p. 208).

Weed Orchards, 43 Mt. Zion Rd., Marlboro, NY 12542; (845) 236-2684; weedorchards.com. Visitors to Weed Orchards are welcome to pick their own apples, peaches, pears, plums, grapes, pumpkins, nectarines, watermelons, and vegetables. The Apple Bakery on the farm offers sandwiches and lunch foods as well as home-baked apple pies, turnovers, muffins, cookies, and apple cider doughnuts. Families can picnic by the lake or enjoy a chicken barbecue. The kids can enjoy hayrides, a petting zoo, corn and hay mazes, and plenty of fun activities and crafts. Open all day on weekends in season, starting in July; call ahead to find out about weather conditions and what's ripe.

Milton

Foodie Faves

Ship Lantern Inn, 1725 Rte. 9W, Milton, NY 12547; (845) 795-5400; shiplanterninn.com; Continental; $$$. Ship Lantern Inn preserves Continental dining in all its old-school glory: beautiful decor, impeccable service, perfectly prepared food. Owner John Foglia was one of the original four founders of the Chef Boy-Ar-Dee Company. His restaurant, now in its third generation of family ownership, is decorated with amazing ship models from his personal collection. The carefully restored building itself dates back to the Revolutionary War. The dishes at Ship Lantern Inn are classic in both preparation and presentation. This is one of the very few restaurants in the region—and perhaps an even wider area—that not only knows how to prepare a chateaubriand for two perfectly, but has skilled waiters who know how to serve it. The rest of the menu is comparably timeless, with dishes such as fillet of lemon sole with asparagus and Maryland crabmeat and veal Valdostana. The dessert menu is wonderful—try the Hudson Valley apple fritters with caramel spice ice cream. Reservations strongly recommended.

Henry's Farm to Table Restaurant at Buttermilk Falls Inn, 220 North Rd., Milton, NY 12547; (845) 795-1310; buttermilk fallsinn.com; New American; $$$. Henry's at the posh Buttermilk Falls Inn takes the farm-to-table concept literally: Most of the produce served at the restaurant comes from their own 40-acre Milestone Farm (they don't eat the llamas you see as you go past). What they can't grow at the farm is sourced from local organic farmers and producers, including **Hepworth Farms** (see p. 252). Because the menu is based on what's fresh from the farm, it focuses on just a handful of beautifully prepared appetizers, entrees, and specials and changes often. This is a lovely place to eat: The dining room is spacious and serene and the windows look out onto beautiful countryside. Henry's offers cooking classes on a regular basis; the classes include the lesson, recipes, and a sit-down dinner with the chef, along with a wine pairing. Check the website for details. Henry's is open for lunch on Fri and Sat, brunch on Sun, and dinner Wed through Sun. Reservations suggested.

Farm Bounty

Heart of the Hudson Valley Farmers' Market, Cluett-Schantz Park, 1801-1805 Rt. 9W, Milton, NY 12547; (845) 464-2789; hhvfarmersmarket.com. Sat, 9 a.m. to 2 p.m., mid-June through mid-Oct, plus Thanksgiving market in Nov.

Hepworth Farms, 506 South Rd., Milton, NY 12547; (845) 795-2007; hepworthfarms.com. The land at Hepworth Farms has been in production since 1818; the seventh generation is now farming it. Today Hepworth Farms is certified as an organic farm by the Northeast Organic Farming Association. The produce here mostly goes to local restaurants and a number of community-supported agriculture (CSA) programs in New York City. In the area, Hepworth Farms organic produce is sold at the **Heart of the Hudson Valley Farmers' Market** in Milton—see p. 251.

Prospect Hill Orchards, 40 Clarkes Ln., Milton, NY 12547; (845) 795-2383; prospecthillorchards.com. Prospect Hill Orchards has been a family farm ever since Nathaniel Clarke moved to Milton in 1817. Today the farm offers pick-your-own cherries, peaches, nectarines, apples, pears, and pumpkins in season. Picking is available only on weekends, usually starting in late July for peaches and nectarines. Call ahead to find out what's ripe and how the weather is.

Modena

Farm Bounty

Hurds Family Farm, 2187 Rte. 32, Modena, NY 12548; (845) 883-7825; hurdsfamilyfarm.com. One of the better-known u-pick operations, Hurds Family Farm offers apple and pumpkin picking, along with a lot of family-friendly activities, including hayrides, a cornfield maze, and a petting zoo. Refreshments are sold in a restored 18th-century Dutch barn. Open in season Mon through Fri from 9 a.m. to 5 p.m.; weekends 10 a.m. to 6 p.m. Call ahead for hours, weather conditions, special events, and what's ripe.

Karl Family Farms, 2207 Rte. 32, Modena, NY 12548; (845) 443-6963; karlfamilyfarms.com. A small family farm raising pastured, humanely treated meat on 130 acres in the shadow of the Shawangunks. Beef, goat, lamb, pork, and poultry are sold at the farm, through a CSA, and at some local farmers' markets. To purchase products at the farm, call ahead to check on availability and cuts.

New Paltz

Foodie Faves

A Tavola Trattoria, 46 Main St., New Paltz, NY 12561; (845) 255-1426; atavolany.com; Italian; $$$. This relatively new Italian restaurant (it opened only in 2011) has very quickly become an award winner and regional foodie destination. The Tuscan-inspired food here is based on what's available from the many outstanding farms and purveyors in the area. The menu is short and focused on a handful of seasonally appropriate antipasti, pastas, and modern takes on classic entrees, such as veal saltimbocca and chicken under a brick. The appetizers include a remarkable poached octopus served with chickpeas, roasted peppers, and Taggiasca olives. The appetizer specials change every day. All the specials are seasonal, of course, and consistently excellent. Dishes such as braised rabbit, truffled mac and cheese, and monkfish meatballs show off the remarkable skills of chefs Bonnie and Nathan Snow. The homemade pasta dishes at A Tavola are especially delicious: dishes such as pappardelle Bolognese or goat cheese tortellini with blueberries and mushrooms are cooked and presented beautifully. The bar here is unusually good and serves some amazing house special cocktails—try the gin and jam. The excellent bread, pastries, and ice cream at A Tavola are all made in-house. The wonderful food here tastes even better for being served in a rustic, candlelit atmosphere with attentive, professional waiters. The restaurant is open for dinner only Thurs through Mon. Reservations recommended.

Hokkaido Japanese Restaurant, 18 Church St., New Paltz, NY 12561; (845) 256-0621; hokkaidonewpaltz.com; Japanese; $$. A bit off the beaten New Paltz track, Hokkaido is an excellent choice for fresh, well-constructed sushi and rolls; the menu also offers a good choice of traditional Japanese favorites, such as *gyoza*, udon, and unusually good miso soup and salads. This is a small restaurant, with maybe a dozen tables. The service here is professional, with a very helpful staff who never rush the customers. Open for lunch on weekdays only; dinner every night. Reservations suggested for dinner, especially on weekends.

Il Gallo Giallo, 36 Main St., New Paltz, NY 12561; (845) 255-3636; ilgallogiallowinebar.com; Italian; $$$. Il Gallo Giallo is an Italian wine bar—a sort of Italian tapas bar, with lots of really good small plates and good drinks, a solid beer list, and perfect wine pairings. The menu has a broad array of great choices, starting with small dishes such as grilled shrimp spiedini over polenta and deviled eggs in pancetta cups. The *salumi* (cured meats) at Il Gallo Giallo are unusually good and varied, including excellent bresaola. More substantial dishes include well-prepared paninis, burgers, and pastas. *Porchetta* (roasted pork) is something of a house specialty. It's especially good as a sandwich on chewy ciabatta with fresh mozzarella, arugula, and aioli. The restaurant has a pleasant outdoor patio in back. It's a great place to watch the sunset over the 'Gunks while enjoying a glass of Italian wine and a small plate of something good. Live jazz on Sun and Thurs.

The Gilded Otter, 3 Main St., New Paltz, NY 12561; (845) 256-1700; gildedotter.com; Pub Grub; $$. This large, sunny brewpub makes its own beer on the premises—the machinery is part of the modern bi-level decor. The food here is standard brewpub fare. The burgers and pizzas are excellent and the rest of the menu is at least good, but you don't go here for the food. At the Gilded Otter, the brews are the main attraction. Most beers are available year-round, including the Huguenot Street American lager, the Three Pines India pale ale, Stone House Irish stout, and the New Paltz Crimson lager. Other beers are seasonal, such as the Belgian Spring Wit, Mayday Maibock, Oktoberfest, blueberry beer, and pumpkin ale. Eight-beer samplers let you try most of the offerings. The Gilded Otter is a very popular spot for hikers coming in from the nearby trails at the Mohonk Preserve (mohonkpreserve.org), the Wallkill Valley Rail Trail (wrvrt.org), and Minnewaska State Park (nysparks.com). It can get crowded, but this is also one of the largest restaurants in town and there's always room for a few more beer lovers.

Mohonk Mountain House, 1000 Mountain Rest Rd., New Paltz, NY 12561; (845) 255-1000; mohonk.com; Traditional American; $$$$. Mohonk Mountain House is one of America's oldest resorts. Founded in 1869 and still run by members of the original Smiley family, today Mohonk Mountain House is a National Historic Landmark. The seven-story Victorian lodge on beautiful Lake Mohonk is surrounded by 26,000 of acres of secluded forest preserve. Overnight guests at the Mohonk Mountain House usually eat in one of the three gracious dining rooms. Day guests are welcome for lunch, dinner, and weekend and holiday brunch. The food at Mohonk is well-prepared standard American. It's good to very good, but the ambience and service, not the food, are the primary reasons to eat here. Lunch at Mohonk requires resort casual attire. Dinner is on the formal side. Jackets and ties are suggested for male guests over 12; women should dress accordingly. For decades, in keeping with their Methodist beliefs, the Smiley family refused to serve alcohol to their guests. That policy has changed, and today Mohonk offers a full bar at lunch and dinner along with an outstanding wine list. The Sunday brunch buffet at Mohonk Mountain House is very popular with day guests. Reservations required for all meals.

Rock and Rye Tavern, 215 Huguenot St., New Paltz, NY 12561; (845) 255-7888; rockandrye.com; New American; $$$. The name of this restaurant is a bit misleading. Rock and Rye Tavern does indeed take beer and cocktails seriously, but it takes food seriously, too. The restaurant is located on historic Huguenot Street (huguenotstreet.org), the oldest street in America. Follow the tree-lined drive to the building, which dates back to a 1759 tavern (some will remember this place as the former Locust Tree Inn); inside, the space has many period details, a lovely bar, and two very pleasant, candlelit dining rooms. The site may be historic, but the cuisine served here is very contemporary and very good. Starters such as mint-scented spring pea flan with a carrot vinaigrette and smoky pea tendrils are highly imaginative and make great use of fresh local produce. Rock and Rye is so proud of its association with local farms that their names are often in the dish titles—for example, Jamaican jerked Karl Family Farms chicken, served with orange tea–scented jasmine rice with cashews and spiced sweet potato puree. Several specials are offered most evenings, such as grilled **Rykowski Livestock** (see p. 271) pork chop with **Huguenot Street Farm** (see p. 265) collard greens, RSK Farms potato medley, and a sweet and sour Dijon sauce. The bar offers an interesting selection of historic classics, house cocktails, and modern classics, all expertly mixed. The service at Rock and Rye is highly professional, adding to the enjoyable ambience. Open for dinner only every night. Reservations recommended.

Suruchi, 5 Church St., New Paltz, NY 12561; (845) 255-2772; suruchiindian.com; Indian; $$. One of the better Indian restaurants in the region, Suruchi offers an authentic menu of mostly vegetarian and vegan choices, with some chicken and shrimp dishes as well. Only organic ingredients are used. Most dishes are also gluten-free, making this restaurant a great choice for people with dietary restrictions. The *dosas* (Indian filled crepes) are extremely good here; so are the samosas (Indian turnovers). Suruchi is a very serene restaurant, with good Indian music, good service, and nice artwork on the walls. Unusually for the region, it has some traditional Indian-style seating, the kind where you take off your shoes and sit at a low table.

Cafes & Quick Bites

Gomen Kudasai Noodle Shop, 232 Main St. (Rite Aid Plaza), New Paltz, NY 12561; (845) 255-8811; gomenkudasainy.com; Japanese; $. Gomen Kudasai is a point of culinary light in a drab strip mall. Fabulous homemade Japanese noodles in all their many delicious forms make up the menu here. This is comfort food, the sort of dishes your grandmother would make for you if she happened to be Japanese. The soba (buckwheat) and udon (thick wheat) noodles are the stars here, ranging from big bowls of noodles in flavorful dashi broth to cold noodles and stir-fried noodles with eggs. The traditional Japanese rice balls and *donburi* (rice bowls) are also very good. Many dishes here are good choices for vegetarians and vegans. The list of gluten-free dishes is unusually long and interesting.

Hudson Coffee Traders, 139 Main St. (Trailways bus station); New Paltz, NY 12561; (845) 255-7800; hudsoncoffeetraders.com; **Coffeehouse; $.** The same menu as the Kingston branch; open 6 a.m. to 6 p.m. every day. See listing description on p. 239.

Kosiner Brothers Organic Hot Dog Cart, 10 Main St. (Water Street Market), New Paltz, NY 12561; kosinerbrothers.com; **Hot Dogs; $.** You can get a regular Sabrett hot dog at this cart, or you can order an organic Applegate dog or a veggie dog. They all come with a choice of homemade toppings, such as zucchini relish, spicy peanut sauce, meat or veggie chili, nori flakes, and others. The dozen different specialty dogs include the Blue Ribbon, made with Dijon mustard, blue cheese, and *herbes de Provence,* the Bangcock, made with spicy peanut sauce, diced cucumbers, and nori strips, and the Hound Dog, made with bacon, bananas, peanut butter, and honey. The cart is mostly parked at the Water Street Market every day from noon to 6 p.m., but it also moves about quite a bit—look for it at local events.

La Stazione, 5 Main St., New Paltz, NY 12561; (845) 256-9447; lastazioneny.com; **Italian; $$.** La Stazione is located at the foot of Main Street in a renovated former train station dating back to the early 1900s, when the Wallkill Valley Railroad served the area. The railroad had been gone for decades when the old railbed was converted in 1993 into a wonderful 12-mile foot and bike trail (wvrta.org) that runs from its northern terminus in New Paltz to its southern end in Gardiner. La Stazione is conveniently close to the trail—its popular outdoor patio is adjacent to it, making this restaurant a popular place among trail users for a meal or a drink. The food here is standard Italian favorites, with good pasta choices (Tuesday and Wednesday are pasta nights here) and good daily specials. Open every day for lunch and dinner.

Main Street Bistro, 59 Main St., New Paltz, NY 12561; (845) 255-7766; mainstreetbistro.com; Traditional American; $. Great breakfast food and lunch sandwiches make Main Street Bistro a favorite for quick meals. The breakfast menu offers several good signature dishes in addition to excellent egg choices. The Zoo Canoe is very popular. Made with scrambled eggs, bacon, and tomato stuffed into a slab of walnut citron bread, and topped with melted cheese and Hollandaise sauce, it comes with home fries. At lunch, check the extensive list of creative sandwiches, wraps, and burgers. They're all good, plus many are good choices for vegetarians and vegans.

The Village TeaRoom, 10 Plattekill Ave., New Paltz, NY 12561; (845) 255-3434; thevillagetearoom.com; New American; $$$. Open for breakfast, lunch, and dinner, the Village TeaRoom is in a charming, 200-year-old building in the heart of the village. The bake shop sells wonderful homemade pastries. They're all good, but the chocolate chubbies, Shaker lemon pie, and adorable honeybee cake are top choices. The cozy restaurant part has two dining rooms, one upstairs (not accessible) and one downstairs. The menu here is based on seasonal, organic ingredients from local farms and suppliers. It's uniformly flavorful and good. At breakfast, order sides of the hand-cut slab bacon and potato pancakes no matter what else you order. The lunch menu has good sandwiches and other standard options, but try the Dingle pies, Irish-style lamb pies that are an enjoyable alternative to the usual lunch choices. At dinner, the entrees feature heartier fare, such as beef carbonnade and vegetarian chickpea stew. The most enjoyable meal at the Village TeaRoom, however, is afternoon tea. This can range from the simple cream tea, served with a scone, clotted cream, raspberry jam, and a pot of tea to the more elaborate version, which adds on an assortment of delicious finger sandwiches and plate of cookies. An impressively large tea selection adds to the enjoyment. Closed Mon.

Adair Vineyards, 52 Allhusen Rd., New Paltz, NY 12561; (845) 255-1377; adairwine.com. Adair Vineyards has 10 acres of vines and a small winery inside a classic red barn. Production here is about 20,000 bottles a year, made from their own grapes and grapes from a nearby associated grower. The winery produces red and white varietal blends, but Adair is best known for *kir*. The tasting room at Adair is open on weekends from 11 a.m. to 6 p.m. May through Oct, and from 11 a.m. to 5 p.m. in Nov and into mid-Dec. At other times, call to arrange purchases. The vineyard is a member of the **Shawangunk Hudson Valley Wine Trail** (see p. 208).

CandyCandy, 10 Main St. (Water Street Market), New Paltz, NY 12561; (845) 255-6506; candycandyny.com. With over 300 candies on hand, including many hard-to-find and retro brands, CandyCandy is an old-fashioned shop that evokes childhood memories for many visitors. The walls of this fun store are lined with bins selling many of the candies in bulk.

The Cheese Plate, 10 Main St. (Water Street Market), New Paltz, NY 12561; (845) 255-2444; cheeseplatenewpaltz.com. The Cheese Plate sells artisan chocolates and charcuterie and has a cafe area offering ice cream and an interesting menu of cheese sandwiches that can be eaten on the patio overlooking the Shawangunk Ridge. The cheese selection, however, is why customers keep coming back. This well-stocked store has one of the broadest selections in the area. It includes many local, regional, and national varieties as well as a broad range of international cheeses.

Gadaleto's Seafood Market, 246 Main St., New Paltz, NY 12561; (845) 255-1717; gadaletos.com. Gadaleto's is known throughout the region as the primary source for fresh, high-quality seafood. The store is a major purveyor to restaurants and also has an excellent retail market. Shopping for seafood here is fun. The store offers by far the largest selection of wild-caught and sustainably farmed seafood in the region. The broad selection is nicely displayed and the staff are very knowledgeable and helpful. The market also has a good selection of specialty grocery items and smoked fish. People in a hurry can call ahead and get their order from the drive-through window (said to have started when an errant car accidentally plowed a hole in the wall). The attached restaurant is a popular spot for local seafood lovers. It's very casual and reasonably priced. Diners pick the fish they want and how they want it prepared—grilled, blackened, fried, or broiled—or enjoy good fish-and-chips, pasta dishes, soups, and shellfish.

Jack's Meats and Deli, 79 Main St., New Paltz, NY 12561; (845) 255-2244. Jack's Meats is a reliable source for natural, free-range poultry and meat, sourced from the many local producers. These products are often hard to find outside of local farmers' markets or directly at the farm. The store also carries unusual meats, such as ostrich and buffalo. Open daily from 8 a.m. to 8 p.m.

Kettleborough Cider House, 277 State Rte. 208, New Paltz, NY 12561; (845) 419-3774; kettleboroughciderhouse.com. A small producer using apples from **Dressel Farm** (see p. 265), Kettleborough produced its first batch of cider in 2012 and very quickly sold out. The tasting room is open on weekends, but call ahead to be sure the cider is in stock. It's available at local farmers' markets and selected local wine shops and liquor stores.

Krause's Chocolates, 2 Church St., New Paltz, NY 12561; (845) 255-1272; krauseschocolates.com. See listing description on p. 278.

Lagusta's Luscious, 25 N. Front St., New Paltz, NY 12561; (845) 255-8VEG (8834); lagustasluscious.com. The chocolates at Lagusta's Luscious are 100 percent vegan—no animal products are used in them, ever. The chocolates here are so good that you never notice the lack of butter, cream, or milk. The confections are made from 100 percent fair trade and organic chocolate, often flavored by products from local farms. They're packed in 100 percent post-consumer recycled boxes. Only here could beet coriander truffles or sour sorrel caramels with candied asparagus even be imagined, much less become popular hits. Other flavors include candied orange and cranberry bonbons, white chocolate strawberry bark, and saffron and wild lime bonbons. The store also offers wonderfully imaginative collections, bars, toffees, and caramels.

Moxie Cupcake, 184 Main St. New Paltz, NY 12561; (845) 255-CAKE (2253); moxiecupcake.com. Moxie cupcakes are small, edible works of art. They're made fresh daily, using only the finest ingredients, including local milk, eggs, fruit, and other products. Moxie makes excellent traditional cupcakes in traditional flavors, such as chocolate, vanilla, lemon, and red velvet. The bakers also let loose with imaginative combinations such as tequila lime, pistachio honey, and witty designs such as Campfire Song, made with chocolate cake with chocolate chips and graham cracker bits topped with a toasted marshmallow. The icing designs are simply beautiful—it's a shame to eat them, and yet somehow everyone does. The shop offers cupcakes and other baked sweets, along with bread from Bread Alone in Woodstock. Enjoy them with a cup of coffee or tea in the cafe area. Moxie Cupcakes are available at some regional restaurants and coffee shops as well.

Robibero Family Vineyards, 714 Albany Post Rd., New Paltz, NY 12561; (845) 255-9463; rnewyorkwine.com. One of the newest boutique winemakers in the region, Robibero Family Vineyards began production in 2010. The output of varietals and blends is small, only 2,500 cases a year, and is sold in the tasting room and online. Selected wine shops and restaurants in the region also carry Robibero wines. Tastings and tours of the wine cellar are available most weekends; call or check the website for hours. In the warmer weather, Robibero sponsors live music almost every weekend. Special events such barbecues and pig roasts are also offered regularly over the summer. The winery is very family-friendly and dog-friendly. Bring a picnic and enjoy it on the beautiful 42-acre property. Robibero Family Vineyards is a member of the **Shawangunk Hudson Valley Wine Trail** (see p. 208).

Russo's Italian Deli, 164 Main St., New Paltz, NY 12561; (845) 255-1485; russofamilydeli.com. A family-owned deli with a large selection of Italian specialties, Russo's is best known for great specialty sandwiches. They all have names, like My Cousin Luca (prosciutto, chicken cutlet, provolone, lettuce, onion, mayo) and The Vinchenz (ham, pepperoni, sopressata, provolone, lettuce, onion, oil and vinegar, mayo, Italian seasoning). This is a great place to pick up a sandwich for lunch while enjoying one of the many nearby hiking/biking trails. Russo's also serves a good breakfast (try the breakfast grilled 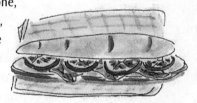 cheese sandwich) until noon each day. In the afternoon, Russo's offers Coffee Happy Hour from 2 to 5 p.m., with discounts on all the home-baked desserts. The small seating area has free Wi-Fi.

Scarborough Fare, 8 N. Front St., New Paltz, NY 12561; (845) 255-0061; scarboroughfarenp.com. At the center of this shop is a large bar topped with a row of stainless steel fusti containers holding a variety of wonderfully aromatic olive oils and balsamic vinegars. The rest of the shop is given over to more olive oils and balsamic vinegars, along with a great selection of cheeses, Italian cured meats, German sausages, pastas, and other gourmet items, domestic and imported. The olive oil bar is both a tasting station and a fill station—bring your own container and fill it up with your favorite olive oil or vinegar.

Farm Bounty

Apple Hill Farm, 124 Rte. 32 S., New Paltz, NY 12561, (845) 255-1605; applehillfarm.com. Pick your own apples here, choosing from varieties such as McIntosh, Macoun, Mutsu, Red Delicious, Golden Delicious, Cortland, and Empire. Apples are also sold at the farm stand. Pick your own starts right after Labor Day weekend and runs to the end of October. Enjoy the restored 1859 barn, hayrides, fresh apple cider, and apple cider doughnuts. Open daily in season from 10 a.m. to 6 p.m. Call ahead to check on the weather and what apples are ripe for picking.

Bradley Farm, 317 Springtown Rd., New Paltz, NY 12561; (845) 255-8769; raybradleyfarm.com. Back in 2000, Bradley Farm was just an abandoned 27-acre property. Owner Ray Bradley has turned an eyesore into a thriving organic farm raising pork and eggs as well as seasonal produce and specialty products, including pickles, herbs, honey, and ground paprika. The farm products are sold to restaurants, at greenmarkets in New York City, and at the farm store in season. In the summer, Ray (formerly a chef at Bouley), or a guest chef cooks up Sunday summer dinners at the farm. Each prix-fixe dinner has five courses featuring seasonal produce; wine pairings are additional. With only 50 seats per dinner, they sell out quickly; check the website for details and reservations.

Brook Farm Project, 60 Gatehouse Rd., New Paltz, NY 12561; (845) 255-1052; brookfarmproject.wordpress.com. Brook Farm is a 20-acre nonprofit, sustainable farm raising vegetables, herbs, berries, flowers, and free-range eggs and livestock. Most produce goes to the CSA members; some is sold at the New Paltz farmers' market and at the farm stand. Call ahead for farm stand hours. Brook Farm is a very hands-on CSA, with a lot of member involvement and volunteer work. The farm also has an active education program and works closely with college students from nearby SUNY New Paltz.

Dressel Farms, 271 Rte. 208, New Paltz, NY 12561; (845) 255-0693; dresselfarms.com. Over 275 acres of apple trees are grown at Dressel Farms. While commercial apples are the main business (the farm packs and ships around 100,000 bushels, or about 4 million pounds, every year), it also offers a popular u-pick operation and nice farm stand. Visitors can pick their own strawberries on weekends starting in mid-June. Apple picking is on weekends in Sept and Oct, from 10 a.m. to 5 p.m. The farm stand sells strawberries, apples, apple cider, and other products; it's open every day from 9:30 a.m. to 5:30 p.m. In the warmer weather, check out the ice cream stand. Call ahead to check on the weather and what's ripe. *Note:* cash only.

Huguenot Street Farm, 205 Huguenot St., New Paltz, NY 12561; (845) 419-2164; huguenotfarm.com. Huguenot Street Farm grows over 125 varieties of vegetable, fruits, and flowers on 77 acres of protected land in the heart of New Paltz. The farm is primarily a community-supported agriculture (CSA) operation, but some produce goes to local restaurants and farmers' markets. Huguenot Street Farm is a longtime pioneer in local organic farming—it's certified by NOFA-NY (see p. 6).

Jenkins–Lueken Orchards, 69 Yankee Folly Rd., New Paltz, NY 12561; (845) 255-0999; jlorchards.com. Apples (McIntosh, Empire, Fortune, Fuji, Jonagold, Macoun, Golden Delicious, Red Delicious, Ida Red) are the main draw here, but you can also pick your own peaches, blackberries, raspberries, pumpkins and vegetables. Picking starts weekends in mid-July; the apples begin coming in early September. The farm stand carries apples and produce along with farm honey, maple syrup, fruit pies, preserves, and other goodies. The farm stand is open daily 9 a.m. to 6 p.m.; closed Wed in the winter. Call ahead for u-pick hours, weather conditions, and what's ripe.

Meadow View Farm, 105 Phillies Bridge Rd., New Paltz, NY 12561; (845) 255-6093; meadowviewfarmstand.com. All the produce and animal products sold at this farm stand are certified naturally grown—no chemicals are used and all livestock is treated humanely. The farm stand carries a wide variety of freshly picked produce from the 55-acre farm, along with grass-fed beef, fresh eggs, and fresh Goat Cheese. Meadow View Also Sells At The New Paltz Farmers' Market. The farm stand is open every day Apr through Nov from 9 a.m. to 8 p.m.

New Paltz Farmers' Market, 24 Main St., New Paltz, NY 12561; (845) 255-5995; newpaltzfarmersmarket.com. Sun, 10 a.m. to 3 p.m., mid-May through mid-Nov.

Taliaferro Farms, 187 Plains Rd., New Paltz, NY 12561; (845) 256-1592; taliaferrofarms.com. Taliaferro Farms has been providing certified organic produce since 1995. CSA members here enjoy 90 varieties of certified organic produce. The farm also sells its products to local restaurants, at farmers' markets, and at a farm stand on the property. The farm stand is open weekends in season: Thurs 8 a.m. to 7 p.m.; Fri 9 a.m. to 6 p.m.; and Sat 9 a.m. to 3 p.m.

Veritas Farms, 32 Rousner Ln., New Paltz, NY 12561; (845) 384-6888; veritasfarms.com. Veritas Farms raises heritage breed beef, pork, and poultry, all on open pasture. The animals are humanely treated; the vegetables are grown organically. Veritas Farm products are available at the farm, through their buyers' club, and at some local retailers and farmers' markets. To purchase directly from the farm, call first to set up a time.

Wallkill View Farm Market, 15 Rte. 299 W., New Paltz, NY 12561; (845) 255-8050; wallkillviewfarmmarket.com. A year-round farm market offering home-grown produce (including apples and berries), fresh-cut flowers, annuals and perennials, Jane's ice cream (see p. 245), and pick-your-own pumpkins in the fall. In October, Wallkill View offers lots of family fun, including a corn maze. Open every day mid-Mar through Christmas, 9 a.m. to 6:30 p.m.

Winter Sun Farms, 195 Huguenot St., New Paltz, NY 12561; (845) 255-1699; wintersunfarms.com. Local CSAs, farmers' markets, and farm stands are all bursting with fresh produce in the spring, summer, and fall. Come winter, however, and locally grown produce is hard to find. Winter Sun Farms partners with local Hudson Valley farms to supply frozen, preserved, and stored vegetables and fruit all winter long—in fact, for 5 months. Winter Sun Farms operates as a CSA with a number of distribution sites in the region.

Rosendale

Bywater Bistro, 419 Main St., Rosendale, NY 12472; (845) 658-3210; bywaterbistro.com; International/Fusion; $$. Well-known for interesting fusion cuisine, Bywater Bistro is also a very enjoyable place to eat. The dining room is pleasantly cozy and the flower-filled streamside garden is beautiful in the warm weather. The menu here relies heavily on fresh, local products, such as beef and lamb from Sir William Angus Farm in Craryville, Dutchess County. Dishes such as grilled leg of lamb, marinated in juniper and fennel and served with couscous, are always well-prepared and served by a very capable staff. The beer menu contains a good choice of local microbrews. Open for dinner every night except Wed.

Market Market, 1 Madeline Ln. (Route 32N), Rosendale, NY 12472; (845) 658-3164; marketmarketcafe.com; International/ Fusion; $$. A casual little restaurant with an intriguingly mixed menu, Market Market is also a popular local performance venue, with live music on weekend evenings and some other nights as well. The decor here isn't much, but the food is very worthwhile. From the snack bar menu, try the avocado on toast. The cafe menu is mostly sandwiches and burgers, including a very good *banh mi;* the breakfast menu is served until 5 p.m. The dinner menu is more ambitious and includes many dishes made with local products, such as the spicy Korean-style Campanelli Farm fried chicken, served with Asian slaw and potato salad. The short but extremely interesting wine list is drawn from around the world, including Romania and Argentina.

Rosendale Cafe, 434 Main St., Rosendale, NY 12472; (845) 658-09048; rosendalecafe.com; Vegetarian; $$. The Rosendale Cafe specializes in vegetarian food; it's consistently rated as one of the best vegetarian restaurants in the area. The dishes here are imaginative and prepared using the fresh, local ingredients. The menu offers good salads and appetizers and an interesting selection of sandwiches, including a vegetarian Reuben that uses baked tempeh instead of corned beef. The entrees are where the cafe shines, however, with choices such as a huge spinach and goat cheese burrito. The dinner specials offer good alternatives to the basic menu. The cafe carries six microbrews on tap. On the weekends, Rosendale Cafe has a busy schedule of live music; Thursday night is Latin dance night. Open for lunch and dinner every day.

Cafes & Quick Bites

Twisted Foods and Pretzel Roll Factory, 466 Main St., Rosendale, NY 12472; (845) 658-9121; facebook.com/twistedfoods .pretzelrollfactory; Sandwich Shop; $. The fabulous pretzel rolls and croissants at Twisted Foods are sold on their own to take home, or as the basis for a range of great breakfast and lunch sandwiches eaten on the spot at this cozy cafe. The shop also has breakfast plates and sandwiches and a good range of prepared foods to take out; the coffee here is always perfect. On a nice day, enjoy your food outside under the bower, where dogs are welcome. Inside, the cafe area is very kid-friendly.

Alternative Baker, 407 Main St., Rosendale, NY 12472; (845) 658-3355; lemoncakes.com. There are a lot of good reasons to stop by the Alternative Baker, but the delectable lemon cakes here are why people drive miles out of their way. Made from a 1930s recipe with nothing but the purest natural ingredients, these cakes have a rich lemon flavor with a delicate shell of sugar icing. Other artisanal baked goods here include cookies, cakes, scones, baguettes, boules, challah (Friday only), and much more. For all that the lemon cakes bring people back here time and again, the Alternative Baker gets its name from the extensive array of tasty alternative baked goods, including gluten-free, dairy-free, sugar-free, egg-free, and vegan choices, all created by master baker Essell Hoenshell-Watson. The shop also has a cafe area serving breakfast and lunch; the menu features, of course, fresh baked breads and treats. Closed Tues and Wed.

The Big Cheese, 402 Main St., Rosendale, NY 12472; (845) 658-7175; facebook.com/thebigcheese. The Big Cheese lives up to its name by carrying hundreds of different domestic and international cheeses. In addition to the expected varieties, The Big Cheese is also a great source of interesting, hard-to-find cheeses, including a range of goat's milk and sheep's milk cheeses and raw cheeses. The cheese part of the store is complemented by a prepared foods case and a small cafe area serving breakfast and lunch. Cheese features heavily on the menu, of course, but other delights, such as such as homemade lamb sausages, paninis, wraps, and baklava are also available.

Farm Bounty

Rosendale Summer Farmers' Market, Rosendale Community Center, 1055 Rte. 32, Rosendale, NY 12472; (845) 658-3467; rosendalefarmersmarket.com. Sun, 9 a.m. to 2 p.m., June through end Oct.

Rosendale Winter Farmers' Market, Rosendale Community Center, 1055 Rte. 32, Rosendale, NY 12472; (845) 658-3467; rosendalefarmersmarket.com. First Sun of the month, 10 a.m. to noon, Nov through May.

Rykowski Livestock, 233 Creeklocks Rd., Rosendale, NY 12472; (845) 658-3632; rykowskilivestock.com. Rykowski Livestock raises free-range polled Hereford cattle, pastured Yorkshire pigs, and Cornish Cross meat birds. The meat is all hormone- and antibiotic-free. Rykowski products are sold at the Rosendale farmers' market and at the farm. For farm pickup and for custom beef and pork cuts, call ahead.

Saugerties

Foodie Faves

Cafe Mezzaluna, 626 Rte. 212, Saugerties, NY 12477; (845) 246-5306; cafemezzaluna.com; Argentinian; $$. The distinctive double-gabled Cafe Mezzaluna building, trimmed in purple, is a local destination for good food, good art, and good live performances. The food here is infused with Latin American influences, most notably in the wonderful Cubano on homemade bread and in the paninis. Breakfast and brunch here are local favorites—the french toast and eggs Benedict are the most popular items in the morning. The bistro is open for lunch and dinner, but at this funky place the performances take precedence. The hours and menu aren't firmly fixed—call ahead.

'cue Shack, 136 Partition St., Saugerties, NY 12477; (845) 246-4CUE (4283); cueshack.com; Barbecue; $$. A new contender among the barbecue restaurants in the area, 'cue Shack serves Texas-style brisket, ribs, pork, and chicken. Texas barbecue is served dry—the homemade sauces on the table are very good. The sides here are nicely done. The collards, for instance, are authentically smoky, with nuggets of ham nestled in the greens. For dessert, try the strawberry shortcake. In the warmer weather, enjoy your food on the large outdoor patio overlooking lively Partition Street. Live music is offered here most weekends. The 'cue Shack food truck, offering the same food as the restaurant, is a popular attraction at many outdoor events in the area.

Dutch Ale House, 255 Main St., Saugerties, NY 12477; (845) 247-2337; dutchalehouse.com; Pub Grub; $$. Two things make the Dutch Ale House a go-to destination in the region: great beer and great burgers. In fact, the bacon, egg, and cheese burger is one of the best in the Hudson Valley, closely followed by the Moody Blue burger, made with smoked blue cheese, caramelized onions, bacon, and balsamic reduction. The rest of the food here is the usual gastropub range of well-prepared contemporary American options, including an extensive appetizers list and very good sandwiches. Fifteen taps, changed often, serve craft brews at the antique bar, and many more are available by the bottle. Dutch Ale House started brewing its own beers in 2012; they're often available on tap. The restaurant hosts frequent beer promotion nights and beer-tasting dinners, plus live music, karaoke, and trivia nights. Check the website to learn what's coming up.

Miss Lucy's Kitchen, 90 Partition St., Saugerties, NY 12477; (845) 246-9240; misslucyskitchen.com; New American; $$$. The country decor and mismatched tables at Miss Lucy's are part of the bigger farm-to-table picture here. The menu is so attuned to the seasons and the local produce that it changes daily. Silky asparagus bisque is made only when the local asparagus are harvested in the spring; the goat cheese onion tart with tomatoes is made only when the local tomatoes are ripe. A dinner entree such as cider braised pork belly with fingerling potatoes, roasted sunchokes, and maple whiskey glaze might appear one night, and then disappear again for days if the ingredients aren't freshly available. Some things do remain constant at Miss Lucy's, however. At lunch, good egg dishes, inventive sandwiches, such as Jamaican jerk chicken salad with banana chutney, and well-executed burgers are regulars on the menu. So are the flaky, delicious cheddar cheese biscuits. The dessert menu features some unusual items, such as chocolate hazelnut dacquoise and rhubarb and pistachio brittle icebox cake. The service at Miss Lucy's is pleasant and professional; the uncrowded dining room and beautiful bar make this a very pleasant space to enjoy a good meal.

New World Home Cooking, 1411 Rte. 212, Saugerties, NY 12472; (845) 246-0900; ricorlando.com/nwhc; International/Fusion; $$$. Chef Ric Orlando has been cooking up his own brand of fusion cuisine in the Hudson Valley for more than 20 years. He's a well-known, longtime advocate of local, sustainable cooking that's clean, casual, and fun. At New World Home Cooking, his destination restaurant, Chef Ric believes that the freshest local ingredients taste even better when they're very spicy. In fact, dishes on the menu are rated according to their spiciness on the Ric-ter scale. Be sure to discuss your heat preferences with your server before ordering—dishes such as Purple Haze Shrimp are aptly named. The creative cooking here is drawn from the flavors and kitchen techniques of the whole world, or at least that part of the world that believes in spicy food. The menu ranges from classic Italian risotto to Cuban-style *ropa vieja* to mouth-searing Jamaican jerk chicken. New World Home Cooking is the very rare restaurant that offers full menus of gluten-free and vegan choices. These dishes, such as the vegan blue-corn crusted seitan medallions with tomatillo salsa, are taken just as seriously as those on the regular menu; the servers are very knowledgeable and helpful for guests with special dietary needs. Eating at New World Home Cooking is fun: The atmosphere is casual and unhurried, the staff is friendly and helpful, and there's a good chance you'll eat something that you've never eaten before.

The Red Onion, 1654 Rte. 212, Saugerties, NY 12477; (845) 679-1223; redonionrestaurant.com; New American; $$$. One of the finest and most popular restaurants in the region, The Red Onion offers contemporary American cuisine served in a restored farmhouse. The sight of this lovely old building, set back from the road and surrounded by gardens, is a portent of a great meal to come. The inside is warm and inviting, with a small, friendly bar; the large front porch is a dining area in the warmer weather. The food here is outstanding across the menu. It's almost unfair to the chef to point out some favorites, but the house-cured sardines, mussels in all variations, house-made goat cheese ravioli, *steak frites,* and hamburgers are fabulous. Even vegetable-hating meat eaters have been known to swap their rib eye with bleu cheese butter for the Thai vegetable curry. The desserts are all very good, especially the vanilla crème brûlée. The service at the Red Onion is friendly and professional, yet another reason this restaurant is a favorite for special occasions. Open every night for dinner only; reservations recommended.

Tavern at Diamond Mills, 25 S. Partition St., Saugerties, NY 12477; (845) 247-0700; diamondmillshotel.com; New American;

$$$$. Diamond Mills is a recently opened boutique hotel right on the Esopus Falls. Once an abandoned factory (hence the name), the building has been restored and rebuilt to have 30 beautiful guest rooms. Within the hotel, the Tavern restaurant offers an elegant menu of contemporary American dishes, served in an spacious dining room or on the large terrace overlooking the falls. The dishes here rely heavily on fresh, locally sourced ingredients whenever possible. Executive Chef Giuseppe Napoli's menus are consistently interesting. The flatbread appetizer, for instance, is offered in six different ways, including chicken confit with ricotta, leeks, olives, and fontina. Entrees are equally creative. The spring lamb trio serves tender lamb three entirely different yet complementary ways: fennel-dusted loin of lamb, lamb bacon, and lamb tortellini. Lovely surroundings, an outstanding wine list, and a very professional staff add to the ambience. A good choice for a special occasion or celebration, Tavern is open nightly for dinner. Lunch is served Wed through Sun; brunch on weekends only. Reservations recommended.

Cafes & Quick Bites

Chef Shack, 208 Ulster Ave., Saugerties, NY 12477; (845) 453-2675; Food Truck; $. Unusually for a food truck, Chef Shack offers New American cuisine using local produce. The lunch specials, which include french fries and a soft drink, include dishes such as smoked salmon on a bed of fresh greens, grass-fed burgers, and smoked chicken apple salad on greens. Open Tues, Wed, and Thurs from 11 a.m. to 3 p.m.

Dallas Hot Wieners, 215 Main St., Saugerties, NY 12477; (845) 246-4080; dallashotwieners.com; Hot Dogs; $. The Saugerties branch of the Kingston institution; see listing description on p. 237.

Love Bites, 85 Partition St., Saugerties, NY 12477; (845) 246-1795; Breakfast/Brunch; $. This tiny restaurant is one of the best places for breakfast in the area. Start with the coffee, which is without question unsurpassed by any other restaurant in the Hudson Valley. Follow it with any of the breakfast choices, such as the carrot bread french toast or any of the many egg dishes—the zucchini fritters topped with poached eggs are unusual and delicious. The lunch menu is short, with a focus on salads and sandwiches made with very good bread. Many dishes at Love Bites are vegetarian or vegan. Open every day but Wed, 8:30 a.m. to 3:30 p.m.

Lox of Bagels, 3103 Rte. 9W, Saugerties, NY 12477; (845) 246-0594; lox-of-bagels.com; Breakfast/Brunch; $. Good bagels are very scarce in the Hudson Valley, which makes Lox of Bagels a favorite among locals and visitors. The bagels here are large and correctly chewy on the inside—they have actual flavor instead of tasting like round bread. Some 14 different varieties are on the menu, including a spinach bagel that's surprisingly good. The shop sells a number of hand-mixed cream cheeses to go along, including chopped lox and an interesting vanilla pecan. Lox of Bagels makes fantastic breakfast egg sandwiches on their bagels. The line to get one can be out the door in the morning, but it's very friendly and moves quickly. The dining area at Lox of Bagels offers a standard menu of breakfast choices. The lunch choices are primarily sandwiches, wraps, and burgers. They come with a choice of breads, although just about everyone seems to order a sandwich on a bagel. The coffee here is excellent and the Wi-Fi is free, making this a favored spot for a coffee or travel break. Open 6 a.m. to 4 p.m. Mon through Sat; 6 a.m. to 3 p.m. on Sun. Closed Christmas Day.

Tango, 216 Main St., Saugerties, NY 12477; (845) 246-4333; tango food.com; Argentinean; $. The cuisine of Argentina makes its way to the Hudson Valley at Tango. This small, informal restaurant serves an eclectic mix of standard American and Argentinean dishes for breakfast and lunch. The Argentine part of the menu includes tasty empanadas and paninis, such as the Milonga, made with grilled ham on a toasted garlic baguette with tomatoes, honey mustard and brie, and the Lomo Argentino, made with grilled steak in chimichurri sauce in a pita with lettuce, tomatoes, onions, fried egg, ham, and melted cheddar. Standard American breakfast fare is also made here. Lunch brings salads, paninis, wraps, and burgers. The coffee bar is very good, with a full range of hot coffee drinks and also *coco Argentino,* dark chocolate melted in steamy milk. Open 8 a.m. to 5 p.m. every day but Tues.

Tin Cantina, 1776 Rte. 212, Saugerties, NY 12477; (845) 863-9429; facebook.com/thetincantina; Food Truck; $. A tiny camper converted to a food service truck, the Tin Cantina is usually parked in the Fiber Flame lot on Route 212 starting at noon and staying until about 7 p.m. most days. The menu is short and leans toward the vegetarian: chicken burritos, black bean burritos, black bean and sweet potato burritos, jack cheese quesadillas with optional chicken or black beans. Fish tacos make an occasional appearance. The guacamole here is heavenly; the homemade hot sauce is powerful.

 *Specialty Stores & Producers*

Brine Barrel, 237 Partition St., Saugerties, NY 12477; (845) 247-3016; brinebarrel.com. The home of pickle on a stick, the Brine Barrel sells home-fermented pickles of all kinds. The barrel-cured sours, half-sours, and dills are great—fresh, flavorful, and crispy. The sliced pickles are equally good, especially the tangy sweet horseradish pickles. The shop also sells sauerkraut, a good range of olives, pickle relishes, pickled peppers, homemade tapenade, and cheese. What goes best with pickles? Sandwiches, of course, and Brine Barrel offers a good selection of subs and deli sandwiches to go or eat in. Closed Mon.

Hudson Valley Dessert Company, 264 Main St., Saugerties NY 12447; (845) 246-1545; hudsonvalleydessertcompany.com. This small artisan bakery specializes in outstanding biscotti, cupcakes, cakes, and cookies. The Espressly Chocolate cookies are wonderful, as is the signature gingerbread. Custom orders are taken for wedding cakes, birthday cakes, pies, and cookie platters. Open 8 a.m. to 6 p.m. daily; closed Wed.

Krause's Chocolates, 41 S. Partition St., Saugerties, NY 12477; (845) 246-8377; krauseschocolates.com. Family members have been making confections at Krause's Chocolates since 1929; the Saugerties shop was opened in 1972. Today the shop offers more than 50 highest-quality, handmade, hand-dipped chocolates, along with fudge, really good peanut brittle, and fabulous chocolate bark with almonds. The sea salt caramels are addictively delicious. The shop is open Mon through Fri from 9:30 a.m. to 6 p.m., Sat from 9:30 a.m. to 5 p.m., and on Sun from noon to 5 p.m. If you can't visit, the website has a full selection for online ordering.

Lucky Chocolates, 115 Partition St., Saugerties, NY 12477; (845) 246-7337; luckychocolates.com. The fortunate residents of Saugerties rejoice in not one but two outstanding chocolatiers: the long-established **Krause's** (see above) and more recently, Lucky Chocolates. This chocolateria, as it calls itself, crafts artistic small-batch delights from organic and fair-trade chocolate. The barks, brittles, toffees, truffles, and turtles are all delicious, as are the intensely flavored and imaginative assortments. Whimsical chocolate Buddhas and dogs are a specialty at Lucky Chocolates. Vegan chocolates are also made here. The shop has a small cafe and juice bar that's a good stop for a quick lunch—chocolate for dessert, of course. Open Tues, Wed, and Thurs from 10 a.m. to 6 p.m.; Fri and Sat from 10 a.m. to 8 p.m., and Sun from 10 a.m. to 6 p.m. Closed Mon.

Mother Earth's Storehouse, 249 Main St., Saugerties NY, 12477; (845) 246-9614; motherearthstorehouse.com. See listing description on p. 247.

Partition Street Wine Shop, 102 Partition St., Saugerties, NY 12477; (845) 246-9463; partitionstreetwineshop.com. The selection at Partition Street Wine Shop isn't as broad as it is in larger shops, but it's so intelligently chosen that exactly the right bottle for you is certain to be there. The shop carries organic wines and many local vintages. The knowledgeable staff will happily help you select a wine that is perfect for your desires. The wines at Partition Street are chosen to be drunk as an ordinary part of a good meal, which means most bottles are reasonably priced. The shop sponsors many tastings and live music events; check the website to see what's coming up.

SmokeHouse of the Catskills, 724 Rte. 212, Saugerties, NY 12477; (845) 246-8767; smokehouseofthecatskills.com. SmokeHouse of the Catskills is a true *deutsche Metzgerei,* or German butcher shop. The shop is widely known for excellent German hot dogs, kielbasa, smoked pork chops, homemade beef jerky, Westphalian ham, and perfectly spiced German-style sausages: bratwurst, knockwurst, liverwurst, *weisswurst,* and more. This is probably the cleanest food shop in the entire region. The owners are very friendly and helpful; come early before holidays to avoid the crowds. Open Thurs through Sat from 8 a.m. to 6 p.m.; Sun 9 a.m. to 4 p.m.

Sunporch Baked Goods, 113A Partition St., Saugerties, NY 12477; (845) 866-2253; facebook.com/sunporchbakedgoods. Located in the alley behind Lucky Chocolates, Sunporch Baked Goods makes gluten-free sweet treats. They're surprisingly good—it's hard to believe they're made without wheat flour or other gluten-containing ingredients. The baked goods include brownies, carrot cake bundts, chocolate cake bundts, chocolate chip cookies, and oatmeal cookies. Sunporch also bakes up muffins, pies, banana bread, zucchini bread, and lemon cakes. If nobody's home at the bakery, you can buy the products at Lucky Chocolates instead.

Farm Bounty

Boice's Farm and Garden Stand, 600 Kings Hwy., Saugerties, NY 12477; (845) 246-7426. The farm stand offers fresh fruits and vegetables from the Boice's 80-acre farm. The garden shop area sells high-quality perennials and annuals. Open daily from May to mid-Dec, 9 a.m. to 6 p.m.

Platte Creek Maple Farm, 808 Glasco Tpke., Saugerties, NY; (845) 853-4240; facebook.com/plattecreekmaplefarm. This Certified Naturally Grown (see p. 6) maple farm taps maple trees in the Woodstock and Saugerties area. The modern evaporator in the sugar shack is wood-fired. The farm participates in Maple Weekend (see pp. 22, 301) each year with tours, pancake breakfasts, and activities for the kids. Platte Creek products are sold at local retailers and at the farm.

Saugerties Summer Farmers' Market, 115 Main St., Saugerties, NY 12477; (917) 453-2082; saugertiesmarket.com. Sat from 10 a.m. to 2 p.m., Memorial Day weekend through mid-Oct.

Saugerties Winter Farmers' Market, 207 Market St. (Senior Center), Saugerties, NY 12477; (917) 453-2082; saugerties market.com. Last Sun of the month, starting in Oct and ending in Apr from noon to 4 p.m.

Vinnie's Farm Market, 3689 Rte. 32, Saugerties, NY 12477; (845) 532-2012. A bit more than a farm market selling a good range of local produce, Vinnie's also carries homemade baked goods and preserves, free-range eggs, cheese, honey, maple syrup, and a range of other edibles. Vinnie's also sells good prepared Italian specialties to take out or eat on the patio.

West Park

Foodie Faves

Global Palate, 1746 Rte. 9W, West Park, NY 12493; (845) 384-6590; globalpalaterestaurant.com; International/Fusion; $$$. Global Palate is one of the most consistently good and interesting restaurants in the area. The menu here is hard to describe. Chef Jessica Winchell takes the slogan "think globally, act locally" and applies it to cooking. That means the dishes are drawn from cuisines around the world but are made with fresh, local organic ingredients. Some of the produce comes from the restaurant's own garden; the rest is sourced from nearby farms. The eggs, poultry, and meat are all hormone-free and come from local producers. The menu rotates often with the seasons. A typical dish in early spring might be five-spice marinated grilled pork loin with spicy almond-cilantro sauce, served with green bamboo rice and a shrimp and vegetable spring roll. Diners looking for something more familiar could choose the grilled half chicken with roasted vegetables, mushroom stuffing, and dandelion greens *agrodolce*. On Wed and Thurs, Global Palate offers a very good three-course prix-fixe menu; it changes weekly. Open for dinner Wed through Sun; brunch on Sun from 10 a.m. to 2 p.m.; closed Mon and Tues.

Specialty Stores & Producers

Coppersea Distillery, West Park, NY 12493; (845) 444-1044; coppersea.com. Coppersea Distillery, founded in 2011, produces hand-crafted spirits using heritage distilling methods. They malt their own grains, mill them themselves, make the mash using water from their own well, and ferment it in an American-made wooden tank. The distilling happens in hand-hammered alembic copper stills. The barley, corn, and rye they use is sourced from nearby sustainable farms. The end result of all this painstaking work is outstanding whiskey, including the signature Raw Rye. Coppersea products are sold at the Kingston Farmers' Market and at select retailers in the area.

Greene County

The small towns that hug the west bank of the Hudson in Greene County back onto the Catskill Mountains. Much of the county is still very rural—the population of 50,000 is scattered over some 660 square miles, much of it within the protected Catskills Park and outside the geographic scope of this chapter. The towns of Catskill and Athens offer some good dining and interesting purveyors; there are some good local farms in the small area close to the Hudson. Because this is an area that now depends on tourism more than long-gone industries, the river towns have put some effort into upgrading. They're still very quiet—the busiest intersection in Athens doesn't have a stoplight—but they've become a lot more interesting. The walkable downtowns now have a lot of worthwhile galleries, shops, and eateries. They're easily accessible from Saugerties to the south and Hudson across the river, making them in some ways extensions of these popular towns.

Athens

 *Foodie Faves*

Cameo's, 7 Second St., Athens, NY 12015; (518) 945-2375; cameos ofathens.com; Italian; $$. Eating at Cameo's will remind diners of

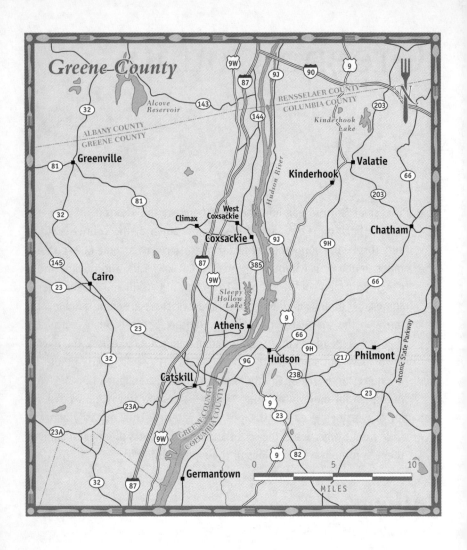

Greene County

9W 87 9J 90 9

143 Alcove Reservoir

32

RENSSELAER COUNTY
COLUMBIA COUNTY

144

Kinderhook Lake

203

ALBANY COUNTY
GREENE COUNTY

81 **Greenville**

Kinderhook **Valatie**

66

203

81

Climax West Coxsackie

Coxsackie

Chatham

32

9J

9H

87

385

66

145

Cairo

9W

23

Sleepy Hollow Lake

9

32

Athens

66

9H

23

9G

Hudson

21 **Philmont**

Catskill

23B

23

23A

9 23

9W

23A

9 82

Germantown

0 5 10

MILES

32 87

Taconic State Parkway

Hudson River

GREENE COUNTY
COLUMBIA COUNTY

eating at a traditional corner restaurant in the Little Italy section of a big city—except this restaurant is in the small Catskills village of Athens. The Italian fare here is fairly standard, but it isn't ordinary. The fried calamari appetizer is very good, as is the fried ravioli, a dish that isn't seen on menus as often as it should be. The pastas and main dishes are all well-prepared traditional choices, such as fettuccine Alfredo, chicken marsala, and veal cardinale—dishes that are classics for a reason. Cameo's also offers very good pizza and calzones, but for takeout and delivery only. If that's right for you, try the excellent vodka sauce pizza.

Crossroads Brewing Company, 21 Second St., Athens, NY 12015; (518) 945-BEER (2337); crossroadsbrewingco.com; Pub Grub; $$. Crossroads Brewing Company brews its own craft beers on the premises. The beer is the star here, with the food playing a supporting role. The brewery and restaurant are located inside the renovated historic 1893 Opera House, once a central attraction in Athens. The short menu offers well-prepared pub food, including good sandwiches, burgers, and simple entrees such as grilled flatbread pizza. On Wiener Wednesday, Crossroads serves up **Northwind Farms** (see p. 135) hot dogs; Friday is fish fry night. The taps rotate six main beers along with several that are available only seasonally. If you can't decide which beer to sample, try a beer flight of six tastes. Closed Tues.

Farm Bounty

Black Horse Farms, 10094 Rte. 9W, Athens, NY 12015; (518) 943-9324; blackhorsefarms.com. Located in remodeled historic barn dating back to 1864, the Black Horse Farms market carries mostly produce grown on the nearby 800-acre family farm. The market is locally famed for its fresh corn and tomatoes. Strawberries, raspberries, and apples come from the farm; other fruit is delivered daily by local growers. The bakery here makes excellent bread, cookies, and pies. Open Mar to Dec, 9 a.m. to 6 p.m. Sun through Thurs; until 7 p.m. on Fri and Sat.

Catskill

Foodie Faves

Barnwood Restaurant, 14 Deer Ln. (Route 23 and Cauterskill Road), Catskill, NY 12414; (518) 943-2200; barnwooddining.com; Traditional American; $. American comfort food done with attention is the main attraction at Barnwood Restaurant. The fried chicken here is excellent—tender, crispy, not at all greasy. The hot sandwiches (try the pulled pork), meat loaf, and burgers are also very good. Sides such as onion rings and baked beans are all homemade and very flavorful. Large portions and very reasonable prices, along with friendly, skilled service make a meal at Barnwood a very enjoyable experience. Note: Some many remember this restaurant as Good Eats, which had reasonably good food. Barnwood has improved the quality of the food and service quite a bit. Open every day for lunch and dinner.

La Conca d'Oro, 440 Main St., Catskill, NY 12414; (518) 943-3549; facebook.com/laconcadoro; Italian; $$. A beloved local institution, La Conca d'Oro serves classic Italian food in a casual atmosphere. The menu includes many well-prepared standards, such as fettuccine carbonara and fried calamari, along with some new ideas, such as the shrimp and scallop salad. A bit surprisingly for a restaurant so far from salt water, the seafood here is always fresh and good. Try the clams Posillipo—this dish of clams in a light tomato/fish broth sauce, once common at Italian-American restaurants, has sadly fallen out of favor. A very popular favorite here is *zuppa de pesce* over linguine. Warning: Portions here are very generous—consider sharing or having an appetizer as a main course. The service at La Conca d'Oro is friendly and professional; families are welcome. A historical note: The cornerstone of the building has Hebrew writing on it—the site was once a synagogue. Open for dinner every night but Tues; open for lunch Wed, Thurs, and Fri. Reservations suggested.

Cafes & Quick Bites

Retriever Roasters, 394 Main St., Catskill, NY 12414; (518) 943-5858; retrieverroasters.com; Coffeehouse; $. A really good cup of freshly made coffee is a rare delight in the area around Catskill. Retriever Roasters offers the best cup locally and for a considerable area beyond that. The coffee here comes from around the world; it's roasted on the spot in the batch roaster and ground just before brewing. The end result of this special effort is a good range of carefully prepared hot and cold coffee drinks, including drip coffee, espresso, latte, cappuccino, and other refreshing choices. If you want something special to drink or a blend of beans to take home, the very knowledgeable and personable owners are happy to help. Retriever Roasters also prepares hot chocolate and teas of all sorts and has a fun selection of hard-to-find (especially in the Catskills) Italian sodas. A good assortment of fresh baked goods is available to go along with the drinks. Open Mon through Fri, 8 a.m. to 2:30 p.m.

Sweet Sensations Chocolate, 388 Main St., Catskill, NY 12414; (518) 943-0600; sweetsensationschocolate.com. This small shop offers a big range of fresh, handmade chocolates and confections. The pecan turtles, truffles, peanut butter cups, chocolate fudge, chocolate caramels, truffles, chocolate-covered pretzels, chocolate-covered marshmallows, shaped chocolates, and other delights here are all crafted in small batches by the chocolatier owners. The shop also offers a range of candies, including jelly beans, old-fashioned candy sticks, and caramel apples. Sweet Sensations also carries Hershey's ice cream and makes ice cream cakes to order.

Farm Bounty

Pathfinder Farms, 2433 Old Kings Rd., Catskill, NY 12414; (518) 943-7096; pathfinderfarms.com. Raising pastured beef on over 400 acres of field and woods, Pathfinder Farms is dedicated to sustainable practices and ecological land stewardship. To order by the half or for pieces by cuts, call or e-mail the farm.

Story Farms, 4640 Rte. 32, Catskill, NY 12414; (518) 678-9716; facebook.com/storyfarms. Story Farms is one of the largest family-owned farms in the area. At the well-stocked and busy farm stand, Story Farms offers its own fresh fruits and vegetables in season. The corn, peaches, apples, and strawberries here are particularly delectable. Pick your own strawberries and raspberries in June and July. Call ahead for u-pick details, including hours, weather conditions, and what's ripe. The farm stand is open every day, 8 a.m. to 6 p.m., from Memorial Day to Thanksgiving.

Climax

Farm Bounty

Boehm Farm, 233A County Rte. 26, Climax, NY 12042; (518) 731-8846; facebook.com/boehmfarmllc. Boehm Farm lets you pick your own peaches starting in mid-August; apples begin in September and go through the end of October. If you don't want to do any picking, you can buy beautiful fruits and vegetables from the farm stand instead. Open every day in season from 10 a.m. to 6 p.m. Call ahead to check on the weather, the hours, and what's ripe.

Coxsackie

Foodie Faves

Cask and Rasher, 245 Mansion St., Coxsackie, NY 12051; (518) 444-8016; thecaskandrasher.com; Pub Grub; $$. Sixteen tap lines for a rotating range of craft brew beers suggests that food isn't the top priority at Cask and Rasher. It isn't, really, but the straightforward bar fare here is actually pretty good. The menu has the usual sliders, mozzarella sticks, and onion rings as starters. The wings are excellent, nice and crispy and served with flavorful sauces. After a few beers, the asbestos-mouthed might want to try the Satan Wing, seasoned with superhot Indian ghost chiles, or the even hotter Necro-Wing, rated at 7.2 million Scoville units. The Caskadillas—soft tortilla shells stuffed with cheddar jack and a choice of fillings—are an interesting take on the quesdilla. The sandwiches, salads, seafood platters, and burgers that make up the rest of the menu are all well prepared; so are the nightly specials. Live music most weekends.

Storm King, 10 Reed St., Coxsackie, NY 12051; (518) 731-DINE (3463); stormkingrestaurant.com; New American; $$$. A recent upscale addition to the area, Storm King has a nicely executed contemporary American menu with international overtones. The starters and small plates, for example, include choices such as tempura fried onion rings and a cheese platter featuring domestic and international artisan cheeses. Main courses at Storm King include roasted monkfish in a Thai sauce containing lime leaf and lemongrass and a free-range lamb burger topped with goat cheese, roasted portobello mushroom, crispy risotto cake, and a poached local duck egg. The restaurant name comes from a steamship freighter called *Storm King* that sank at its moorings on the Coxsackie riverfront in 1938. Except at high tide, the wreck can still be seen along the shore. Dinner Wed through Sun; brunch on Sun. Reservations suggested.

Farm Bounty

Coxsackie Farmers' Market, Riverside Park (1 Betke Blvd.), Coxsackie, NY 12501; (518) 731-2718. Wed, 4 p.m. to 7 p.m., end of May to mid-Sept.

Hudson Valley Farmers' Markets

Cold Spring Indoor Farmers' Market, Philipstown Recreation Center; 107 Glenclyffe, Garrison, NY 10524; csfarmmarket .org. Sat from 8:30 a.m. to 1:30 p.m., mid-Nov through early May.

Cold Spring Outdoor Farmers' Market, Boscobel House & Gardens, 1601 Rte. 9D, Garrison, NY 10524; csfarmmarket.org. Sat from 8:30 a.m. to 1:30 p.m., mid-May through mid-Nov.

Putnam Valley Farmers' Market, Grace United Methodist Church, 337 Peekskill Hollow Rd., Putnam Valley NY 10579. Fri, 3 p.m. to 7 p.m., June through Sept.

St. Christopher's Inn Farmers' Market, St. Christopher's Inn Thrift Shop, 21 Franciscan Way (Graymoor building), Garrison, NY 10524; (845) 335-1141. Fri, 10 a.m. to 2:30 p.m., mid-Apr through late Nov.

Dutchess County

Amenia Indoor Farmers' Market, Town Hall (4988 Rte. 22), Amenia, NY 12501; ameniafarmersmarket.com. First and third Sat, 10 a.m. to 2 p.m., Oct through Apr.

Amenia Outdoor Farmers' Market, Town Hall (4988 Rte. 22), Amenia, NY 12501; ameniafarmersmarket.com. Fri, 3 to 7 p.m., mid-May through Oct.

Arlington Farmers' Market, Alumnae House Lawn (Raymond Avenue at Fulton Avenue), Poughkeepsie, NY 12601; (845) 559-0023. Mon and Thurs, 3 p.m. to 7 p.m., June through Oct.

Beacon Farmers' Market, Beacon Sloop Club dock; Beacon, NY 12508; thebeaconfarmersmarket.com. Every Sun, 11 a.m. to 3 p.m.

Fishkill Farmers' Market, Main Street Plaza, Fishkill, NY 12524; (845) 897-4430. Thurs, 9 a.m. to 4 p.m., late May through late Oct.

Hudson Valley Farmers' Market at Greig Farm, 229 Pitcher Ln., Red Hook, NY 12571; greigfarm.com. Every Sat, 10 a.m. to 3 p.m.

Hyde Park Farmers' Market, Town Hall parking lot, Route 9, Hyde Park, NY 12538; (845) 229-9336; hydeparkchamber.org. Sat, 9 a.m. to 2 p.m., beginning of June through mid-Oct.

LaGrangeville Farmers' Market, M&T Bank plaza (1100 Rte. 55), LaGrangeville, NY 12540. Fri, 3 p.m. to 7 p.m., early June through end Oct.

Milan Farmers' Market, Wilcox Memorial Town Hall parking lot, Route 199, Milan, NY 12571; facebook.com/MilanFarmersMarket. Fri, 3 p.m. to 7 p.m., mid-May through mid-Oct.

Millbrook Farmers' Market, Tribute Garden parking lot, Front Street and Franklin Avenue, Millbrook, NY 12545; millbrooknyfarmersmarket .com. Sat, 9 a.m. to 1 p.m., mid-May through mid-Oct.

Millerton Farmers' Market, Railroad Plaza (off Main Street), Millerton NY 12546; millertonfarmersmarket.org. Sat, 9 a.m. to 1 p.m., end of May through last week of Oct.

Red Hook Outdoors Farmers' Market, 7467 S. Broadway (municipal parking lot), Red Hook, NY 12571; (845) 464-3598; facebook.com/RedHookOutdoorsFarmersMarket. The outdoor market is every Sat, June through Nov, 10 a.m. to 2 p.m.

Red Hook Winter Farmers' Market, 7562 N. Broadway, Red Hook, NY 12571; (845) 943-8699; heartyroots.com. The indoor market is held the second Sat of the month, Dec through Feb, 10 a.m. to 2 p.m. at the historic Elmendorph Inn. The market is organized by **Hearty Roots Community Farm** (see p. 159).

Rhinebeck Farmers' Market, 61 E. Market St. (municipal parking lot), Rhinebeck, NY 12572; rhinebeckfarmersmarket.com. Founded in 1994, this is the market that began the farmers' market movement in the region. It's still the best. The outdoor market is open every Sun from 10 a.m. to 2 p.m. from Mother's Day to Thanksgiving. The winter market is held every other Sun from 10 a.m. to 2 p.m. from Dec through Apr at the Rhinebeck Town Hall, 80 E. Market St.

Wappingers Falls Farmers' Market, Mesier Park, Wappingers Falls, NY 12590; (845) 529-7283. The market is set up in lovely Mesier Park, in the center of the village, every Fri from 4 p.m. to 7 p.m. from June through Oct.

Columbia County

Chatham Farmers' Market, 15 Church St. (Route 203), Chatham, NY 12037; (518) 392-3353; chathamrealfoodcoop.net. Early June to mid-Oct, Fri, 4 p.m. to 7 p.m.

Clermont Farmers' Market, 1820 Rte. 9, Clermont, NY 12526; (845) 464-3598; clermontny.org. This market is located where the old Hettling's Farm stand used to be. It's open Fri, 3:30 p.m. to 7:30 p.m., from Memorial Day through the end of Oct.

Copake Farmers' Market, Church Street (next to First Niagara Bank), Copake, NY 12516;. (518) 329-0384; facebook.com/copake farmersmarket. Every Sat, June through Oct, 9 a.m. to 1 p.m.

Hillsdale Farmers' Market, Roe Jan Park, 9140 Rte. 22, Hillsdale, NY 12529; (518) 325-4165; facebook.com/hillsdalefarmers market. Sat, 9 a.m. to 1 p.m., beginning of June through mid-Oct.

Hudson Farmers' Market, 6th and Columbia Streets, Hudson NY 12534; hudsonfarmersmarketny.com. Open from the beginning of May to Thanksgiving, Sat, 9 a.m. to 1 p.m.

Kinderhook Farmers' Market, 7 Hudson St. (Village Green at Route 9), Kinderhook, NY 12106; (518) 755-9293; kinderhook farmersmarket.com. Open from early May through mid-Oct, Sat, 8:30 a.m. to 12:30 p.m.

Philmont Farmers' Market, 93 Main St. (Tripp Center parking lot), Philmont, NY 12565; pbinc.org/revitalization. Open from mid-June through mid-Oct, Sun, 10 a.m. to 1 p.m.

Orange County

Cornwall Farmers' Market, 183 Main St. (Town Hall lawn), Cornwall, NY 12558; (845) 527-1084; cornwallcoop.com. Memorial Day through the end of Oct, Wed, 9 a.m. to 1 p.m.; Sat, 10 a.m. to 2 p.m.

Cornwall Winter Farmers' Market, 66 Clinton St. (St. John's Episcopal Church), Cornwall, NY 12558; (845) 527-1084; cornwall coop.com. Nov through Apr, first and third Sat, 11 a.m. to 3 p.m.

Newburgh Farmers' Market, Downing Park, Route 9W and South Street, Newburgh, NY 12550; (845) 565-5559. Fri, 10 a.m. to 4 p.m., July through the end of Oct.

Newburgh Farmers' Market, 131 Broadway, Newburgh, NY 12550. Tues, 10 a.m. to 4 p.m., July through the end of Oct.

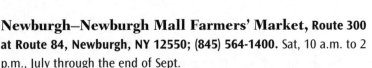

Newburgh–Healthy Orange Farmers' Market, Broadway between Johnston Street and Lander Street, Newburgh, NY 12550; (845) 568-5247. Tues, 10 a.m. to 3 p.m., July through the end of Oct.

Newburgh–Newburgh Mall Farmers' Market, Route 300 at Route 84, Newburgh, NY 12550; (845) 564-1400. Sat, 10 a.m. to 2 p.m., July through the end of Sept.

West Point–Town of Highlands Farmers' Market, parking lot across from West Point Visitors Center (45 Main St., Highland Falls, NY 10928); (917) 509-1200; facebook.com/West pointtownofhighlandsfarmersmarket. Sun, 9 a.m. to 2 p.m., mid-June through end Oct.

Heart of the Hudson Valley Farmers' Market, Cluett-Schantz Park, 1801-1805 Rte. 9W, Milton, NY 12547; (845) 464-2789; hhvfarmersmarket.com. Sat, 9 a.m. to 2 p.m., mid-June to mid-Oct, plus Thanksgiving market in Nov.

Highland Farmers Market, Route 9W and Haviland Rd., Highland, NY 12528; (845) 691-2144. Wed from 3 p.m. to 7 p.m., mid-June through mid-Oct.

Kingston Farmers' Market Midtown, Broadway between Henry and Cedar Streets, Kingston, NY 12401; (845) 535-3185; kingstonfarmersmarket.org. Tues, 3 p.m. to 7 p.m., end of May to end Sept.

Kingston Farmers' Market Uptown, Wall Street between Main and John Streets, Kingston, NY 12401; (845) 535-3185; kingston farmersmarket.org. Sat, 9 a.m. to 2 p.m., May through Nov.

Kingston Winter Market, Bethany Hall at the Old Dutch Church, 272 Wall St., Kingston, NY (845) 535-3185; kingstonfarmersmarket.org. First and third Sat of the month, 10 a.m. to 2 p.m.

New Paltz Farmers' Market, 24 Main St., New Paltz, NY 12561; (845) 255-5995; newpaltzfarmersmarket.com. Sun, 10 a.m. to 3 p.m., mid-May through mid-Nov.

Rosendale Summer Farmers' Market, Rosendale Community Center, 1055 Rte. 32, Rosendale, NY 12472; (845) 658-3467; rosendalefarmersmarket.com. Sun, 9 a.m. to 2 p.m., June through end Oct.

Rosendale Winter Farmers' Market, Rosendale Community Center, 1055 Rte. 32, Rosendale, NY 12472; (845) 658-3467; rosendalefarmersmarket.com. First Sun of the month, 10 a.m. to noon, Nov through May.

Saugerties Summer Farmers' Market, 115 Main St., Saugerties, NY 12477; (917) 453-2082; saugertiesmarket.com. Sat from 10 a.m. to 2 p.m., Memorial Day weekend through mid-Oct.

Saugerties Winter Farmers' Market, 207 Market St. (Senior Center), Saugerties, NY 12477; (917) 453-2082; saugertiesmarket.com. Last Sun of the month, Oct through Apr from noon to 4 p.m.

Greene County

Coxsackie Farmers' Market, Riverside Park (1 Betke Blvd.), Coxsackie, NY 12501; (518) 731-2718. Wed, 4 p.m. to 7 p.m., end of May through mid-Sept.

Food Events, Festivals & Celebrations

Monthly

Festival of Farmers' Markets, sponsored by *Edible Hudson Valley* **magazine; ediblehudsonvalley.com.** Rotating weekly among participating regional markets, Festival offerings include special events, live music, giveaways, tastings, cooking demonstrations, and more. The Festival runs from July to mid-Oct.

Hudson Valley Food Truck Festival, Fiber Flame Studio, 1776 Rte. 212, Saugerties, NY 12477; (845) 399-2222; facebook .com/hvfoodtrucks. On the third Thursday of the month (except the winter months), from 3:30 p.m. to 9:30 p.m., food trucks from up and down the Hudson Valley form an aromatic corral in the parking area of the Fiber Flame Studio and serve up their wares. The festival has live music under a tent with picnic seating; there are also lots of kids' activities. A word of warning: Be careful crossing Route 212. Part of the charm of the Food Truck Festival is that it's a little improvised. The vendors and activities are unpredictable but always fun. Check ahead on Facebook to see which trucks are expected and if inclement or cold weather has canceled the event.

March

Hudson Valley Beer & Cheese Fest, hudsonvalleybeerand cheeseweek.com. This big party takes place at Keegan Ales in Kingston (see p. 245). Beer and cheese go together, so it's a perfect pairing of regional cheesemakers, regional brewers, and happy consumers.

Hudson Valley Restaurant Week, hudsonvalleyrestaurant week.com. Organized by *The Valley Table* (see p. 8) and with many regional sponsors, Hudson Valley Restaurant Week is actually 2 weeks long. During this time, over 150 participating restaurants in the region offer a special three-course prix-fixe lunch ($20.95) or dinner ($29.95)—beverage, tax, and gratuity are extra. The list of restaurants and their special menus are posted on the website. Many restaurants also advertise their participation. To enjoy a great meal (the restaurants use this opportunity to show themselves off) at a very reasonable price, just contact the restaurant and mention Hudson Valley Restaurant Week when you make your reservation—no tickets or coupons needed.

Maple Weekend, mapleweekend.com. Sponsored by the New York State Maple Producers Association (nysmaple.com), Maple Weekend is a time for maple syrup producers across the state, including many in the Hudson Valley region, to showcase their sugarhouses and their products; many offer pancake breakfasts on the weekend. The website lists the participating producers and events.

April

Hudson Valley Pizza Fest, Arbor Ridge Catering and Banquet Hall, 17 Rte. 376 (at Route. 52), Hopewell Junction, New York 12533; (845) 590-1915. A relatively new event, the Hudson Valley Pizza Fest brings together pizza makers in a friendly competition for the best pizza in the region. Among the competitions: best pie, best Sicilian, best specialty pie, pizza tossing, and fastest pie made. There's also a pizza eating competition.

Ramp Fest, rampfesthudson.com. The ramp, that pungent member of the onion family, is the first spring green to be forageable in the

Hudson Valley. In this celebration, chefs from the region and beyond converge on the foodie city of Hudson to cook up dishes using ramps as the primary ingredient. The event is actually a big street fair centered on the Basilica, a performance space at 100 Front St., across from the Amtrak station. A cash bar and lots of free entertainment round out the food. Tickets are limited; purchase them in advance through the website. The fest takes place rain or shine.

Taste of Rhinebeck, (845) 871-3505; health-quest.org/taste. An annual fundraiser for the Northern Dutchess Hospital Foundation, Taste of Rhinebeck lets visitors stroll through the village and sample dishes from over 25 Rhinebeck restaurants, caterers, and gourmet food producers. Tastings are set up in the restaurants or are hosted by village shops. This is a good way to check out the many great restaurants in this foodie town. Tickets are pricey; for a discount, purchase in advance through the website.

May

Gardiner Cupcake Festival at Wright's Farm, 699 Rte. 208, Gardiner, NY 12525; (845) 255-5300; gardinercupcakefestival .com. More than 30,000 cupcakes are consumed at this family-friendly event. It's technically out of the region covered in this book, but too much fun to leave out. Cupcakes, prizes, good food, live music, local vendors, wine tastings, activities for children, the 5K Cupcake Classic run, and a beautiful setting on the historic 453-acre farm.

Hudson Berkshire Wine & Food Festival, Columbia County Fairgrounds, Route 66, Chatham, NY 12037; (518) 732-7317;

hudsonberkshireexperience.com. This 2-day event was inaugurated in 2013 and was a huge success despite torrential rain. The festival showcases the many outstanding food, wine, beer, and distilled spirits producers in the Hudson–Berkshire region. It's sponsored by the trade organization the Hudson Berkshire Experience, which also sponsors the **Hudson–Berkshire Beverage Trail** (see p. 147).

June

Beacon Sloop Club Strawberry Festival, Riverfront Park, **1 Flynn Dr., Beacon, NY 12508; beaconsloop.org.** The Beacon Sloop Club is home to the sloop *Woody Guthrie* and is active in protecting the Hudson through environmental advocacy. The annual Strawberry Festival features the club's famous strawberry shortcake, plus strawberries in lots of other forms. Live music, educational and environmental exhibits, vendors, kids' activities, and free sails on the *Woody*. The festival takes place rain or shine. Free admission. Riverfront Park is right on the Hudson, just across from the Beacon Metro-North railroad station.

July

Blueberry Festival, Old Austerlitz, 11550 Rte. 22, Austerlitz, **NY 12017; (518) 392-0062; oldausterlitz.com.** The Austerlitz Historical Society sponsors the Blueberry Festival every year on the last Sunday in July. The event is held on the grounds of Old Austerlitz, a living history museum of historic buildings. The event offers blueberries in every way, a blueberry pancake breakfast (additional charge), live music, crafts demonstrations and vendors, and more. Kids under 12 admitted free; no pets allowed.

Bounty of the Hudson, Shawangunk Hudson Valley Wine Trail, shawangunkwinetrail.com. An annual weekend event featuring all the wineries on the Shawangunk Wine Trail, plus a few others, along with lots of good food from local restaurants, producers, and farms. Also, live music and entertainment. The event is held at a different winery on the Trail each year.

Friends of the Farmer Festival, Copake Country Club, 44 Golf Course Rd., Copake Lake, NY 12521; (518) 325-9437; friends ofthefarmer.com. Regional farmers and growers, chefs, specialty food producers, winemakers, brewers, and distillers all come together at this festival to celebrate and support the next generation of Hudson Valley farmers. Lots of food and drink sampling, live music, and fun for kids in the Little Farmers tent. Children under 10 get in free. Proceeds support the Farm On! Foundation, which funds agriculture education, scholarships, and curriculum for Hudson Valley students. This event is one of the many in the region sponsored by the nonprofit organization Hudson Valley Bounty (hudsonvalleybounty.com).

August

Beacon Sloop Club Corn Festival, Riverfront Park, 1 Flynn Dr., Beacon, NY 12508; beaconsloop.org. The Beacon Sloop Club is home to the *Woody Guthrie,* a wooden replica of a gaff-rigged Hudson River ferry sloop. The annual Corn Festival raises funds for the upkeep of the sloop and for the club's environmental advocacy activities. Corn is a buck an ear; there's also live music, food and merchandise vendors, educational and environmental exhibits, kids' activities, and free sails on the *Woody*. The festival takes place rain or shine. Admission is free. Riverfront Park is right on the Hudson, just across from the Beacon Metro-North railroad station.

Dutchess County Fair, Dutchess County Fairgrounds, 6550 Spring Brook Ave. (Route 9), Rhinebeck, NY 12572; (845) 876-4000; dutchessfair.com. First held in 1845, the annual Dutchess County Fair is the second largest county fair in New York State. (The largest is in Erie County near Buffalo.) Building D is full of specialty food vendors selling products such as maple syrup and honey. The Harvest Kitchen in Building E has demonstrations by master chefs and TV cooking show celebrities; it's a good place to sit down for a rest. The fair has a huge food court with all the usual fairground foods, plus a number of very good food stands operated by local churches and organizations. The best thing to eat at the fair, however, is one of the amazingly good milk shakes made by the kids from 4H. Look for them at the 4H exhibit building off the dairy barn area—the milk comes from the contented cows you can visit there.

Hudson Valley Ribfest, Ulster County Fairgrounds, 249 Libertyville Rd., New Paltz, NY 12561; (845) 306-4381; hudsonvalleyrib fest.org. Enjoy great barbecue and other food as fifty teams compete in the New England Barbecue Society Grilling Contest and the Kansas City Barbeque Society Contest. Lots of live music, plenty of vendors, and good activities for the kids—those under 12 get in free. Important note: No pets.

The Taste of Hudson Valley Bounty, (518) 432-5360; hudsonvalleybounty.com. This moveable feast celebrates the farms, food producers, and restaurants of the region and Hudson Valley Bounty's efforts to support them. The event features dishes prepared by local Hudson Valley Bounty member chefs, using locally grown and produced food and products from more than 30 local Hudson Valley Bounty member farms. The dinner is usually at a different location within the region each year.

September

Hudson River Craft Beer Festival, Riverfront Park, 1 Flynn Dr., Beacon, NY 12508; hudsonrivercraftbeerfestival.com. At this celebration of New York State microbrew craft beers, visitors can sample beer from over 30 regional breweries. Lots of vendors sell food to enjoy with the beer; merchandise and craft vendors and live music as well. Riverfront Park is right on the Hudson, just across from the Beacon Metro-North railroad station. Order tickets online in advance if possible. No one under 21 admitted. This event takes place rain or shine.

Hudson Valley Garlic Festival, Cantine Field, Washington Avenue Extension, Saugerties, NY 12477; (845) 246-3090; hvgf.org. This is one of the most popular food events in the region—well over 45,000 people attend the 2-day festival. The Hudson Valley Garlic Festival brings together hundreds of vendors selling garlicky food (including garlic ice cream, garlic marshmallows, and garlic shortbread), garlic growing stuff, garlic merchandise, garlic crafts, lectures and demonstrations by top chefs and growers, and more. Lots of live entertainment and good kids' stuff make this an excellent family event. To avoid delays, purchase tickets online in advance. The festival is sponsored by the Saugerties Kiwanis Club; proceeds go to community activities. The festival goes on rain or shine. Important note: No pets allowed.

Hudson Valley Harvest Festival, Ulster County Fairgrounds, 249 Libertyville Rd., New Paltz, NY 12561; hudsonvalleyharvest festival.com. The third weekend of September is the date for the annual Hudson Valley Harvest Festival. This event benefits both the Cornell Cooperative Extension of Ulster County and Family of Woodstock, a nonprofit organization that provides shelters, food pantries, counseling, and other services to area residents. The festival offers a massive two-day farmers' market, crafts artisans, a wide array of food vendors, music on three stages, a pie bake-off and a cupcake contest, CCEUC classes, and lots of fun activities for kids and adults. The Wool Room, which demonstrates the entire process of making wool from sheep to finished product, is always worth a visit. Don't miss the milkshake stand operated by the local 4H kids. Kids under 12 free; parking is free. Important note: No pets.

Hudson Valley Wine & Food Fest, Dutchess County Fairgrounds, 6550 Spring Brook Ave. (Route 9), Rhinebeck, NY 12572; (845) 658-7181; hudsonvalleywinefest.com. Held on the weekend following Labor Day, the Hudson Valley Wine & Food Fest is a major foodie event. The event highlights Hudson Valley wineries; most in the region participate every year. Also on hand are many regional gourmet and specialty food vendors, a restaurant showcase area, a food truck corral, wine seminars, and cooking demonstrations. Starting in 2013, this event also includes the annual Hudson Valley Craft Beer Fest (hudsonvalleycraftbeerfest.com). Order tickets in advance online if possible. The price includes parking.

Taste of New Paltz, Ulster County Fairgrounds, 249 Libertyville Rd., New Paltz, NY 12561; (845) 255-0243; atasteofnewpaltz.com. The main event at this big festival is food. Local restaurants serve tastings; local farmers, food producers, food artisans, and wineries all offer samples of their wares. Also on hand are many other vendors, including crafts, antiques, and much more. Lots of kids' activities as well. The festival goes on rain or shine (it's all under tents). Kids under 12 free; parking is free. Important note: No pets.

Beacon Sloop Club Pumpkin Festival, Riverfront Park, 1 Flynn Dr., Beacon, NY 12508; beaconsloop.org. The Beacon Sloop Club supports protection of the Hudson River through environmental advocacy; it's also the home of the replica sloop *Woody Guthrie*. The annual Pumpkin Festival features fresh-baked pumpkin pie, apple cider, pumpkin soup, and other treats. The Beacon Farmers' Market vendors are on hand with their products. Good food, live music, and educational and environmental booths, plus free sails on the *Woody*. The festival takes place rain or shine. Admission is free. Riverfront Park is right on the Hudson, just across from the Beacon Metro-North railroad station.

Cider Week, ciderweekny.com; many events in New York City and the Hudson Valley. Recent changes to the laws in New York State have led to an upsurge in the production of cider (the alcoholic kind) in the region, much as they have for beer and spirits production. Glynwood (glynwood.org), a nonprofit organization that supports environmentally sustainable agriculture and the growth of new agricultural markets, is the driving force behind Cider Week. Over the course of the week, nearly 200 restaurants, bars, shops, and markets in New York City and the Hudson Valley feature regional, orchard-based hard ciders through tastings, flights, and other events.

Heart of the Hudson Valley Bounty Festival, Cluett Schantz Memorial Park, 1801 Rte. 9W, Milton, NY 12547; (845) 616-7824; hvbountyfestival.com. An all-day celebration of the rich agricultural heritage of the Hudson Valley. This event includes a large farmers' market, many food vendors, crafts and merchandise vendors, and a lot of fun entertainment and kids' activities. This is a wonderful family event that culminates with fireworks at 7 p.m.

Warwick Applefest, 2 Bank St., Warwick, NY 10990; www.warwickapplefest.com. Over 35,000 people attend this annual celebration of the apple harvest in the heart of apple-growing country (technically, Warwick is outside the scope of this book, but some vendors mentioned here participate). Dozens of food vendors, over 200 craft vendors, a large farmers' market, live music and entertainment all day long, activities for the kids, and, naturally, an apple pie contest. This is a very enjoyable event that takes place within easy walking distance of the shops and restaurants in the charming village of Warwick. The event is sponsored by the Warwick Valley Community Center and the Warwick Valley Chamber of Commerce; proceeds go to some 50 local nonprofit organizations. Free admission. Parking is in satellite areas only and costs $5; free shuttle buses bring you to the event. The Applefest happens rain or shine. Important note: No pets.

November

International Pickle Festival, Town of Rosendale Recreation Center, 1055 Rte. 32, Rosendale, NY 12472; picklefest.com. Sponsored by the Rosendale Chamber of Commerce every year since 1998, this festival celebrates the pickle in all its myriad forms. Over 5,000 people come to sample pickles and other food, hear live music, and enjoy events such as pickle judging, the pickle toss, and the pickle juice drinking contest. If you like pickles, this is the event for you.

Taste of the Hudson Valley, (845) 431-8707; tastehv.org. An annual food and wine event that benefits St. Francis Hospital in Poughkeepsie, home of the busiest Level II trauma center in New York State. The event involves some 80 regional restaurants, wineries, and purveyors, leading to many outstanding food and wine pairings. It's held at the Grandview Hotel in Poughkeepsie. Tickets are pricey and need to be purchased in advance through the website. No one under 21 admitted.

Recipes

Glynwood Apple Soup

Glynwood Farm in Cold Spring (see p. 17) is a nonprofit foundation dedicated to promoting sustainable agriculture in the Hudson Valley region. Among other innovative work, Glynwood sponsors the Apple Project, which seeks to preserve apple orchards in the Hudson Valley by promoting the production of hard cider and apple spirits and working to create markets for these products. This recipe from Chef Jason Wood, Glynwood's first culinary director, uses apples and hard apple cider to make a really delicious and very simple soup. Chef Jason says to try to buy Cortland apples. They work well in this soup—they have a nicely tart and sweet flavor, and they just melt in the pan. Any type of apples will work, though; you can even mix and match to get different but wonderful results every time. If possible, make this soup the day before you serve it. Soup is always better the next day!

Serves 5

1 lemon	Dry hard cider or dry white wine
Apples (1 medium-size apple per serving)	Parchment paper
4 tablespoons (½ stick) butter for every 5 apples	Salt

Fill a bowl with enough water to cover the apples and squeeze the juice of the lemon into it.

Peel, core, and slice the apples very thinly. The thinner the slices, the better the consistency of the soup. Drop the slices into the lemon water as you go—this will prevent them from oxidizing.

When all your apples are sliced, melt the butter over medium heat in a soup pot (but do not brown the butter). You want the fat to balance the hard cider/white wine, so use at least half a stick of butter per 5 apples. When the butter is melted, add your apples and stir them so they are all coated. Cut a piece of parchment paper that is a little bigger than the circumference of the pot and cut an X into the middle. Press it down into the pot to cover the surface of the apples. This will poach the apples in the butter.

Cook the apples, stirring occasionally, until they are falling apart (at least 20 minutes). Discard the parchment paper once the apples are cooked through. Add enough hard cider or white wine to cover the apples by one inch. Bring to a boil and then reduce to a simmer.

Add salt to taste. Cook until the alcohol taste is gone, but it's still nicely acidic. Puree the soup in a blender and add it back to a clean soup pot. Adjust seasoning: You want to taste the apples, hard cider/white wine, and butter. If your soup is too acidic, add a bit more butter; if it's not tart enough, add more hard cider or wine. If you add more hard cider or white wine, cook off the alcohol taste again.

Courtesy of Crown Maple Syrup (see p. 44)

Magic Soup

At Great Song Farm (see p. 59), Magic Soup is a fall and winter favorite that sometimes sneaks in during the summer months. It's very simple and quick to make—so simple that there really isn't a recipe in the sense of giving accurate measurements. Just use whatever vegetables are at hand. The variations on the basic recipe are endless. Cut the vegetables into chunks about 1 inch square so that they cook quickly and evenly but still have some bite to them. Use only the very best organic salted butter. For the miso, use South River brand if possible; hearty dark brown rice or barley miso works well, but so does lighter chickpea or adzuki miso. If you don't have miso, make the soup anyway—it's still good. Make it a day in advance if you can.

Serves 4

Onions
Lots of butter (no skimping here)
Salt to taste
Garlic (chopped)
Carrots
Water

Turnips, rutabagas and/or other root vegetables, such as radishes or winter squash (cut into 1-inch chunks)
Leafy greenish things, such as Chinese cabbage, kale, spinach, bok choi, or tat-soi (coarsely chopped)
Miso to taste

Halve the onions and cut them lengthwise into chunks. In a large soup pot, gently sauté them in a few tablespoons butter and some salt. Add chopped garlic as the onions soften. Add the carrots and more butter and salt along with a little bit of water. Simmer the carrot mixture for a few minutes. Add the turnips or other root vegetables as the carrots begin to soften. Add more butter and salt and a bit more water if needed to steam the vegetables. In a separate pot, bring enough water to a boil to cover the vegetables by a few inches. As the turnips begin to soften, add leafy greenish things to the pot of vegetables; add more butter, salt, and water if needed. Simmer for a few minutes, then add the boiling water and miso. Simmer for another 10 to 15 minutes or a bit longer if you're using a lot of root vegetables.

Courtesy of Great Song Farm (see p. 59)

Spaghetti Squash Gratin

Spaghetti squash is low in carbs, high in fiber, and actually pretty easy to prepare, but it's hard to find good recipes that use it creatively. This one, from Rockerbox Garlic in Millbrook (see p. 64) is simple and really delicious. It can be made in a single large baking dish or cooked in individual ramekins.

Serves 4

- 1 2- to 3-pound spaghetti squash
- 2 tablespoons olive oil
- ½ teaspoon salt
- ¼ teaspoon coarsely ground black pepper
- 1 tablespoon Rockerbox Garlic Flakes or 3 cloves fresh garlic, chopped

- 1 tablespoon fresh thyme
- 2 tablespoons chopped Italian parsley
- 8 ounces crème fraîche
- 1 cup shredded Asiago cheese (about 1 cup)

Preheat the oven to 400°F.

Cut the squash in half lengthwise and remove the seeds. Brush the cut sides of the squash with the oil, and sprinkle with salt and pepper to taste. Place the squash halves, cut-side down, on a rimmed baking sheet. Roast until tender, about 45 minutes. Let cool slightly on sheet on a wire rack, about 10 minutes.

Turn the oven up to 450°F.

Run the tines of a fork lengthwise over the cut surfaces of the squash to loosen the spaghetti-like strands. Scoop them out and drain off any excess liquid if necessary. Set aside in large bowl.

Combine the garlic, thyme, parsley, more salt and pepper, the crème fraîche, and ⅔ cup of the cheese in small bowl. Fold the mixture into the squash strands. Spread the squash evenly in a shallow, ovenproof baking dish. Top with the remaining cheese.

Bake for 20 minutes or until slightly browned.

Courtesy of Rockerbox Garlic (see p. 64)

Sour Cream Onion Dip

The popular dip made from sour cream mixed with a packet of dried onion soup isn't really onion dip—it's a chemically flavored slurry that often has a bitter flavor. The true onion dip is made with fresh onions, cooked slowly until they caramelize and take on a rich color and sweet flavor. They're then combined with the finest, creamiest sour cream available to make a memorable dip. This recipe, courtesy of Hudson Valley Fresh (see p. 89), calls for 2 cups of sour cream. If that's too much, the recipe can easily be halved.

Makes 2 cups

2 tablespoons olive oil
1½ cups finely diced onions
1 teaspoon coarse salt

2 cups Hudson Valley Fresh
  sour cream
¼ teaspoon garlic powder

Heat the olive oil in a sauté pan over medium heat. Add the onions and ½ teaspoon salt. Cook, stirring often, until the onions are caramelized, about 20 minutes. Let cool.

Put the sour cream into a medium-size mixing bowl. Add the remaining salt, the garlic powder, and the onions. Stir well to mix, then refrigerate for at least 1 hour before serving.

Courtesy of Hudson Valley Fresh (see p. 89)

Sour Cream Pancakes

In this unusual pacake recipe, from the dairy cooperative Hudson Valley Fresh (see p. 89), sour cream is substituted for the more usual milk and eggs. Because sour cream is naturally high in butter fat, these pancakes have a smooth texture and rich, very slightly sour flavor.

Makes approximately 12 pancakes

**2 cups Hudson Valley Fresh
  sour cream**
1 cup flour
2 tablespoons sugar

2 teaspoons baking soda
1 teaspoon salt
4 eggs
1 teaspoon vanilla

Mix first 5 ingredients together in a large bowl. In a separate bowl, beat the eggs and vanilla together. Add egg mixture to ingredients in large bowl and mix well.

Heat a greased griddle to 400°F. When hot, pour about ¼ cup of the batter on griddle for each pancake. Cook about 2 minutes, until bubbles form on the top, then flip and cook 2 more minutes.

Courtesy of Hudson Valley Fresh (see p. 89)

Basil Pesto

This recipe from Great Song Farm in Milan (see p. 59) is an excellent way to use and also preserve fresh basil when it is abundant in the summer. If you don't like cheese or don't eat animal foods, substitute a teaspoon or so of chickpea miso. The traditional use for basil pesto is on pasta, but try stirring a spoonful into a bowl of vegetable soup or chicken soup. It adds the flavor of summer.

Makes 1 cup

2 cups packed fresh basil
    leaves
2 cloves garlic
¼ cup pine nuts or walnut
    pieces

⅔ cup extra-virgin olive oil
Coarse salt
Freshly ground black pepper
½ cup grated pecorino cheese

Combine the basil, garlic, and nuts in a food processor and pulse until the ingredients are coarsely chopped. Add ½ cup of the olive oil and process until the oil is fully incorporated and the mixture is smooth. Season to taste with salt and pepper.

If using immediately, add all the remaining oil and pulse some more, until the mixture is smooth. Transfer the pesto to a large mixing bowl and stir in the grated cheese. Use immediately.

To freeze, make the pesto but leave out the cheese. Put the pesto into an airtight container and dribble olive oil over the top (this keeps the pesto from turning black from exposure to the air). To use, thaw and then stir in the cheese. The pesto keeps well frozen for up to 3 months.

Courtesy of Great Song Farm (see p. 59)

Bootlegger's Swizzle

During Prohibition, bootlegger Dutch Schultz made his whiskey at a farm in rural Dutchess County. Dutch was busted and the distillery destroyed, but his legacy lives on. Today Dutch's Spirits (see p. 75), based at Dutch's old farm distillery, produces whiskey once again. This simple cocktail is one Dutch himself might have drunk.

Makes 1 cocktail

2 ounces Dutch's Sugar Wash Moonshine or corn whiskey
½ ounce fresh lemon or lime juice

1 bar spoon superfine sugar
¼ ounce chilled seltzer
Lemon wedge, lime wedge, or mint sprig, for garnish

Pour all ingredients except garnish into a rocks glass over crushed ice. Swizzle ingredients to mix. Garnish with a lemon wedge, lime wedge, or mint sprig.

Courtesy of Dutch's Spirits (see p. 75)

Fire Cider Margarita

There are margaritas and then there are amazing margaritas. This recipe from Field Apothecary and Herb Farm (see p. 159) falls into the amazing class. The basic recipe for Fire Cider can be used for anything that calls for cider vinegar—it's great in salad dressing.

Fire Cider

Makes 4 cups

¼ cup grated fresh horseradish
¼ cup grated fresh ginger
1 medium onion
1 head garlic, peeled and chopped

Cayenne pepper to taste
1 quart organic apple cider vinegar
¼ cup honey

Fill a clean glass jar with all solid ingredients. Pour in the apple cider vinegar and honey and cap with an acid-proof lid. Store in a warm place for 4 weeks, shaking the jar a few times a week. Strain the mixture, rebottle, and refrigerate.

Fire Cider Margarita

Makes 1 cocktail

1½ ounces tequila
½ ounce Grand Marnier
1 ounce lime juice
½ ounce Fire Cider

Salt or sugar with cayenne pepper to rim the glass
Lime wedge for garnish

Pour all the liquid ingredients into a cocktail shaker with ice cubes. Shake well. Salt or sugar the rim of a chilled margarita glass. Pour contents, with the ice, into the glass. Garnish with lime wedge.

Courtesy of Field Apothecary and Harb Farm (see p. 159)

Frozen Raspberry Mojito

In the Hudson Valley, Jane's Ice Cream (see p. 245) has a devoted following. Adults and kids love it and will drive miles for a Jane's cone. On a hot summer's night, though, grown-ups sometimes want something even more refreshing. This recipe uses Jane's richly flavorful raspberry sorbet, but any sorbet—or combination of sorbets—can be substituted. Mango and/or lemon are good choices.

Makes 2 cocktails

½ pint Jane's raspberry sorbet
¼ cup simple syrup (liquid
   sugar)
¼ cup fresh lime juice
15 mint leaves

4 ounces rum
2 cups ice
Extra mint leaves, for garnish
Lime slices, for garnish

Combine all ingredients except garnishes in a blender and blend on high until smooth. Serve garnished with mint leaves and a lime slice.

Courtesy of Jane's Ice Cream (see p. 245)

Hawthorne Valley Farm Rye Strudel

Hawthorne Valley Farm (see p. 161) is the spiritual home for the many organic farmers in the Hudson Valley. In operation since 1972, the farm runs on organic and biodynamic principles and is very active in educating farmers and the public. The farm store sells Hawthorne Valley's legendary sauerkraut, fermented on the premises, along with farm-made cheese. This recipe is the home cook's version of the very popular strudel made at the farm bakery.

Makes 1 strudel

For the dough:

1 package active dry yeast
¼ cup warm water (110–120°F)
¼ cup milk, lukewarm
1 tablespoon sugar
½ teaspoon salt
¼ cup molasses
1 tablespoon butter, softened
1½ cups rye flour
1¼ cups bread flour

For the filling:

1 (15-ounce) jar Hawthorne Valley Farm caraway sauerkraut
8 ounces Hawthorne Valley Farm Alpine cheese or swiss cheese, coarsely grated
3 tablespoons spicy brown mustard
1 tablespoon caraway seeds

To finish:

¼ cup milk
Caraway seeds to taste

Dissolve the yeast in warm water. In a large bowl combine the milk, sugar, and salt. Use a mixer to beat in the molasses, butter, yeast mixture, and 1 cup of rye flour. Use a wooden spoon to mix in the remaining rye flour.

Stir in bread flour until the dough is stiff enough to knead.

Knead for 5 to 10 minutes. If the dough sticks to your hands or the board, add more flour. Cover dough and let rise 1 to 1½ hours, or until the dough has doubled in size.

To make the filling, drain the sauerkraut in a colander. Combine the sauerkraut and the remaining ingredients in a bowl and mix well

Plaiting the dough:

Preheat oven to 425°F.

Plaiting the dough makes this dish beautiful. However, if plaiting seems too complicated, you can just spread the mixture down the middle of the dough, fold the dough over from either side, and pinch closed. Make slashes in the top with a sharp knife.

Punch down risen dough and roll into a rectangle about 18 inches long and 8 inches wide. Spread sauerkraut, cheese, and mustard mixture down the middle third, allowing 2½ inches at the top and bottom ends.

With a knife, cut lines inward in the dough on either side of the mixture to form strips ¾-inch wide. Cut the corners of the dough rectangle off to form semicircles at the top and bottom.

Gently fold the semicircles of dough at the top and bottom of the mixture, forming a "hood" and a "slipper."

Fold the first left strip diagonally over the "hood" and sauerkraut mixture at an angle toward your right. Next, fold the first right-hand strip diagonally over the left one.

Repeat, always covering the ends of the previously folded strips with the next strip. When you get to the bottom, tuck the ends of the last strips under the bottom of the dough.

Use two spatulas to lift the strudel onto a cookie sheet. Brush on a milk wash and sprinkle caraway seeds on top.

Bake for 15 to 20 minutes until lightly browned.

Courtesy of Hawthorne Valley Farm (see p. 161)

Hudson Valley Raclette

The traditional Swiss raclette, made with potatoes and sauerkraut topped with freshly melted cheese, gets a Hudson Valley makeover in this recipe from the Amazing Real Live Food Co. (see p. 74). The recipe calls for a tomme-style cheese—a cheese that is round, with a gray-brown rind, a creamy semi-soft interior, and a delicious nutty flavor. At Amazing Real Live Food Co., this would be their raw-milk Stella Vallis cheese, but any cheese you like can be used. This recipe is a great way to use the freshly baked breads, homemade fruit jams, and grainy mustards sold at many farm stands in the region.

Serves 4

3 pounds fingerling potatoes   Toast triangles
Olive oil   Whole-grain mustard
2 cups sauerkraut, drained   Whole-fruit jam
½ pound tomme-style cheese

Preheat oven to 425°F. Peel the potatoes if you wish (not necessary) and cut them into pieces roughly 1½ inches long. Parboil in water to cover until they are about half cooked. Drain, let air-dry briefly, and then roll the pieces in the olive oil. Arrange on a baking dish or cookie sheet and roast in the oven until lightly browned, about 20 minutes.

When the potatoes are ready, divide them evenly among serving plates. Place half a cup of sauerkraut on each plate next to the potatoes.

Heat a griddle or shallow pan over low heat. Hold the edge of the cheese against the hot surface until it begins to melt, then use a spatula or knife blade to remove the melted cheese and place it on top of the potatoes. Repeat until all the potatoes are nicely covered with melted cheese.

Serve with the toast triangles, mustard, and jam on the side. Alternate bites of the cheesy potatoes and sauerkraut with bites of toast spread with mustard or jam.

Courtesy of Amazing Real Live Food Co. (see p. 74)

Porcini Mushroom Sauce

Rich and creamy, this sauce from La Bella Pasta in Kingston (see p. 247) is perfect over freshly made filled pasta such as ravioli. This recipe calls for spinach ravioli, but any of the 16 other raviolis from La Bella Pasta would also work well. Try it over their lobster ravioli or their exceptional pumpkin and ricotta ravioli.

Serves 4

⅓ ounce dried porcini
   mushrooms
2 tablespoons unsalted butter
1 medium onion, chopped
⅓ ounce sundried tomatoes,
   chopped
¼ cup chopped fresh mush-
   rooms (any kind, but porcini preferred)

2 pints heavy cream
½ teaspoon nutmeg
Salt to taste
Black pepper to taste
2 12-ounce packages fresh
   spinach ravioli

Bring a large pot of salted water to a boil.

Soak the dried mushroom for 10 minutes in enough warm water to cover. Remove the mushrooms, reserving the liquid. Coarsely chop the mushrooms.

Melt the butter in a medium pan; add the chopped onions and sauté lightly for a few minutes. Add the chopped dried porcini mushrooms, the sundried tomatoes, and the fresh mushrooms and sauté for another 10 minutes. Add some of the dried porcini soaking liquid if the mixture gets dry.

Add the cream, nutmeg, salt, and pepper and cook gently over low heat until the mixture thickens, about 5 to 10 minutes.

When the sauce is nearly ready, add the ravioli to the boiling water and cook for four minutes. Drain in a colander and place in a pasta dish. Add the sauce and serve at once.

Courtesy of La Bella Pasta (see p. 247)

Simple Fresh Garden Pasta Sauce

This recipe comes from Mark Adams, a member of the extended family that owns the Adams Fairacre Farms stores. The original store, located in Pough-keepsie (see p. 95), has been joined over the years by three others in Wappingers Falls, Kingston, and Newburgh. The Adams stores are prized in the region for their high-quality products and their support of local farmers and food artisans.

Serves 4

¼ pound ground beef, browned
    and drained or ¼ pound
    Andouille sausage
3 tablespoons olive oil
1 medium onion, coarsely
    chopped

1 pound fresh tomatoes, peeled
    and seeded
15 fresh basil leaves, chopped
¼ cup fresh oregano, chopped

If using ground beef, brown it in a teaspoon of olive oil and drain it. If using Andouille sausage, slice the sausage very thinly and brown the slices in a teaspoon of olive oil.

In a saucepan, soften the onions in the remaining olive oil. Add the tomatoes, basil, oregano, and ground beef or sausage. Cook over low heat just until the tomatoes are just soft. Serve over pasta, topped with grated Parmesan cheese.

Courtesy of Adams Fairacres Farms (see p. 95)

Adams's Own Tattooed Rosemary Potatoes

Sue Adams, a member of the illustrious Adams Fairacre Farms family (see p. 95), created this attractive approach to potatoes. It's easy to make and looks really beautiful when it's served. You can mix and match sprigs of any fresh herb, such as oregano, parsley, sage, or thyme, for the rosemary. Figure on two potatoes per person (more for hearty eaters).

Serves 2

2 small potatoes per person
⅓ to ½ cup olive oil
1 to 2 teaspoons kosher salt

½ teaspoon ground black pepper
1 sprig rosemary or other herb per each potato half

Preheat the oven to 400 degrees.

Cut each potato in half lengthwise.

Add the olive oil into a glass baking dish, reserving 1 tablespoon.

Press a rosemary or other herb sprig onto the cut side of each potato. Position the potatoes cut-side down in the baking dish. Don't crowd them.

Brush the tops of the potatoes with the reserved olive oil. Sprinkle with the salt and pepper.

Bake for 30 minutes, or until the potatoes are browned and sizzling (poke them with a knife to be sure they're done). Use a spatula to carefully lift the potatoes from the dish—you'll see the lovely herb "tattoo" on the cut side.

Courtesy of Adams Fairacres Farms (see p. 95)

Crown Maple® Blackberry Pork Chops from Madava Farms

Chef Jacob Griffin of Madava Farms (see p. 44) says of this recipe, "I love picking blackberries in the summer in the Hudson Valley and this is one of my favorite dishes, combining Crown maple sugar with the delicious fruit. The tartness of blackberries is enhanced by the rich flavor of maple sugar. The pork and sage bring a balance that makes this dish perfectly savory with balanced sweetness. I also like to add a couple of dried pequin chiles to add some heat."

Serves 4

1 cup Crown maple sugar
⅛ teaspoon ground cloves
1 tablespoon ground black pepper
1 tablespoon kosher salt
6 fresh sage leaves, chopped
2 garlic cloves, chopped
4 thick-cut bone-in pork chops

2 tablespoons vegetable oil
1 cup fresh blackberries
2 pequin or other small, hot chile peppers (optional)
½ cup water
½ cup white wine
1 teaspoon flour

Combine the Crown maple sugar with the cloves, black pepper, salt, sage, and garlic. Set aside a quarter cup of this spice mix.

Rub the remaining spice mixture generously into the pork chops. Let the pork rest for an hour or more; this allows the flavor to build.

Over medium-high heat, sear the pork chops with vegetable oil in a sauté pan until golden brown on each side but not fully cooked. Turn off the heat to avoid burning the searing juices and remove the chops from the sauté pan.

Place the blackberries, remaining spice mix, optional chiles, water, and white wine into the sauté pan and cook over medium heat. Crush the blackberries with a wooden spoon as they heat.

Whisk in the flour. Add the pork chops back into the pan and cook, covered, for 4 to 5 minutes, or until the pork is fully cooked.

Serve pork chops immediately, drizzled with blackberry pan drippings.

Appendices

Appendix A:
Eateries by Cuisine

Codes for Corresponding County Chapters:
(CC) Columbia County
(DC) Dutchess County
(GC) Greene County
(OC) Orange County
(PC) Putnam County
(UC) Ulster County

Argentinian
Cafe Mezzaluna, (UC), 271
Tango, (UC), 277

Asian
Cafe East, (UC), 237
Hudson Food Studio, (CC), 172
Yum Yum Noodle Bar, (UC), 236

Barbecue
American Glory BBQ, (CC), 166
Big W's Roadside BBQ, (DC), 140
Billy Bob's BBQ, (DC), 83
Billy Joe's Ribworks, (OC), 202
'cue Shack, (UC), 272
Fireside Barbecue & Grill,
    (DC), 127

Hickory BBQ and Smokehouse,
    (UC), 233
Max's Memphis BBQ, (DC), 101
RoundUp Texas BBQ, (PC), 14

Black Sea
Art Bar, (DC), 111

Chinese
China Rose, (DC), 113
DimsumGoGo, (DC), 31
Palace Dumpling, (DC), 137

Continental
Calico Restaurant and Patisserie,
    (DC), 112
Canterbury Brook Inn, (OC), 196

Charlotte's, (DC), 60
Hoffman House, (UC), 223, 233
Ship Lantern Inn, (UC), 223, 250
Swiss Hütte Inn and Restaurant,
   (CC), 164

Cuban
Havana 59, (OC), 205

French
Bocuse Restaurant, The, (DC), 55
Brasserie le Bouchon, (PC), 11
Brasserie 292, (DC), 83
Cafe les Baux, (DC), 60
Le Canard Enchaîné, (UC), 230
Le Chambord, (DC), 50
Le Express Bistro and Bar, (DC), 137
Le Petit Bistro, (DC), 115
Stissing House, (DC), 73, 223

German
Gunk Haus Restaurant and
   Biergarten, (UC), 218
Schatzi's Pub and Bier Garden,
   (DC), 90

Indian
Chai Shop, The, (CC), 177
Cinnamon, (DC), 113
Cinnamon Indian Bistro, (DC), 84
Citrus, (OC), 200
Suruchi, (UC), 257
Tanjore Cuisine of India, (DC), 47

International/Fusion
Bywater Bistro, (UC), 268
Egg's Nest Saloon, The, (UC), 220
Global Palate, (UC), 281
Market Market, (UC), 268
New World Home Cooking, (UC), 273
Painter's, (OC), 197

Italian
Aroma Osteria, (DC), 136
A Tavola Trattoria, (UC), 253
Blue Fountain, The, (DC), 49
Brothers' Trattoria, (DC), 30
Cafe Bocca, (DC), 84
Cafe Pitti, (OC), 203
Ca' Mea Ristorante, (CC), 167
Cameo's, (GC), 283
Cathryn's Tuscan Grill, (PC), 11
Cena 2000 Ristorante and Bar,
   (OC), 204
Cosimo's Trattoria, (DC), 85
Cousin's Pizza, (DC), 141
Dominick's Cafe, (UC), 238
Il Barilotto Enoteca, (DC), 46
Il Cenácolo, (OC), 205
Il Gallo Giallo, (UC), 254
La Conca d'Oro, (GC), 286
La Stazione, (UC), 258
Lia's Mountain View Restaurant,
   (DC), 73
Market Street, (DC), 117
Mercato Osteria and Enoteca,
   (DC), 101

Mint, (UC), 234
Portofino Ristorante, (DC), 129
Puccini Ristorante, (DC), 118
Ristorante Caterina de' Medici,
   (DC), 55
River Terrace Bar and Restaurant,
   (DC), 33
Savona's Trattoria, (UC), 234
Tavola Rustica, (DC), 122
Vico Restaurant and Bar, (CC), 175

Japanese
Akari Sushi and Japanese Food,
   (DC), 80
Gomen Kudasai Noodle Shop,
   (UC), 257
Hokkaido Japanese Restaurant,
   (UC), 254
Isamu, (DC), 32
Momiji, (DC), 117
Osaka, (DC), 118, 133

Korean
Seoul Kitchen, (DC), 37
Toro, (DC), 47

Mediterranean
Arielle, (DC), 110
Aurelia, (DC), 59
Ecce Terra, (UC), 232
Gigi Trattoria, (DC), 114
Serevan, (DC), 26

Mexican
Armadillo Bar and Grill, (UC), 229
Avocado, (OC), 196
Cafe Maya, (DC), 137
Casa Villa, (UC), 231
Coyote Flaco, (CC), 152
Destino Cucina Mexicana and
   Margarita Bar, (CC), 149
Gaby's Cafe, (DC), 114
La Puerta Azul, (DC), 61
Maya Cafe, (DC), 46
Mexican Radio Hudson, (CC), 172
Salsa Fresca Mexican Grill, (DC), 67
Santa Fe, (DC), 134
Santa Fe Uptown, (UC), 234
Tito Santana Taqueria, (DC), 38

Middle Eastern
Park Falafel and Pizza, (CC), 178

New American
American Bounty Restaurant,
   (DC), 54
Another Fork in the Road, (DC), 58
Artist's Palate, The, (DC), 81
Beacon Falls Cafe, (DC), 29
Beekman Arms and Delamater Inn,
   (DC), 111, 223
Bird & Bottle Inn, The, (PC), 20, 223
Cafe Amarcord, (DC), 30
Carolina House, (CC), 185
Coyote Grill, (DC), 85
Crave, (DC), 85

Crew Restaurant and Bar, (DC), 86
Crimson Sparrow, The, (CC), 168
CrossRoads Food Shop, (CC), 164
DePuy Canal House, (UC), 219
Duo Bistro, (UC), 231
Farm to Table Bistro, (DC), 45
Fish & Game, (CC), 170
Greens at Copake Country Club,
    The, (CC), 155
Helsinki Hudson, (CC), 171
Henry's Farm to Table Restaurant at
    Buttermilk Falls Inn, (UC), 251
Hopped Up Cafe, (UC), 221
Ice House on the Hudson, (DC), 87
Liberty of Rhinebeck, (DC), 115
Local 111, (CC), 189
Local Restaurant and Bar, The,
    (DC), 116
McKinney & Doyle Fine Foods,
    (DC), 72
Miss Lucy's Kitchen, (UC), 273
Nic L Inn Wine Cellar on the
    Hudson, (DC) 88
No. 9, (DC), 66
Northern Spy Cafe, (UC), 222
North Plank Road Tavern, (OC), 207
Old Chatham Country Store, The,
    (CC), 188
Red Devon Market, Cafe, Bar and
    Restaurant, (DC), 130
Red Dot Restaurant and Bar,
    (CC), 173
Red Onion, The, (UC), 274

River Bank, The, (OC), 197
Riverview Restaurant, (PC), 14
Rock and Rye Tavern, (UC), 256
Ship to Shore, (UC), 235
St. Andrew's Cafe, (DC), 55
Storm King, (GC), 290
Swift and the Roundhouse at
    Beacon Falls, (DC), 34
Swoon Kitchenbar, (CC), 174
Tavern at Diamond Mills, (UC), 274
Tavern at Highlands Country Club,
    (PC), 20
Terrapin, (DC), 119
Troutbeck Inn and Conference
    Center, (DC), 27
2 Taste Food and Wine Bar,
    (DC), 56
Valley at the Garrison, (PC), 21
Vanderbilt House, (CC), 190
Village TeaRoom, The, (UC), 259
Would, The, (UC), 225
Yianni's Restaurant, (CC), 150

Peruvian
Machu Picchu Peruvian Restaurant,
    (OC), 206

Pub Grub
Cask and Rasher, (GC), 289
Crossroads Brewing Company,
    (GC), 285
Dutch Ale House, (UC), 272
Gilded Otter, The, (UC), 255

Hyde Park Brewery and Restaurant,
The, (DC), 52
Mill Street Brewing Company,
(DC), 87
Peint O Gwrw, (CC), 149
Rhinecliff, The, (DC), 119

Scandinavian
DABA, (CC), 169

Seafood
Captain Jake's Riverhouse, (OC), 203
Gadaleto's Seafood Market,
(UC), 260
Gerardo's Seafood Cafe, (DC), 32
Mariner's on the Hudson, (UC), 225

Soul Food
BJ's Restaurant, (DC), 29

South American
El Solar Cafe, (OC), 204
Gabriel's Cafe, (UC), 239

Spanish
Panzúr Restaurant and Wine Bar,
(DC), 133

Steak House
Flatiron, (DC), 160
Hudson's Ribs and Fish, (DC), 45
Joseph's Steakhouse, (DC), 52
Sapore Steakhouse, (DC), 47

Schlesinger's Steakhouse, (OC), 200
Skytop Steakhouse & Brewing
Company, (UC), 236

Tapas
Elephant Wine Bar, (UC), 232
52 Main, (DC), 66
(p.m.) Wine Bar, (CC), 173

Thai
Aroi Thai, (DC), 110
Citrus, (OC), 200
Sukhothai, (DC), 34

Traditional American
Andy's Place, (DC), 81
Babycakes Cafe, (DC), 82
Bangall Whaling Company,
(DC), 130
Barnwood Restaurant, (GC), 286
Beechtree Grill, The, (DC), 82
Blue Plate Restaurant, (CC), 148
Boitson's, (UC), 229
Bread and Bottle, (DC), 100
Cold Spring Depot, (PC), 12
Copperfield's, (DC), 127
Farmer's Wife, The, (CC), 144
Grazin, (CC), 171
High Falls Cafe, (UC), 221
Historic Blue Store Restaurant,
(CC), 187
Hudson House River Inn, (PC),
12, 223

Lakeview House, (OC), 206
Main Street Bistro, (UC), 259
Manna Dew Cafe, (DC), 66
Max's on Main, (DC), 32
Me-Oh-My Cafe and Pie Shop,
   (DC), 103
Miller's Tavern, (CC), 144
Mohonk Mountain House, (UC),
   223, 255
Poppy's Burgers & Fries, (DC), 33
Plumbush Inn at the Parrott House,
   (PC), 13
River Station, (DC), 88

Rusty's Farm Fresh Eatery, (DC), 103
Shadows on the Hudson, (DC), 90
Silver Spoon Restaurant and Bar,
   (PC), 16
Thayer Hotel at West Point, The,
   (OC), 214, 223

Vegetarian

Luna 61, (DC), 132
Murray's, (DC), 133
Rhinebeck Health Foods, (DC), 124
Rosendale Cafe, (UC), 269

Appendix B: Specialty Producers & Shops

Codes for Corresponding County Chapters:
- **(CC) Columbia County**
- **(DC) Dutchess County**
- **(GC) Greene County**
- **(OC) Orange County**
- **(PC) Putnam County**
- **(UC) Ulster County**

Asian Markets

Krishna Grocery, (DC), 97

Phil-Asian Foods, (DC), 98

Pinoy Outlet, (DC), 41

Welcome Oriental Grocery (DC), 98

Bakeries

All You Knead, (DC), 38

Alternative Baker, (UC), 270

Caffe Aurora Pasticceria, (DC), 96

Cake Box Bakery, (UC), 244

Corsino Cakes, (DC), 139

Deising's Bakery, (UC), 244

Ella's Bellas, (DC), 40

Gluten-Free Bakery & Our Daily Bread Cafe, The, (CC), 150

Hudson Valley Dessert Company, (UC), 278

La Deliziosa Italian Pastry Shoppe, (DC), 97

Los Hornitos Bakery, (DC), 139

McKinney & Doyle Fine Foods, (DC), 72

Moxie Cupcake, (UC), 262

Shops at Jones Farm, The, (OC), 199

Sunporch Baked Goods, (UC), 280

Tivoli Bread and Baking, (DC), 135

Bakery Cafes

Bonfiglio & Bread, (CC), 176
Bread Alone, (DC), 122
Cafe Le Perche, (CC), 176
Gigi Market and Cafe, (DC), 105
Me-Oh-My Cafe and Pie Shop,
   (DC), 103
Nolita Bakery and Cafe,
   (CC), 178
Red Devon Market, Cafe, Bar and
   Restaurant, (DC), 130
Village TeaRoom, The, (UC), 259

Breakfast/Brunch

Back in the Kitchen, (DC), 27
Beacon Bagel, (DC), 35
Love Bites, (UC), 276
Lox of Bagels, (UC), 276
Pine Plains Platter, (DC), 74
Tanzy's, (CC), 179

Breweries

Chatham Brewing, (CC), 150
Crossroads Brewing Company,
   (GC), 285
Gilded Otter, The, (UC), 255
Keegan Ales, (UC), 245
Mill Street Brewing Company,
   (DC), 87
Newburgh Brewing Company,
   (OC), 212
Sloop Brewing, (DC), 53, 98

Burgers

Poppy's Burgers & Fries, (DC), 33

Butchers

Fleisher's Meats, (UC), 245
Quattro's Game Farm and Farm
   Store, (DC), 79

Candy Stores

CandyCandy, (UC), 260
Gourmetibles, (DC), 40
Kingston Candy Bar, (UC), 246
Michael's Candy Corner, (UC), 247
Vasilow's Confectionery, (CC), 181

Cheese Shops

Big Cheese, The, (UC), 270
Cheese Louise, (UC), 244
Cheese Plate, The, (UC), 260
Grand Cru Beer and Cheese Market,
   (DC), 123

Chocolatiers

Alps Sweet Shop, (DC), 39, 48
Christopher Norman Chocolates,
   (CC), 180
Commodore Chocolatier, (OC), 211
Hudson Chocolate Bar, (CC), 180
Hudson Chocolates, (DC), 96
Kokokobi, (UC), 246
Krause's Chocolates, (UC), 261, 278
Lagusta's Luscious, (UC), 262
Lucky Chocolates, (UC), 278

Oliver Kita Chocolates, (DC), 123
Sweet Sensations Chocolate, (GC), 288

Cider
Annandale Cidery, (DC), 105
Bad Seed Cider Company, (UC), 226
Breezy Hill Orchard and Cider Mill,
    (DC), 129
Kettleborough Cider House, (UC), 261
Mister Cider, (CC), 188

Coffee and Coffeehouses
Bank Square Coffeehouse, (DC), 35
Caffe Macchiato, (OC), 210
Cold Spring Coffee Pantry, (PC), 15
Crafted Kup, The, (DC), 91
Ground Hog, The, (DC), 138
Hudson Coffee Traders, (UC),
    239, 258
Irving Farm Coffee House, (DC), 67
J.B. Peel Inc., (DC), 106
Monkey Joe Roasting Company,
    (UC), 241
Retriever Roasters, (GC), 287
Samuel's of Rhinebeck, (DC), 121
Taste Budd's Chocolate and Coffee
    Cafe, (DC), 104

Delis
Jack's Meats and Deli, (UC), 261
Joe's Italian Marketplace, (DC), 48
Russo's Italian Deli, (UC), 263
Tavola Rustica, (DC), 122

Distilleries
Coppersea Distillery, (UC), 282
Dutch's Spirits, (DC), 75, 319
Harvest Spirits Farm Distillery,
    (CC), 192
Hillrock Estate Distillery, (CC), 145

Food Trucks
Bubby's Burritos, (DC), 102
Chef Shack, (UC), 275
El Danzante on Wheels, (UC), 236
Ixtapa Taco Truck, (OC), 211
Mr. Grumpy's, (DC), 57
Tin Cantina, (UC), 277
Tortillaville, (CC), 180

Gourmet Shops
Adams Fairacre Farms, (UC), 95, 138
Olde Hudson Specialty Food,
    (CC), 181
Otto's Market, (CC), 158
Slammin' Salmon, (DC), 62

Health Food Stores
Beacon Natural Market, (DC), 39
Chatham Real Food Market, (CC), 152
Mother Earth's Storehouse, (UC), 98,
    247, 279
Rhinebeck Health Foods, (DC), 124

Hot Dogs
Dallas Hot Wieners, (UC), 237,
    238, 275

Kosiner Brothers Organic Hot Dog Cart, (UC), 258
Pete's Hot Dogs, (OC), 211
Savana's Gourmet Hot Dogs and Sausages, (DC), 93
Soul Dog Restaurant, (DC), 93

Ice Cream/Yogurt
Artigiani del Gelato, (DC), 120
Beacon Creamery, (DC), 36
Boice Brothers Ice Cream, (UC), 237
Cherry Top Dairy Bar, (OC), 210
Debra T's Ice Cream Cafe, (DC), 91
Frozenberry, (PC), 15, 48
Frozen Caboose, (UC), 226
Go-Go Pops, (PC), 15
Holy Cow, (DC), 102
Jane's Ice Cream, (UC), 245, 321
Letti's Ice Cream, (DC), 58
Lick, (CC), 178
Mickey's Igloo, (UC), 241
Moo-Moo's Creamery, (PC), 16
Village Scoop, (CC), 165
Zora Dora Paletaria, (DC), 38

Kitchenware
Blue Cashew Kitchen Pharmacy, (DC), 122
Utensil Kitchenware, (DC), 44
Warren Kitchen and Cutlery, (DC), 125

Olive Oil
Pure Mountain Olive Oil, (DC), 124
Scarborough Fare, (UC), 41, 263

Pasta
Andrea's Pasta di Casa, (DC), 28
La Bella Pasta, (UC), 247

Pickles
Brine Barrel, (UC), 277
Spacey Tracy's Pickles, (DC), 124

Pizza
Baba Louie's Pizza, (CC), 175
Brothers' Trattoria, (DC), 30
Cousin's Pizza, (DC), 141
Park Falafel and Pizza, (CC), 178
Pizzeria Posto, (DC), 121
Two Boots, (DC), 104

Sandwich Shops
Babette's Kitchen, (DC), 61
Carne, (DC), 36
Cascades, The, (CC), 177
Dolce, (UC), 238
Farmer's Wife, The, (CC), 144
Homespun Foods, (DC), 37
Joe Beez Famous Sandwiches, (UC), 240
Kavos Gyros, (DC), 91
Last Bite, The, (UC), 224
Lola's Cafe and Gourmet Take Out, (DC), 92

Lunch Box, The, (UC), 240

Old Chatham Country Store, The,
(CC), 188

Pine Plains Platter, (DC), 74

Rosticceria Rossi and Sons, (DC), 92

Rusty Tomato Snack Bar, (DC), 62

Sissy's Cafe, (UC), 243

Slammin' Salmon, (DC), 62

Twisted Foods and Pretzel Roll
Factory, (UC), 269

Sausages

Elia's Catering Company & House of
Sausage, (UC), 227

SmokeHouse of the Catskills,
(UC), 279

Specialty Shops

Block Factory Tamales, (CC), 157

Gadaleto's Seafood Market, (UC),
260

Terni's Store, (DC), 68

Wild Hive Farm, (DC), 43

Tacos

El Danzante on Wheels, (UC), 239

Tito Santana Taqueria, (DC), 38

Tea and Tearooms

Cup & Saucer Restaurant and Tea
Room, (DC), 31

Drink More Good, (DC), 40

Harney & Sons Fine Teas, (DC), 68

Verdigris Tea, (CC), 182

Wine, Beer, and Spirits Shops

Arlington Wine and Liquor, (DC), 95

Artisan Wine Shop, (DC), 39

Grand Cru Beer and Cheese Market,
(DC), 123

Half Time Beverage, (DC), 96

Hudson Wine Merchants, (CC), 181

Partition Street Wine Shop,
(UC), 279

Viscount Wines and Liquor,
(DC), 139

Wineries

Adair Vineyards, (UC), 260

Benmarl Winery, (UC), 248

Cascade Mountain Winery, (DC), 28

Clinton Vineyards, (DC), 42

Glorie Farm Winery, (UC), 249

Hudson–Chatham Winery, (CC),
147, 161

Millbrook Vineyards and Winery,
(DC), 62

Oak Summit Vineyard, (DC), 63

Robibero Family Vineyards,
(UC), 262

Stoutridge Vineyard, (UC), 249

Tousey Winery, (CC), 147, 158

Appendix C: Farm Bounty

Codes for Corresponding County Chapters:
- **(CC) Columbia County**
- **(DC) Dutchess County**
- **(GC) Greene County**
- **(OC) Orange County**
- **(PC) Putnam County**
- **(UC) Ulster County**

Cheesemakers

Amazing Real Live Food Co., (DC), 74, 324

Coach Farm, (DC), 75

Creamery at Twin Maple Farm, The, (CC), 160

Edgwick Farm, (OC), 199

Hawthorne Valley Farm, (CC), 161, 322

Sprout Creek Farm, (DC), 99

Community Supported Agriculture (CSA)

Brook Farm Project, (UC), 265

Clove Valley CSA at Outback Farm, (UC), 224

Common Hands Farm, (CC), 153

Farm at Miller's Crossing, The, (CC), 187

Fishkill Farms, (DC), 51

Glynwood Farm, (PC), 17, 312

Great Song Farm, (DC), 59, 314, 318

Hearty Roots Community Farm, (CC), 159

Hepworth Farms, (UC), 252

Huguenot Street Farm, (UC), 265

Obercreek Farm, (DC), 49

Poughkeepsie Farm Project, (DC), 99

Red Oak Farm, (CC), 191

Roxbury Farm, (CC), 186

Shoving Leopard Farm, (DC), 109

Sisters Hill Farm, (DC), 131

Slow Roots Farm, (UC), 248

Sol Flower Farm, (DC), 69

Sparrowbush Farm, (CC), 184
Taliaferro Farms, (UC), 266
Threshold Farm, (CC), 191

Dairies

Hawthorne Valley Farm, (CC), 322
Hill-Over Farm, (CC), 156
Hudson Valley Fresh, 89,
    316, 317
Ronnybrook Dairy, (CC), 146
Shunpike Dairy, (DC), 65

Farmers' Markets

Amenia Indoor Farmers' Market,
    (DC), 28, 292
Amenia Outdoor Farmers' Market,
    (DC), 28, 292
Arlington Farmers' Market, (DC),
    99, 293
Beacon Farmers' Market, (DC),
    42, 293
Chatham Farmers' Market, (CC),
    152, 295
Clermont Farmers' Market, (CC),
    155, 295
Cold Spring Indoor Farmers'
    Market, (PC), 17, 292
Cold Spring Outdoor Farmers'
    Market, (PC), 17, 292
Copake Farmers' Market, (CC),
    156, 295
Cornwall Farmers' Market, (OC),
    199, 296

Cornwall Winter Farmers' Market,
    (OC), 199, 296
Coxsackie Farmers' Market, (GC),
    290, 298
Fishkill Farmers' Market, (DC),
    49, 293
Heart of the Hudson Valley
    Farmers' Market, (UC), 251, 297
Highland Farmers Market, (UC),
    228, 297
Hillsdale Farmers' Market, (CC),
    165, 295
Hudson Farmers' Market, (CC),
    183, 295
Hudson Valley Farmers' Market at
    Greig Farm, (DC), 108, 293
Hyde Park Farmers' Market, (DC),
    57, 293
Kinderhook Farmers' Market, (CC),
    186, 295
Kingston Farmers' Market Midtown,
    (UC), 248, 297
Kingston Farmers' Market Uptown,
    (UC), 248, 297
Kingston Winter Market, (UC),
    248, 297
LaGrangeville Farmers' Market, (DC),
    57, 293
Milan Farmers' Market, (DC), 59, 293
Millbrook Farmers' Market, (DC),
    64, 293
Millerton Farmers' Market, (DC),
    69, 294

Newburgh Farmers' Market, (OC),
213, 296
Newburgh Farmers' Market
Downing Park, (OC), 213, 296
Newburgh–Healthy Orange
Farmers' Market, (OC),
213, 296
Newburgh–Newburgh Mall
Farmers' Market, (OC), 213, 296
New Paltz Farmers' Market, (UC),
266, 297
Philmont Farmers' Market, (CC),
191, 295
Putnam Valley Farmers' Market,
(PC), 292
Red Hook Outdoors Farmers'
Market, (DC), 109, 294
Red Hook Winter Farmers Market,
(DC), 109, 294
Rhinebeck Farmers' Market, (DC),
126, 294
Rosendale Summer Farmers'
Market, (UC), 271, 297
Rosendale Winter Farmers' Market,
(UC), 271, 297
Saugerties Summer Farmers'
Market, (UC), 280, 298
Saugerties Winter Farmers' Market,
(UC), 281, 298
St. Christopher's Inn Farmers'
Market, (PC), 23, 292
Wappingers Falls Farmers' Market,
(DC), 140, 294

West Point–Town of Highlands
Farmers' Market, (OC), 215, 296

Farm Stands

Berry Farm, The, (CC), 151
Black Horse Farms, (GC), 285
Boehm Farm, (GC), 289
Boice's Farm and Garden Stand,
(UC), 280
Bradley Farm, (UC), 264
Brook Farm Project, (UC), 265
Common Hands Farm, (CC), 153
Dubois Farms, (UC), 227
Eger Brothers, (CC), 182
Fishkill Farms, (DC), 51
Golden Harvest Farms, (CC), 192
Greig Farm, (DC), 106
Hahn Farm, (DC), 128
Hardeman Orchards, (DC), 108
Hawk Dance Farm, (CC), 165
Hawthorne Valley Farm, (CC),
161, 322
Holmquest Farms, (CC), 183
Jenkins–Lueken Orchards, (UC), 266
Lawrence Farms Orchards, (OC), 212
Loveapple Farm, (CC), 163
McEnroe Organic Farm Market,
(DC), 69
Mead Orchards, (DC), 135
Meadowbrook Farm, (DC), 140
Meadow View Farm, (UC), 266
Migliorelli Farm Stand, (DC),
108, 126

Montgomery Place Orchards,
    (DC), 108
Overlook Farm Market and Country
    Store, (OC), 213
Samascott Orchards, (CC), 186
Shops at Jones Farm, The, (OC), 199
Shortcake Farm, (CC), 183
Silamar Farm, (DC), 69
Sprout Creek Farm, (DC), 99
Story Farms, (GC), 288
Taliaferro Farms, (UC), 266
Terhune Orchards, (DC), 128
Thompson-Finch Farm, (CC), 148
Vera's Philipstown Fruit and
    Vegetable Market, (PC), 17
Vinnie's Farm Market, (UC), 281
Walbridge Farm Market, (DC), 65
Wallkill View Farm Market,
    (UC), 267
White Oak Farm, (CC), 166
Wigsten's Farm Market, (DC), 80
Wilklow Orchards, (UC), 228
Winter Sun Farms, (UC), 267
Wonderland Florist, Nursery, and
    Farm Market, (DC), 126
Yonder Fruit Farms, (CC), 193

Garlic
Rockerbox Garlic, (DC), 64, 315

Herbs
Field Apothecary and Herb Farm,
    (CC), 159, 320

Honey and Maple Syrup
Bumble & Hive, (DC), 123
Cronin's Maple Farm, (DC), 22, 51
Hummingbird Ranch, (DC), 22, 159
Madava Farms, (DC), 22, 44, 326
Niese's Maple Farm, (PC), 22, 23
Platte Creek Maple Farm, (UC),
    22, 280
Remsburger Maple Farm and
    Apiary, (DC), 22, 79

Meat, Poultry, Eggs
Arch River Farm, (DC), 64
Black Sheep Hill Farm, (DC), 78
Cool Whisper Farm, (CC), 162
Fox Hill Farm, (CC), 146
Grazin Angus Acres, (CC), 162
Hahn Farm, (DC), 128
Herondale Farm, (CC), 146
Highland Farm, (CC), 159
Karl Family Farms, (UC), 253
Kinderhook Farm, (CC), 163
Knoll Krest Farm, (DC), 42
Meadowland Farm, (DC), 43
Meadow View Farm, (UC), 266
Millbrook Venison Products,
    (DC), 64
Mountain Brook Farm, (CC), 166
Northwind Farms, (DC), 135, 325
Pathfinder Farms, (GC), 288
Pigasso Farms, (CC), 156
Rykowski Livestock, (UC), 271
Second Chance Farm, (DC), 59

Sir William Farm Stand, (CC), 157
Staron Farm Stand, (CC), 193
Temple Farm, (DC), 65
Thunder Hill Farm, (DC), 132
Van Wie Natural Foods, (CC), 184
Veritas Farms, (UC), 267

Pick-Your-Own

Apple Hill Farm, (UC), 264
Barn, The, (CC), 182
Barton Orchards, (DC), 50
Berry Farm, The, (CC), 151
Boehm Farm, (GC), 289
Brittany Hollow Farm, (DC), 125
Cedar Heights Orchard, (DC), 126
Dressel Farms, (UC), 265
Dubois Farms, (UC), 227
Fishkill Farms, (DC), 51
Fix Brothers Fruit Farm, (CC), 182
Fraleigh's Rose Hill Farm, (DC), 106
Golden Harvest Farms, (CC), 192

Greig Farm, (DC), 106
Hurds Family Farm, (UC), 252
Jenkins–Lueken Orchards, (UC), 266
Klein's Kill Fruit Farm, (CC), 159
Lawrence Farms Orchards, (OC), 212
Liberty View Farm, (UC), 228
Loveapple Farm, (CC), 163
Mead Orchards, (DC), 135
Oriole Orchards, (DC), 109
Philip Orchards, (CC), 153
Prospect Hill Orchards, (UC), 252
Samascott Orchards, (CC), 186
Secor Strawberries, (DC), 140
Shortcake Farm, (CC), 183
Smith Farms, (CC), 183
Story Farms, (GC), 288
Taconic Orchards, (CC), 184
Terhune Orchards, (DC), 128
Thompson-Finch Farm, (CC), 148
Weed Orchards, (UC), 250
Wilklow Orchards, (UC), 228

Appendix D: Land Trusts

Land trusts, also known as land conservancies, play a crucial role in preserving agriculture in the Hudson Valley. These nonprofit organizations help farmers protect their livelihoods through permanent easements on their land, the sale of development rights, and other methods that give the farmers financial security and let them pass the farm down to the next generation. By making it possible for farmers to stay on their land, the conservancies keep farms in production and avoid turning productive farmland into subdivisions and suburban sprawl. Most land trusts also protect historic and natural areas in their region through parks and preserves that are open to the public. The trusts sponsor many tours, walks, classes, and other events. Most are free and family friendly—they're a great way to enjoy the beauty of the region.

Columbia Land Conservancy, 49 Main St., Chatham, NY 12037; (518) 392-5252; clctrust.org. The Columbia Land Conservancy has been a pioneer in preserving farmland and the beautiful rural character of the county. Overall, the CLC protects 29,500 acres of land and holds conservation easements on 22,900 acres—an astonishing 25 percent of all privately conserved land in the Hudson Valley. The conservancy has established 5,750 acres of public land and manages 10 public conservation areas. As part of its strong commitment to agriculture, the CLC has helped raise over $7 million to ensure the protection of 5,800 acres of working farmland. The CLC also created a highly successful match program that brings together landowners and farmers. The program has worked so well that it has been extended to Dutchess County through cooperative arrangements with the Dutchess

Land Conservancy and the Winnakee Land Trust (see below). As part of its public outreach, the CLC has an extensive educational program and sponsors many free events at its public conservation areas.

Dutchess Land Conservancy, 4289 Rte. 82, Millbrook, NY 12545; (845) 677-3002; dutchessland.org. Dutchess Land Conservancy is an outstanding example of how a land trust can help agriculture. Through an active purchase of development rights (PDR) program, DLC has completed projects that protect over 3,400 acres of working farmland in the county. DLC also partners with Columbia Land Conservancy on a farmer/landowner match program in the county. The program brings together landowners who want to have their property farmed and farmers seeking land. DLC sponsors hikes, tours, classes, and other events.

Greene Land Trust, 270 Mansion St., Coxsackie, NY 12051; (518) 731-5544; greenelandtrust.org. The agricultural lands and family farms of rural Greene County are under as much development pressure as land in more developed areas. Greene Land Trust helps preserve the county's farmland, grasslands, and open spaces.

Kingston Land Trust, Box 2701, Kingston, NY 12402; (845) 877-5263; kingstonlandtrust.org. The Kingston Land Trust is devoted to protecting and preserving open space, historic sites, and the environment in the city of Kingston and the surrounding region. The trust has been very active in supporting urban agriculture by promoting community-based, small-scale, entrepreneurial farming in Kingston.

Open Space Institute, 1350 Broadway, NY, NY, 10018; (212) 290-8200; osiny.org. Don't let the Manhattan address fool you: The Open Space Institute is very active in land preservation in the Hudson Valley (and also in New Jersey, New England, and parts of the southeast). For more than 40 years, OSI has been protecting land in New York, including the Catskills, Capital District, and lower Hudson Valley. OSI protects family farms, open space, recreation areas, and historic sites with both direct acquisitions and conservation easements. In the mid-Hudson region alone, OSI has preserved close to 15,000 acres; in all, OSI has protected over 116,000 acres of land in the state.

Orange County Land Trust, 23 White Oak Dr., Sugar Loaf, NY 10981; (845) 469-0951; orangecountylandtrust.org. Since its founding in 1993, the Orange County Land Trust has permanently protected nearly 4,700 acres of scenic ridgelines, working farmland, and wildlife corridors. The trust operates six preserves that are open to the public; check the website for the active calendar of fun and free events at the preserves.

Putnam County Land Trust: Save Open Spaces, Box 36, Brewster, NY 10509; (845) 278-2808; pclt.net. One of the oldest land trusts in New York, Putnam County Land Trust was founded in 1969. It focuses on preserving natural resources and environmentally sensitive areas that can be used for passive recreation. The trust has preserved 835 acres of diverse habitat. In addition, through its sponsorship of county legislation, the trust has helped preserve more than 2,000 acres as Putnam County Conservation Areas.

Rondout-Esopus Land Conservancy, Box 144, Accord, NY 12404; (917) 974-8467; relandconservancy.org. The Rondout-Esopus Land Conservancy works with landowners to preserve special sites in Ulster County in the area around the Rondout and Esopus creeks. The conservancy holds easements on 40 properties comprising nearly 3,200 acres.

Scenic Hudson, 1 Civic Center Plaza, Poughkeepsie, NY 12601; (845) 473-4440; scenichudson.org. Scenic Hudson has been fighting to preserve and protect the natural beauty and environment of the Hudson River Valley since it was founded in 1963 in the fight to save Storm King Mountain — northern gateway to the fabled Hudson Highlands — from a proposal to build a hydroelectric plant at its base. Scenic Hudson launched the grass-roots environmental movement, winning the right of citizens to speak out and initiate lawsuits to protect their environment. As a powerful force in the region for protecting agriculture and the environment, Scenic Hudson has since created or enhanced more than 50 parks, preserves, and historic sites and conserved nearly 30,000 acres. Since 1992, Scenic Hudson has protected more than 9,600 acres of farmland in ten communities throughout Columbia, Dutchess, Orange, and Ulster counties. All Scenic Hudson sites are open to the public at no charge. It's the rare weekend in the Hudson Valley when Scenic Hudson isn't offering a fun and free event such as a guided hike or program of some sort at one of its sites.

Wallkill Valley Land Trust, **64 Huguenot St., New Paltz, NY 12561; (845) 255-2761; wallkillvalleylt.org.** Preserving open space in southern Ulster County, the Wallkill Valley Land Trust was founded in 1987. Today it preserves about 1,800 acres of land, including a lot of working farmland—the Huguenot Street Farm CSA in New Paltz is a good example (see page 265). The Trust is also the organization behind the remarkable Wallkill Valley Rail Trail, a wonderful recreational resource that stretches for just over 12 miles between the towns of Gardiner and New Paltz (wvrta.org). Wallkill Valley Land Trust sponsors house tours and numerous free walks and talks throughout the year.

Winnakee Land Trust, **187 E. Market St., Rhinebeck, NY 12572; (845) 876-4213; winnakeeland.org.** The Winnakee Land Trust protects farmland and natural habitats in northern Dutchess County from development. Winnakee also provides public recreational opportunities through two parks and has established miles of public access trails in the area. A major fundraiser every year in late September or early October is a tour of historic barns and working farms—an excellent opportunity to visit unique properties that are not normally open to the public. Winnakee also partners with Dutchess Land Conservancy and the Columbia Land Conservancy on an important landowner/farmer match program.

Index

A

Adair Vineyards, 260
Adams Fairacre Farms, 95, 138
Akari Sushi and Japanese Food, 80
Alexis Diner, 202
All You Knead Bakery, 38
Alps Sweet Shop, 39, 48
Alternative Baker, 270
Amazing Real Live Food Co., 74, 324
Amenia Indoor Farmers' Market,
    28, 292
Amenia Outdoor Farmers' Market,
    29, 292
American Bounty Restaurant, 54
American Glory BBQ, 166
Andrea's Pasta di Casa, 28
Andy's Place, 81
Annandale Cidery, 105
Another Fork in the Road, 58
Apple Hill Farm, 264
Apple Pie Bakery Cafe, 54
Applewood Winery, 208
Arch River Farm, 64
Arielle, 110
Arlington Farmers' Market, 99, 293
Arlington Wine and Liquor, 95
Armadillo Bar and Grill, 229
Aroi Thai, 110
Aroma Osteria, 136

Art Bar, 111
Artigiani del Gelato, 120
Artisan Wine Shop, 39
Artist's Palate, The, 81
A Tavola Trattoria, 253
Aurelia, 59
Avocado, 196

B

Baba Louie's Pizza, 175
Babette's Kitchen, 61
Babycakes Cafe, 82
Back in the Kitchen, 27
Bad Seed Cider Company, 226
Baldwin Vineyards, 209
Bangall Whaling Company, 130
Bank Square Coffeehouse, 35
Barn, The, 182
Barnwood Restaurant, 286
Barton Orchards, 50
Beacon Bagel, 35
Beacon Creamery, 36
Beacon Falls Cafe, 29
Beacon Farmers' Market, 42, 293
Beacon Natural Market, 39
Beacon Sloop Club Corn
    Festival, 304
Beacon Sloop Club Pumpkin
    Festival, 307

Beacon Sloop Club Strawberry
Festival, 303
Beechtree Grill, The, 82
Beekman Arms and Delamater
Inn, 111, 223
Benmarl Winery, 248
Berry Farm, The, 151
Big Cheese, The, 270
Big W's Roadside BBQ, 140
Billy Bob's BBQ, 83
Billy Joe's Ribworks, 202
Bird & Bottle Inn, The, 20, 223
BJ's Restaurant, 29
Black Horse Farms, 285
Black Sheep Hill Farm, 78
Block Factory Tamales, 157
Blueberry Festival, 303
Blue Cashew Kitchen
Pharmacy, 122
Blue Fountain, The, 49
Blue Plate Restaurant, 148
Bocuse Restaurant, The, 55
Boehm Farm, 289
Boice Brothers Ice Cream, 237
Boice's Farm and Garden
Stand, 280
Boitson's, 229
Bonfiglio & Bread, 176
Bounty of the Hudson, 304
Bradley Farm, 264
Brasserie 292, 83
Brasserie le Bouchon, 11
Bread Alone, 122

Bread and Bottle, 100
Breezy Hill Orchard and Cider
Mill, 129
Brimstone Hill Winery, 209
Brine Barrel, 277
Brittany Hollow Farm, 125
Broadway Lights Diner, 242
Brook Farm Project, 265
Brookview Station Winery, 147
Brotherhood Winery, 209
Brothers' Trattoria, 30
Bubby's Burritos, 102
Bumble & Hive, 123
Bywater Bistro, 268

C
Cafe Amarcord, 30
Cafe Bocca, 84
Cafe East, 237
Cafe Le Perche, 176
Cafe les Baux, 60
Cafe Maya, 137
Cafe Mezzaluna, 271
Cafe Pitti, 203
Caffe Aurora Pasticceria, 96
Caffe Macchiato, 210
Cake Box Bakery, 244
Calico Restaurant and Patisserie, 112
Ca' Mea Ristorante, 167
Cameo's, 283
CandyCandy, 260
Canterbury Brook Inn, 196
Captain Jake's Riverhouse, 203

Carne, 36
Carolina House, 185
Casa Villa, 231
Cascade Mountain Winery, 28
Cascades, The, 177
Cask and Rasher, 289
Cathryn's Tuscan Grill, 11
Cedar Heights Orchard, 126
Cedar Ridge Farm, 162
Cena 2000 Ristorante and Bar, 204
Chai Shop, The, 177
Charlotte's, 60
Chatham Brewing, 53, 150
Chatham Farmers' Market,
    152, 295
Chatham Real Food Market, 152
Cheese Louise, 244
Cheese Plate, The, 260
Chef Shack, 275
Cherry Top Dairy Bar, 210
China Rose, 113
Christopher Norman
    Chocolates, 180
Cider Week, 308
Cinnamon, 113
Cinnamon Indian Bistro, 84
Citrus, 200
Clearview Vineyard, 209
Clermont Farmers' Market,
    155, 295
Clinton Vineyards, 42
Clove Valley CSA at Outback
    Farm, 224

Coach Farm, 75
Cold Spring Coffee Pantry, 15
Cold Spring Depot, 12
Cold Spring Indoor Farmers'
    Market, 17, 292
Cold Spring Outdoor Farmers'
    Market, 17, 292
College Diner, 242
Commodore Chocolatier, 211
Common Hands Farm, 153
Community-supported
    agriculture, 18
Continental Organics, 201
Cool Whisper Farm, 162
Copake Farmers' Market, 156, 295
Copperfield's, 127
Coppersea Distillery, 282
Cornwall Farmers' Market,
    199, 296
Cornwall Winter Farmers' Market,
    199, 296
Corsino Cakes, 139
Cosimo's Trattoria, 85
Cousin's Pizza, 141
Coxsackie Farmers' Market,
    290, 298
Coyote Flaco, 152
Coyote Grill, 85
craft breweries, 53
Crafted Kup, The, 91
Crave, 85
Creamery at Twin Maple Farm,
    The, 160

Crew Restaurant and Bar, 86
Crimson Sparrow, The, 168
Cronin's Maple Farm, 22, 51
Crossroads Brewing Company,
    53, 285
CrossRoads Food Shop, 164
'cue Shack, 272
Culinary Institute of America, 54
Cup & Saucer Restaurant and Tea
    Room, 31

D
DABA, 169
Daily Planet, The, 70
Dallas Hot Wieners, 237, 238, 275
Debra T's Ice Cream Cafe, 91
Deising's Bakery, 244
Demarest Hill Winery, 209
DePuy Canal House, 219
Destino Cucina Mexicana and
    Margarita Bar, 149
Dietz Stadium Diner, 242
DimsumGoGo, 31
Dolce, 238
Dominick's Cafe, 238
Dressel Farms, 265
Drink More Good, 40
Dubois Farms, 227
Duo Bistro, 231
Dutch Ale House, 272
Dutchess County Fair, 305
Dutchess Wine Trail, 43
Dutch's Spirits, 75, 319

E
Ecce Terra, 232
Edgwick Farm, 199
Eger Brothers, 182
Egg's Nest Saloon, The, 220
El Danzante on Wheels, 239
Elena's Restaurant and Diner, 242
Elephant Wine Bar, 232
Elia's Catering Company & House
    of Sausage, 227
Ella's Bellas, 40
El Solar Cafe, 204
Eveready Diner, 70

F
Farm at Miller's Crossing, The, 187
farm distilleries, 76
Farmer's Wife, The, 144
Farm to Table Bistro, 45
Festival of Farmers' Markets, 300
Fiddlestix Cafe, 198
Field Apothecary and Herb Farm,
    159, 320
52 Main, 66
Fireside Barbecue & Grill, 127
Fish & Game, 170
Fishkill Farmers' Market, 49, 293
Fishkill Farms, 51
Fix Brothers Fruit Farm, 182
Flatiron, 100
Fleisher's Meats, 245
Fox Hill Farm, 146
Fraleigh's Rose Hill Farm, 106

Friends of the Farmer Festival, 304
Frozenberry, 15, 48
Frozen Caboose, 226
Furnace Brook Winery at Hilltop
    Orchards, 147

G

Gabriel's Cafe, 239
Gaby's Cafe, 114
Gadaleto's Seafood Market, 260
Gardiner Cupcake Festival at
    Wright's Farm, 302
Gerardo's Seafood Cafe, 32
Gigi Market and Cafe, 105
Gigi Trattoria, 114
Gilded Otter, The, 255
The Gilded Otter, 53
Global Palate, 281
Glorie Farm Winery, 249
Gluten-Free Bakery & Our Daily
    Bread Cafe, The, 150
Glynwood Farm, 17, 312
Go-Go Pops, 15
Golden Harvest Farms, 192
Gomen Kudasai Noodle Shop, 257
Gourmetibles, 40
Grand Cru Beer and Cheese
    Market, 123
Grazin, 171
Grazin Angus Acres, 162
Great Song Farm, 59, 314, 318
Greens at Copake Country Club,
    The, 155

Greig Farm, 106
Ground Hog, The, 138
Gunk Haus Restaurant and
    Biergarten, 218

H

Hahn Farm, 128
Half Time Beverage, 96
Hardeman Orchards, 108
Harney & Sons Fine Teas, 68
Harvest Spirits Farm Distillery, 192
Havana 59, 205
Hawk Dance Farm, 165
Hawthorne Valley Farm, 161, 322
Heart of the Hudson Valley Bounty
    Festival, 308
Heart of the Hudson Valley
    Farmers' Market, 251, 297
Hearty Roots Community Farm, 159
Helsinki Hudson, 171
Henry's Farm to Table Restaurant
    at Buttermilk Falls Inn, 251
Hepworth Farms, 252
Herondale Farm, 146
Hickory BBQ and Smokehouse, 233
High Falls Cafe, 221
Highland Farm, 159
Highland Farmers Market, 228, 297
Hill-Over Farm, 156
Hillrock Estate Distillery, 145
Hillsdale Farmer's Market, 165, 295
Historic Blue Store Restaurant, 187
Hoffman House, 223, 233

Hokkaido Japanese Restaurant, 254
Holmquest Farms, 183
Holy Cow, 102
Homespun Foods, 37
Hopped Up Cafe, 221
Hop, The, 41
Hudson-Berkshire Beverage
    Trail, 147
Hudson Berkshire Wine & Food
    Festival, 302
Hudson–Chatham Winery, 147, 161
Hudson Chocolate Bar, 180
Hudson Chocolates, 96
Hudson Coffee Traders, 239, 258
Hudson Farmers' Market, 183, 295
Hudson Food Studio, 172
Hudson House River Inn, 12, 223
Hudson River Craft Beer
    Festival, 306
Hudson's Ribs and Fish, 45
Hudson Street Cafe, 198
Hudson Valley Beer & Cheese
    Fest, 300
Hudson Valley Dessert
    Company, 278
Hudson Valley Farmers' Market at
    Greig Farm, 108, 293
Hudson Valley Food Truck
    Festival, 300
Hudson Valley Fresh, 89, 316, 317
Hudson Valley Garlic Festival, 306
Hudson Valley Pizza Fest, 301
Hudson Valley Restaurant

Week, 300
Hudson Valley Ribfest, 305
Hudson Valley Wine & Food
    Fest, 307
Hudson Wine Merchants, 181
Huguenot Street Farm, 265
Hummingbird Ranch, 22, 129
Hurds Family Farm, 252
Hyde Park Brewery and Restaurant,
    The, 52
Hyde Park Farmers' Market,
    57, 293

I
Ice House on the Hudson, 87
I-84 Diner, 70
Il Barilotto Enoteca, 46
Il Cenácolo, 205
Il Gallo Giallo, 254
International Pickle Festival, 309
Irving Farm Coffee House, 67
Isamu, 32
Ixtapa Taco Truck, 211

J
Jack's Meats and Deli, 261
Jane's Ice Cream, 245, 321
J.B. Peel Inc., 106
Jenkins–Lueken Orchards, 266
Joe Beez Famous Sandwiches, 240
Joe's Italian Marketplace, 48
Joseph's Steakhouse, 52

K

Karl Family Farms, 253
Katchkie Farm, 185
Kavos Gyros, 91
Keegan Ales, 53, 245
Kettleborough Cider House, 261
Kinderhook Farm, 163
Kinderhook Farmers' Market,
    186, 295
Kingston Candy Bar, 246
Kingston Farmers' Market Midtown,
    248, 297
Kingston Farmers' Market Uptown,
    248, 297
Kingston Winter Market, 248, 297
Kings Valley Diner, 243
Klein's Kill Fruit Farm, 159
Knoll Krest Farm, 42
Kokokobi, 246
Kosiner Brothers Organic Hot Dog
    Cart, 258
Krause's Chocolates, 261, 278
Krishna Grocery, 97

L

La Bella Pasta, 247
La Conca d'Oro, 286
La Deliziosa Italian Pastry
    Shoppe, 97
LaGrangeville Farmers' Market,
    57, 293
Lagusta's Luscious, 262
Lakeview House, 206

La Puerta Azul, 61
La Stazione, 258
Last Bite, The, 224
Lawrence Farms Orchards, 212
Le Canard Enchaîné, 230
Le Chambord, 50
Le Express Bistro and Bar, 137
Le Petit Bistro, 115
Letti's Ice Cream, 58
Lia's Mountain View Restaurant, 73
Liberty of Rhinebeck, 115
Liberty View Farm, 228
Lick, 178
Local 111, 189
Local Restaurant and Bar,
    The, 116
Lola's Cafe and Gourmet Take
    Out, 92
Los Hornitos Bakery, 139
Loveapple Farm, 163
Love Bites, 276
Lox of Bagels, 276
Lucky Chocolates, 278
Luna 61, 132
Lunch Box, The, 240

M

Machu Picchu Peruvian
    Restaurant, 206
Madava Farms, 22, 44, 328
Main Street Bistro, 259
Mama Theresa's Italian Deli, 201
Manna Dew Cafe, 66

maple syrup, 22
Maple Weekend, 22, 301
Mariner's on the Hudson, 225
Market Market, 268
Market Street, 117
Markristo Farm, 165
Martindale Chief Diner, 154
Max's Memphis BBQ, 101
Max's on Main, 32
Maya Cafe, 46
McEnroe Organic Farm Market, 69
McKinney & Doyle Fine Foods, 72
Mead Orchards, 135
Meadowbrook Farm, 140
Meadowland Farm, 43
Meadow View Farm, 266
Me-Oh-My Cafe and Pie Shop, 103
Mercato Osteria and Enoteca, 101
Mexican Radio Hudson, 172
Michael's Candy Corner, 247
Michael's Diner, 243
Mickey's Igloo, 241
Migliorelli Farm Stand, 108, 126
Milan Farmers' Market, 59, 293
Millbrook Farmers' Market, 64, 293
Millbrook Venison Products, 64
Millbrook Vineyards and Winery, 62
Miller's Tavern, 144
Millerton Farmers' Market, 69, 294
Mill Street Brewing Company, 53, 87
Minard Farms, 219
Mint, 234
Miss Lucy's Kitchen, 273

Mister Cider, 188
Mohonk Mountain House, 223, 255
Momiji, 117
Monkey Joe Roasting Company, 241
Montgomery Place Orchards, 108
Moo-Moo's Creamery, 16
Mother Earth's Storehouse, 98,
    247, 279
Mountain Brook Farm, 166
Moxie Cupcake, 262
Mr. Grumpy's, 57
Murray's, 133

N
Newburgh Brewing Company,
    53, 212
Newburgh Farmers' Market,
    213, 296
Newburgh Farmers' Market
    Downing Park, 213, 296
Newburgh–Healthy Orange
    Farmers' Market, 213, 296
Newburgh–Newburgh Mall Farmers'
    Market, 213, 296
New Paltz Farmers' Market,
    266, 297
New Windsor Coach Diner, 202
New World Home Cooking, 273
Nic L Inn Wine Cellar on the
    Hudson, 88
Niese's Maple Farm, 22, 23
Nolita Bakery and Cafe, 178
No. 9, 66

Northern Spy Cafe, 222
North Plank Road Tavern, 207
Northwind Farms, 135

O
Oakhurst Diner, 71
Oak Summit Vineyard, 63
Obercreek Farm, 49
Old Chatham Country Store,
    The, 188
Old Chatham Sheepherding
    Company, 189
Olde Hudson Specialty Food, 181
Oliver Kita Chocolates, 123
Olympic Diner, 243
Oriole Orchards, 109
Osaka, 118, 133
O's Eatery, 154
Otto's Market, 158
Outdated: An Antique Cafe, 242
Overlook Farm Market and Country
    Store, 213

P
Painter's, 197
Palace Diner, 71
Palace Dumpling, 137
Palaia Vineyards, 209
Panzúr Restaurant and Wine
    Bar, 133
Park Falafel and Pizza, 178
Partition Street Wine Shop, 279
Pathfinder Farms, 288

Peint O Gwrw, 149
Pete's Hot Dogs, 211
Phil-Asian Foods, 98
Philip Orchards, 153
Philmont Farmers' Market,
    191, 295
Pigasso Farms, 156
Pine Plains Platter, 74
Pinoy Outlet, 41
Pizzeria Posto, 121
Platte Creek Maple Farm,
    22, 280
Plaza Diner, 154
Plumbush Inn at the Parrott
    House, 13
Poppy's Burgers & Fries, 33
Portofino Ristorante, 129
Poughkeepsie Farm Project, 99
Prospect Hill Orchards, 252
Puccini Ristorante, 118
Pure Mountain Olive Oil, 124
Putnam Valley Farmers'
    Market, 292

Q
Quattro's Game Farm and Farm
    Store, 79

R
Ramp Fest, 301
Red Devon Market, Cafe, Bar and
    Restaurant, 130
Red Dot Restaurant and Bar, 173

Red Hook Outdoors Farmers'
Market, 109, 294
Red Hook Winter Farmers Market,
109, 294
Red Line Diner, 71
Red Oak Farm, 191
Red Onion, The, 274
Remsburger Maple Farm and
Apiary, 22, 79
Retriever Roasters, 287
Rhinebeck Farmers' Market,
126, 294
Rhinebeck Health Foods, 124
Rhinecliff, The, 119
Ristorante Caterina de' Medici, 55
River Bank, The, 197
River Station, 88
River Terrace Bar and
Restaurant, 33
Riverview Restaurant, 14
Robibero Family Vineyards, 262
Rock and Rye Tavern, 256
Rockerbox Garlic, 64, 315
Ronnybrook Dairy, 146
Rosendale Cafe, 269
Rosendale Summer Farmers'
Market, 271, 297
Rosendale Winter Farmers' Market,
271, 298
Rosticceria Rossi and Sons, 92
RoundUp Texas BBQ, 14
Roxbury Farm, 186
Russo's Italian Deli, 263

Rusty's Farm Fresh Eatery, 103
Rusty Tomato Snack Bar, 62
Rykowski Livestock, 271

S
Salsa Fresca Mexican Grill, 67
Samascott Orchards, 186
Samuel's of Rhinebeck, 121
Santa Fe, 134
Santa Fe Uptown, 234
Sapore Steakhouse, 47
Saugerties Summer Farmers'
Market, 280, 298
Saugerties Winter Farmers'
Market, 281
Saugerties Winter Farmers'
Market, 298
Savana's Gourmet Hot Dogs and
Sausages, 93
Savona's Trattoria, 234
Scarborough Fare, 41, 263
Scenic Hudson, 107
Schatzi's Pub and Bier Garden, 90
Schlesinger's Steakhouse, 200
Second Chance Farm, 59
Secor Strawberries, 140
Seoul Kitchen, 37
Serevan, 26
Shadows on the Hudson, 90
Shawangunk Hudson Valley Wine
Trail, 208
Ship Lantern Inn, 223, 250
Ship to Shore, 235

Shops at Jones Farm, The, 199
Shortcake Farm, 183
Shoving Leopard Farm, 109
Shunpike Dairy, 65
Silamar Farm, 69
Silver Spoon Restaurant and
    Bar, 16
Sir William Farm Stand, 157
Sissy's Cafe, 243
Sisters Hill Farm, 131
Skytop Steakhouse & Brewing
    Company, 236
Slammin' Salmon, 62
Sloop Brewing, 53, 98
Slow Roots Farm, 248
Smith Farms, 183
SmokeHouse of the Catskills, 279
Sol Flower Farm, 69
Soul Dog Restaurant, 93
Spacey Tracy's Pickles, 124
Sparrowbush Farm, 184
Spotty Dog Books and Ale, 179
Sprout Creek Farm, 99
St. Andrew's Cafe, 55
Staron Farm Stand, 193
St. Christopher's Inn Farmers'
    Market, 23, 292
Stissing House, 73, 223
Storm King, 290
Story Farms, 288
Stoutridge Vineyard, 249
Sukhothai, 34
Sunporch Baked Goods, 280

Suruchi, 257
Sweet Sensations Chocolate, 288
Swift and the Roundhouse at
    Beacon Falls, 34
Swiss Hütte Inn and Restaurant, 164
Swoon Kitchenbar, 174

T
Taconic Orchards, 184
Taliaferro Farms, 266
Tango, 277
Tanjore Cuisine of India, 47
Tanzy's, 179
Taste Budd's Chocolate and Coffee
    Cafe, 104
Taste of Hudson Valley Bounty,
    The, 305
Taste of New Paltz, 307
Taste of Rhinebeck, 302
Taste of the Hudson Valley, 309
Tavern at Diamond Mills, 274
Tavern at Highlands Country
    Club, 20
Tavola Rustica, 122
Temple Farm, 65
Terhune Orchards, 128
Terni's Store, 68
Terrapin, 119
Thayer Hotel at West Point, The,
    214, 223
Thompson-Finch Farm, 148
Threshold Farm, 191
Thunder Hill Farm, 132

Tin Cantina, 277
Tito Santana Taqueria, 38
Tivoli Bread and Baking, 135
Toro, 47
Tortillaville, 180
Tousey Winery, 147, 158
Troutbeck Inn and Conference
  Center, 27
Twisted Foods and Pretzel Roll
  Factory, 269
Twisted Soul Food Concepts, 94
Two Boots, 104
2 Taste Food and Wine Bar, 56

U
Utensil Kitchenware, 41

V
Valley at the Garrison, 21
Vanderbilt House, 190
Van Wie Natural Foods, 184
Vasilow's Confectionery, 181
Vera's Philipstown Fruit and
  Vegetable Market, 17
Verdigris Tea, 182
Veritas Farms, 267
Vico Restaurant and Bar, 175
Village Diner, 243
Village Scoop, 165
Village TeaRoom, The, 259
Vinnie's Farm Market, 281
Viscount Wines and Liquor, 139

W
Walbridge Farm Market, 65
Wallkill View Farm Market, 267
Wappingers Falls Farmers' Market,
  140, 294
Warren Kitchen and Cutlery, 125
Warwick Applefest, 308
Warwick Valley Winery, 209
Weed Orchards, 250
Welcome Oriental Grocery, 98
West Point–Town of Highlands
  Farmers' Market, 215, 296
West Taghkanic Diner, 154
Whitecliff Vineyard, 209
White Oak Farm, 166
Wigsten's Farm Market, 80
Wild Hive Farm, 43
Wilklow Orchards, 228
Winter Sun Farms, 267
Wonderland Florist, Nursery, and
  Farm Market, 126
Would, The, 225

Y
Yankee Clipper Diner, 71
Yianni's Restaurant, 150
Yonder Fruit Farms, 193
Yum Yum Noodle Bar, 236

Z
Zora Dora Paletaria, 38

Getaway ideas for the local traveler

Need a day away to relax, refresh, renew?
Just get in your car and go!